Migrants in Chinese Megacities

Producing Transient Urban Spaces in the Pearl River Delta

This book starts from the assumption that there is no single path of migrant integration or incorporation into the megacity. It then asks what kinds of migrant pathways into the Chinese megacity might be discovered by studying migrants' own agency. Based on over one hundred qualitative interviews conducted in the Pearl River Delta, the micro-studies in this volume show how different high-risk migrant groups (voluntary and involuntary, blue-collar and white-collar, internal and international) connect to the megacity through their everyday routines and practices, constituting and appropriating transient urban spaces. It also examines the responsiveness of the Chinese government's migration policies from the perspective of these different migrant groups. The study brings aspects of migration sociology and risk sociology into dialogue with each other and with urban China studies. Linked to ideas of the global risk society and planetary urbanisation, the study provides an empirical and theoretical building block beyond China's national development. Its findings are expected to contribute to current debates on restricting or promoting migration to (Chinese) megacities.

Migrants in Chinese Megacities

Producing Transient Urban Spaces in the Pearl River Delta

Bettina Gransow

Freie Universität Berlin, Germany

World Scientific

NEW JERSEY • LONDON • SINGAPORE • BEIJING • SHANGHAI • HONG KONG • TAIPEI • CHENNAI • TOKYO

Published by

World Scientific Publishing Co. Pte. Ltd.
5 Toh Tuck Link, Singapore 596224
USA office: 27 Warren Street, Suite 401-402, Hackensack, NJ 07601
UK office: 57 Shelton Street, Covent Garden, London WC2H 9HE

Library of Congress Cataloging-in-Publication Data
Names: Gransow, Bettina, author.
Title: Migrants in Chinese megacities : producing transient urban spaces in the Pearl River Delta / Bettina Gransow, Freie Universität Berlin, Germany.
Description: New Jersey : World Scientific, [2025] | Includes bibliographical references.
Identifiers: LCCN 2024056901 | ISBN 9789811275678 (hardcover) | ISBN 9789811275685 (ebook) | ISBN 9789811275692 (ebook other)
Subjects: LCSH: Internal migrants--China--Pearl River Region. | Urbanization--China--Pearl River Region.
Classification: LCC HB2114.P43 G73 2025 | DDC 307.2/4095127--dc23/eng/20250217
LC record available at https://lccn.loc.gov/2024056901

British Library Cataloguing-in-Publication Data
A catalogue record for this book is available from the British Library.

For any available supplementary material, please visit
https://www.worldscientific.com/worldscibooks/10.1142/13394#t=suppl

Desk Editors: Kannan Krishnan/Kura Sunaina

Typeset by Stallion Press
Email: enquiries@stallionpress.com

Preface and Acknowledgements

This book is based on data from successive research projects that were part of a collaborative priority programme called "Megacities – Megachallenges: Informal Dynamics of Global Change" (2007–2014). After the projects had been completed, some of the extensive interview material on various migrant groups remained unprocessed, and I felt that the messages or concerns of the interviewees themselves had not yet been sufficiently explored. It was at this point that Andrea Wolf approached me and asked if I had any ideas for a book project with World Scientific Publishing. Without her encouragement, this book would probably never have been written. I would like to thank her and World Scientific for this opportunity and for being so receptive to my suggestions. I would especially like to thank Kura Sunaina and Kannan Krishnan for their excellent work and cooperation during the production phase of the book.

Without the generous funding of the German Research Foundation (DFG), the database, also for this book, would not have been possible. The trilateral cooperation within the programme, involving universities in Germany, China and Bangladesh, provided numerous workshops in the three countries and stimulating opportunities for transregional and interdisciplinary academic exchange and personal dialogue. As one of thirteen joint international research teams, each working on one of the two mega-urban regions of Dhaka, Bangladesh, and the Pearl River Delta (PRD), China, "PRD 3" focused on informal migration and migrant settlements in the mega-cities of China's PRD. The team consisted of two independent sub-projects, a "Cologne group" based at the Institute of Geography, University of Cologne (led by Frauke Kraas who also led the priority programme), and our "Berlin group" based at the Institute of Chinese Studies, Freie Universität Berlin. I would like to thank Yuan Yuan and Kimiko Suda, who, as research assistants and doctoral students in the Berlin group, were highly committed to the project work and pursued their creative and independent dissertation projects with great vigour. I would also like to thank Frauke Kraas and Tabea Bork-Höffer for the intensive, well-coordinated and effective collaboration.

The Berlin group's main partners were from Sun Yat-sen University in Guangzhou, especially from the Faculty of Sociology and Social Anthropology. I am very grateful to Zhou Daming for his continuous support. I would also like to thank Zhu Jiangang and Cheng Yu, as well as Jack Wing-Kit Chan from the School of Government. I have learned a lot from all of them during my three years of research and teaching at Sun Yat-sen University (SYSU). Without Huang Yuan's support in navigating the daily academic routine, I am sure many things would not have been achieved, and I would like to thank him for that. A workshop was held at SYSU in 2012 on "Outsiders, Migrant Workers, New Citizens - Interpreting qualitative interviews with different groups of migrants in the mega-urban Pearl River Delta/China. What story to tell?" In addition to the project members and partners, Cai He, Deborah Davis, Ellen Friedman, He Shenjing, Jing Xiang, Liu Mengqin, Liu Ye, Amy Zhang, Zheng Guanghuai and others contributed to the success of the workshop with presentations and/or contributions to the discussion. The question of the workshop continued to haunt me for some time. Inspiring international research collaborations have also developed in Guangzhou with both the Sun Yat-sen Center for Migrant Health Policy and the United Nations Research Institute for Social Development (UNRISD) on migration and health in China. None of this would have been possible without Ling Li and Sarah Cook. Looking back, the conditions of fieldwork at the time and the dynamic synergies of international research contexts in and with China seem particularly valuable, and the potential for collaborative knowledge production cannot be overestimated.

Earlier versions of individual chapters of this book were presented at the Urban China Conference 2017 in London, at the Max Planck Institute for Social Anthropology 2018 in Halle, and at two workshops of the project "Social Worlds: Chinese Cities as Places of Worldmaking," a sub-project of the collaborative research initiative "Worldmaking from a Global Perspective: A Dialogue with China" (since 2020). The sub-project is led by Björn Alpermann, University of Würzburg, and Elena

Meyer-Clement, University of Copenhagen, and I would like to thank them both for my time as a temporary fellow in this project. I would also like to thank Chris Hann, Ryanne Flock, Xie Kailing and Michael Malzer for their valuable comments on earlier versions of individual chapters of this book. Many thanks to Marlene Schoofs for checking and correcting the language of earlier versions of several chapters over the years, for her patience and thoughtful comments, and for her stimulating questions and suggestions. Last but not least, I am very grateful to the first readers of the book manuscript, Monika Schädler, Elena Meyer-Clement and Gao Xiaoxue, for taking the time to read it carefully, asking provocative questions and making constructive suggestions. All remaining errors or mistakes are clearly mine.

About the Author

Bettina Gransow has been Associate Professor of Chinese Studies at the Freie Universität Berlin, Germany, since 1999. From 2009 to 2012, she was a Visiting Professor at Sun Yat-sen University in Guangzhou, China. Her research interests include Chinese migrations and the migration–urbanisation nexus, China's infrastructure strategy and social safeguard policies, and the production of knowledge in Chinese sociology. She has published widely in these areas. Her research has had academic and policy impact, including consultancy for the Asian Development Bank and the World Bank. Since 2023, she has been a member of the International Advisory Board of the Urban China Research Network. Her most recent publication was a guest-edited special issue of the *Journal of Current Chinese Affairs* (1/2024) on "Chinese Migrants in Metropolises Abroad: Agency, Interactions, Belonging".

Contents

Chapter 1

Producing and Negotiating Transient Mega-Urban Spaces: Migrant Agency and Migration Governance in China's Risk Society

If I were asked to describe in a few sentences what this book is about, the spontaneous answer would be something like this: It focuses on migrants or groups of migrants in Chinese megacities who – according to the official migration and urbanisation policies of the Chinese government – are not supposed to be there, or who would not be expected to be there. In order to gain a better understanding of their situation, interviews were conducted with migrants who, it turned out, did not necessarily see themselves as "migrants." It should also be noted that one of the most important sources of information for the micro-studies presented in this book is the answers given by the migrants interviewed to questions that were not actually asked – in other words, the respondents' "message in a bottle." And could this message in a bottle – by revealing the perception and production of mega-urban spaces by different migrant groups in Chinese megacities – contain clues to the deeper reasons for a migration and urbanisation policy that repeatedly fails to achieve its goals?

What may sound somewhat puzzling at this point will be explained in this introductory chapter. Starting from the insight that there is no single organisational form of urban integration or incorporation of migrants (Glick Schiller and Caglar, 2011:190, 191), this introductory chapter aims to take a step towards an analytical framework on pathways of (self-)incorporation of different migrant groups in Chinese megacities by producing distinct transient urban spaces out of their own agency. Achieving this goal requires a triangulation of sociological approaches fundamental to the study of the issue, namely, urban sociology, sociology of migration, sociology of space and sociology of risk.

Urban Sociology: "Integration Through Separation"

The topos of the migrant in the megacity takes up the core of all definitions of urbanity: the city as a place where strangers live together (Siebel, 1997:30). The question of how this coexistence can succeed was answered by the classics of urban sociology at the beginning of the 20th century with the seemingly paradoxical formula "integration through separation." While Georg Simmel understood this to mean a process of individualisation characterised by impersonality, indifference and distance, which – according to the rational rules of monetary economics – creates the conditions for personal freedom in the sense of negative integration ("live and let live"), Robert Park focused on integration through community building among immigrants in large cities (Simmel, 1903/1998; Park, 1915; Häußermann, 1997:142). However, as the urban sociologist Hartmut Häußermann has pointed out, this optimism was based on economic growth, which made possible urban indifference as a modern virtue, tolerating and respecting the differences between newcomers and locals. If this basis no longer exists, he warns at the turn of the 21st century, but gives way to conditions of systematic social exclusion, urbanism as a way of life will be endangered (Häußermann, 1997:145, 146).

A Chinese Version of "Integration Through Separation": Urban Villages in China's Megacities

Since the reform and opening-up policy, urban villages or villages in the city (*chengzhongcun*)[1] have developed as a type of migrant settlement in Chinese megacities, which can be understood as another variant of "integration through separation." Basically, two types of rural–urban migrant settlements have emerged in Chinese megacities: homogeneous and heterogeneous urban villages. Homogeneous urban villages are usually

[1] 城中村 or urban villages. Both concepts will be used interchangeably.

named after the provinces of origin of their migrant residents (most of whom come from the same areas and have similar occupations), such as Zhejiang Village or Xinjiang, Henan or Sichuan Villages. Zhejiang Village in Beijing represents a homogeneous type of urban village and was the first to be extensively researched (Wang, 1995; Xiang, 2005; Zhang, 2001). Heterogeneous urban villages were once natural villages that retained their original names (such as Shipai, Liede or Sanyuanli in Guangzhou) but changed markedly as a result of urban expansion (Li, 2020). These "villages in the city" became mixed settlements of migrants from very different places of origin and could well be called "villages of strangers." In a sense, Simmel's and Park's two different understandings of the formula "integration through separation" seem to have materialised in these two types of urban villages. While the homogeneous villages stand in the tradition of Robert Park's "community building of immigrants in big cities," the heterogeneous villages can be seen as places of indifferent coexistence of strangers. At the same time, urban villages are surrounded by high-rise buildings that radiate anonymity and – as in the case of Shenzhen – are likely to be home to other migrants.

As more and more rural migrants flocked to the Pearl River Delta, attracted by the expanding export industries and in search of cheap housing, the former peasants in their now-encircled villages discovered the profitable business of renting to migrants and began to add floors on their houses (Gransow, 2011:81, 82). It was a win-win situation for both the peasant turned landlord on the one hand and the peasant turned migrant in need of affordable housing on the other. But since their emergence, entrepreneurial city governments have been eager to redevelop these informal settlements.[2] This was partly in order to gain access to the villages' valuable land and to realise their plans for a modern, efficient and profitable city through redevelopment projects, and partly because a potentially slum-like development of the urban villages would have run counter to the self-image of a modern socialist city. They explicitly distanced themselves from the "Latin Americanisation" of large cities. Megacities without slums are seen as a kind of socialist seal of approval. Overall, for migrant tenants in the urban villages, redevelopment means increased

[2]For example, Guangzhou's "Three-Olds Redevelopment" policy, starting in 2010, refers to old villages in the city, old industrial areas, and old residential districts and their redevelopment. Press conference on Guangzhou's "Three-Olds Redevelopment" programme, 18 August 2010, www.gz.gov.cn/business/htmlfiles/gzgoven/s7467/20 1101/719458.html.

insecurity, uncertainty and higher risks of being forced to find new housing – more expensive and less convenient – and possibly new jobs. The shrinking supply of low-cost housing in urban villages, the lack of new affordable housing being built, and the slowing economy have created a situation in which migrants find themselves competing for limited resources. This may result in less room for migrants' "integration through separation."

Sociology of Migration: "Integration Through Agency"

Turning to the sociology of migration to further explore the question of migrants' pathways to mega-urban integration, we shall firstly deal with some of its fundamental critiques. These include accusations of predominantly policy-driven mainstream migration research, a lack of migration theorising and, as part of this, a lack of meaningful conceptualisation of how migrants exert agency within broader structural constraints. For example, Stephen Castles has called for migration to be studied in the context and as part of processes of transformation of social structures and institutions (Castles 2010: 1566). He points to the difficulty of separating between a social-scientific and a political understanding of migration. "Claims of academic neutrality", he argues, "can mask a sedentary bias – an unquestioning assumption that migration is a bad thing. Yet theories of global migration should not be based on the normative objective of finding ways of helping people to stay at home. Rather they should be based on the postulate that migration is a normal part of social relations" (Castles, 2010: 1568).

This is not a new demand in the history of migration research, but one that has been neglected time and again.[3] In the sense of such a change in perspective, migration will not be understood in the following as behaviour that deviates from the norm of sedentary societies. Rather, it is assumed that under the conditions of regional and social inequality, migration processes are normal social behaviour in the sense of "human mobility," which is nevertheless controlled and restricted by governments at various levels (cf. Castles, 2010:1568). The tasks that migration

[3] As early as 1958, William Petersen criticised the assumptions of migration research in his general typology of migration, "that man is everywhere sedentary, remaining fixed until he is impelled to move by some force" and countered, "Man migrates because of wanderlust" (Petersen, 1958:258).

policies would then have to fulfil would have to be different from simply opening or closing state (or urban) borders to certain categories of migrants. They would have to aim at overcoming social inequalities and balancing security promises to different groups of the population. Fulfilling these tasks would require a multi-level approach to migration policy (local, national, regional and global) and would have to include international and transnational networks of mobility facilitation. As a consequence, such a migration-oriented approach could also set fundamentally new priorities in international development cooperation and – under the given circumstances – upgrade development cooperation in terms of international relations.

Hein de Haas also complains of a lack of migration theorising. But while Castle's focus is more on the contextualising of migration as part of the transformation process of social structures and institutions, Hein de Haas is more concerned with the agency of migrants. "The main conceptual problem of conventional theoretical accounts of migration," de Haas argues, "remains their inability to meaningfully conceptualise how individual and groups of migrants exert agency within broader structural constraints" (de Haas, 2021:14). Whereas functionalist approaches to migration studies have tended to characterise migrants as "rather soulless individual utility-optimisers," historical-structural accounts would describe migrants as "rather passive victims of global capitalist forces" (*ibid.*). The central challenge for migration theory, according to de Haas, is therefore to develop a conceptual toolkit that takes both structure and agency into account in understanding migration, without ignoring the insights provided by functionalist and neo-Marxist approaches to migration studies (*ibid.*). Moreover, in urban China studies, research on the active agency of migrants in the city has been similarly identified as a research deficit in recent studies (He and Qian, 2017:840).[4]

The present study recognises the legitimate demands for (1) migration research that contextualises migration as part of the processes of transformation in China's economy and society, (2) non-policy-driven migration research, and (3) migration research that begins from the agency of individuals and groups of migrants, while locating them within their broader structural constraints. It first proposes the formula of "integration by migrant agency" as a research path for studying migrants in Chinese

[4]Exceptions were, e.g. Bork-Hüffer (2012) or Liu *et al.* (2015).

megacities from a non-normative perspective. Beyond the formula of "integration through separation" migrants' agency is analysed by drawing on relational sociological approaches to the production or constitution of social space (Lefebvre 1991; Löw 2001; Gao 2021). Second, the study addresses the mismatch between migrants' agency and migration policies that attempt to channel and shape migration processes in China. Third, it identifies this mismatch as a form of risk entanglement, a phenomenon that is characteristic of China's ongoing social transformation process, which goes beyond the transition to a post-Maoist market society and Chinese urbanism (Wu 2022) to include a transformation into a complex risk society as part of an emerging world risk society (Beck 1999, Chang 2017).

Sociology of Space: The Production of Transient Urban Spaces

This study analyses the agency of different groups of migrants in Chinese megacities through their social production of urban spaces, which will be referred to as transient urban spaces in the following. To this end, the micro-studies in the individual chapters are based on a relational understanding of space as developed by Henri Lefebvre as a Marxist-oriented theory of the social production of space and elaborated in Martina Löw's sociological theory of space as a unity of structure and action. Lefebvre's more structurally oriented theory of space finds its concentrated expression in a triadic understanding of space as (1) spatial practice/perceived space; (2) representations of space/conceived space and (3) representational spaces/lived space (associated with images and symbols) (Lefebvre, 1991:30, 38–40). Löw's more action-oriented spatial sociological approach corresponds even more closely to the demand of critical migration sociology and urban China studies to conceptualise migrants' agency in the context of structural constraints.

Löw seeks to understand spaces as products of actions that at the same time exert a structural power. In this sense, she describes three key dimensions of the constitution of space: (1) routinised paths of action (repetitive actions of everyday life); (2) structural dimensions of spatiality (spatial structures); (3) the constitution of places and the emergence of atmospheres (power of spaces) (Löw, 2008:36). Analytically, Löw divides the constitution of space into two different processes, namely, "spacing" and "synthesising" (2001:159, 160). Spacing refers to the constitution of space through the placement of social goods and persons and has to do with building, erecting and positioning, especially the positioning of symbolic markers. The second necessary element in the constitution of space, according to Löw, is synthesising, through which goods and persons are brought together through processes of perception, imagination and memory. While synthesising can take place without the associated spacing – e.g. in planning processes – spacing in practical action is inconceivable without synthesising, for it is perceptual synthesising that makes a space, e.g. the linking of urban buildings (2001:158, 159). Both approaches show that different actors can create very different spaces in the same place, including virtual spaces. Both authors have also formulated their own approaches to sociological urban research, which can be summarised under the keywords "right to the city" (Lefebvre, 1968) and "intrinsic logic of cities" (Berking and Löw, 2008).

The Pearl River Delta (PRD) is predestined as a site for analysing the production of transient urban spaces in the context of human mobility. It has a century-long history of emigration, return, re-emigration, and translocal and transnational ties, which are visible in the region's architectural formations. Since the beginning of the reform policy, it has probably become the most important immigration region in China, with a comparatively high proportion of young women among the migrants. At the same time, the PRD has become a kind of seismograph for the relationship between technological progress, especially in information technology and digitalisation, urban and regional development, and the composition of migrant, post-migrant and local urban populations. The scope, fluidity and scale of these developments, as well as the multiple attempts to control and manage them through migration and urbanisation policies, including the resulting intended and unintended consequences, make the PRD a giant social laboratory par excellence.

At this point, where we are concerned with the social production of mega-urban spaces through the agency of rural–urban migrants, the concept of transient urban spaces will be defined as spaces where mobile subjects in the city arrive, stay or leave (voluntarily or involuntarily), where they can make a living (more or less), often in informal arrangements, where they manage to adapt or not, develop or stagnate, implying upward and downward mobility. Transient urban spaces are shared by people from the same or different places, with similar or very different social networks, often smaller than larger, as comrades or as strangers, with translocal and transnational trajectories, as individuals, groups or families. Transient urban spaces can have the potential to trigger new and transformative uses of urban spaces. In a mega-urban agglomeration such as the PRD in southern China, the high degree of mobility and the influx of large numbers of migrants produce an experiment of the city in which transient actors are bound to the place in different ways and with different levels of tolerable coexistence (see Albrow, 1997:52; Gransow, 2012; Bork-Hüffer *et al.*, 2016). Transient urban spaces cannot be equated with migrant communities or migrant enclaves: What the mobile subjects, presented in the micro-studies, experience is very different from the traditional notion of community based on a shared local history and culture.

Mismatch between Migration and Migration Policy: The Hukou System as a "Sorting Machine"

Although internal rural–urban migration does not involve crossing national borders, the household registration system (known as the *hukou* system) has been a significant barrier to moving from poorer inland regions to the richer urban areas along China's east coast. The distinction between rural and urban residency means that individuals with rural *hukou*, as opposed to those with urban *hukou*, are denied various public services such as health, education and housing in their urban migration destinations. Similar to international borders functioning as a "sorting machine" for migration (Mau, 2021), the *hukou* system acts as a filter for internal Chinese migration to the benefit of entrepreneurial city governments.

Hukou registration has not always had this function. In the early days of the PRC, before the *hukou* system was introduced in 1958, a dual system of rural and urban households emerged. The background to this was a nationwide land reform, which resulted in rural households owning a plot of land (initially private, later collectivised) on the one hand and urban households organised into work units (*danweis*),[5] "small societies" with the right to a job, subsidised housing, access to urban educational institutions and integration into a health and pension system, on the other (Lü and Perry, 1997). With the introduction of the planned economy (1953), it soon became clear that the provision of comprehensive services to the urban population (which at the time represented no more than 15%

[5] 单位.

of the total population) could only be achieved by transferring resources from the countryside to the cities, at the expense of the peasants. There were spontaneous rural–urban migrations, but these were quickly stopped. In the scarcity economy of the Mao era, this dual system of rural and urban households formed the basis for the allocation of resources and subsidies to selected groups of the population, mainly urban dwellers. Rationed food and goods were distributed using a ration coupon system. It was only in this function that the *hukou* system became an effective means of combating spontaneous migration. It was – and remains – an instrument for managing social inequality.

With the transition to a market economy, the ration coupon system disappeared and the "sorting logic" of the *hukou* system changed. Instead of regulating access to rationed food and goods, it now regulated rural–urban migration by opening and closing access to public goods, entitlements, subsidies and other privileges reserved for urban citizens, but now in an environment characterised by competition between cities and their entrepreneurial activities. From 1995 to 2003, the *hukou* system was made effective through the introduction of additional deterrent measures against unwanted migrants. For example, the so-called "three-without population" (*sanwu renyuan*)[6] – migrants without income, accommodation or papers in large cities – could be detained locally by the security authorities and then sent back home. Public outrage, media attention and the support of dedicated lawyers led to the repeal of the regulation on which the detention centres were based.[7] Detention centres were later converted into shelters for the homeless (Gransow, 2011:70, 71). Since then, exclusion from urban social infrastructure has mainly acted as a filter to allow migrant workers, but not costly family members such as schoolchildren, to remain in cities.

While the PRD, as the economic powerhouse of Guangdong province (and beyond), continues to attract many (and different types of) migrants, particularly to its largest megacities, the chances of migrants making the "mobile-to-settled" transition are relatively low (Yang and Chan, 2023:3). There are many factors that discourage migrants from settling down: In addition to the notorious *hukou* system and the growth limits of megacities such as Guangzhou and Shenzhen, these factors include lack of access

[6]三无人员.

[7]This practice came under public criticism after a young graphic artist named Sun Zhigang died in one of those detention centres in March 2003.

to affordable housing; the high cost of living in the city, which is seen as too expensive for raising a family on low wages; finding childcare during long working hours, which is seen as difficult and too expensive; and reluctance to give up rural land rights (related to rural *hukou*) in exchange for an urban *hukou* in a small city with limited social services (Yang and Chan, 2023:6). Despite these discouraging conditions, tens of millions of migrants find their way to the PRD, particularly to Shenzhen and Guangzhou.

In parallel with this development, a migration and urbanisation policy began to emerge in the mid-1990s that aimed to steer rural–urban migrants away from large cities and towards medium-sized and, above all, smaller cities by making the *hukou* system more flexible in order to reduce the pressure on the material and social infrastructure of large cities – albeit with only moderate success. A new urbanisation plan (NUP, 2014–2020) also emphasised smaller cities (Guojia, 2014).[8] It aimed to manage both migration flows to smaller cities and local governments' access to land resources by concentrating residential areas[9] and developing transport infrastructure. One of the aims of this plan was to take a step towards overcoming the inequality between migrants in the city and the local urban population. To this end, the degree of urbanisation of the "permanent population"[10] was to be increased to around 60 per cent by 2020.[11] In addition, the integration of 100 million migrants was to increase the urbanisation rate of the urban *hukou* population from 32.5% in 2010 to 45% in 2020. With its policy of opening up smaller cities to unrestricted immigration and sealing off large megacities from further rural–urban migration, the new urbanisation plan continued the sorting logic of previous migration and urbanisation policies. More specifically than before, the new urbanisation plan called on the governments of major megacities to set population caps.[12] Since 2016, Beijing, Shanghai, Guangzhou,

---

[8] This is evident already in the choice of words for urbanisation 城镇化 (*chengzhenhua*), as opposed to 城市化 (*chengshihua*) where 镇 stands for small towns and 市 for cities.

[9] On *in situ* urbanisation, see Meyer-Clement (2016).

[10] The statistical category of "permanent population" (常住人口 *changzhu renkou*) combines the local *hukou population* and the population without local *hukou* who stay in the city for more than six months.

[11] The degree of urbanisation exceeded the 50% mark for the first time in 2011.

[12] According to a 2014 definition by the State Council, a city-region with a permanent population of five to ten million inhabitants is called a megacity (特大城市 *teda chengshi*)

Shenzhen and other megacities have proposed plans to control population ceilings.[13] The 14th Five-Year Plan (2021–2025, with an outlook to 2035) reaffirmed the policy of the NUP. Some authors have fundamentally criticised the NUP's goal of capping the population of large megacities: "Given the superior economic and educational opportunities in the megacities and super-megacities, scholars question the effectiveness of imposing differentiated *hukou* systems on cities of different sizes as a means of achieving the goal of optimisation" (Chu, 2020; Guojia, 2014:2).

A five-year action plan for a so-called "new people-centred urbanisation strategy (until 2029)", released by the State Council in 2024, addressed some of the issues discussed above, particularly with regard to the provision of public services to rural migrants and their families in large cities. The action plan pursues the implementation of its goals in two different ways: In regions with low rates of urbanisation and large populations, the focus will be on increasing the level of urbanisation; in areas with already high levels of urbanisation rates and continuous agglomeration, modern metropolitan areas (*xiandaihua dushiquan*)[14] should contribute to transform the development mode of megacities so that central cities and surrounding cities can enjoy shared growth (State Council, 2024).

Obviously, the economic resources concentrated in the megacities and the opportunities offered by the labour market attract migrants much more than the smaller cities. This is due to the fact that not only do smaller cities have less economic power and are much further down the social hierarchy of Chinese cities, but they also require access to the local social networks that influence the distribution of resources to a greater extent than in large cities. Without such networks it is hardly possible for outsiders to gain a foothold. The long-standing asymmetry between the planned or expected immigration and the actual, more extensive immigration to the megacities has resulted in a larger number of rural–urban migrants living in the

---

and a city-region with a permanent population of more than ten million inhabitants is called a large megacity (超大城市 *chaoda chengshi*).

[13] It was stipulated that Guangzhou should not exceed the target of 15.5 million permanent residents and Shenzhen should not exceed 14.8 million permanent residents by 2020. Guangzhou proposed to control the size of its population "moderately" and had a permanent population of 18.73 million in 2020; Shenzhen grew from about 10 million in 2010 to 17.56 million in 2020. https://m.21jingji.com/article/20210515/herald/ff7d5ea380301c269fb7bfc5d2205608_zaker.html (accessed June 10, 2024).

[14] 现代化都市圈.

Chinese megacities, inconsistent with the objectives of the urbanisation planning and migration policy.[15] It is these migrants in the PRD megacities that are the main subject of the following micro-studies.

One explanation for the contradictory development of migration practices and migration policies is that they follow different logics, interests and perceptions of risk. This becomes clearer when considering what constitutes risk in the context of migration. While Chinese migration and urbanisation policy perceives risks to the city (or country) as emanating from the mass of migrants and aims to avert high costs, slum-like developments and possible social conflicts from the already vulnerable and overburdened megacities, for the migrants themselves, it is a matter of their own individual risks (or those of their families), risks that they take during an informal stay in a migration-restricted megacity and risks to which they are exposed but of which they have only a limited awareness. It is unclear where these differently defined risks and risk perceptions of migrant actors and migration policymakers intersect. There are also other actors involved, such as residents with urban *hukou* or post-migrant urban residents with permanent residence permits. In order to analyse this relationship between migrants and decision-makers in megacities in more detail, the following section examines approaches to risk research in this context.

Sociology of Risk: Migration as Risk Entanglement

In the migration literature, the concept of risk is not so rare but is rarely theorised (Williams and Balaz, 2012:176). Of fundamental importance in the context of migration are distinctions such as (1) that between risk and uncertainty (*ibid.*), the latter being attributed mainly to insufficient knowledge and the unpredictability of the future; (2) that between "risks taken knowingly" and "risks imposed on people" (Douglas and Wildawsky, 1983: 16); and (3) that between risk and danger, i.e. that possible damage is either attributed to one's own (risk) decision or is seen as externally induced, namely, as a danger (Luhmann, 1991:30, 31). According to Williams and Balaz, risk theoretical considerations that have influenced migration research have mainly been made from an economic viewpoint.

[15]The difference between the 641 million urban *hukou* population and the 902 million permanent urban population in 2020 is 261 million urban migrants, who are more or less excluded from access to urban social infrastructure (Chan, 2021:2).

From this perspective, risks are seen as objectively "real" rather than "socially constructed," with the rational-behaving individual at the centre (Williams and Balaz, 2012:169).

The theoretical conceptualisation of risk in the context of migration and urban development will be explored in three steps: Firstly, the subject will be addressed on the basis of socially constructed approaches to risk research. In a second step, the social relationality of risks will be discussed and illustrated using the example of the lack of controllability of migration in China as described earlier. Finally, in a third step, the question of the connection between social transformation in China and the emergence of a Chinese risk society will be addressed.

A socially constructed understanding of risk, based on the orientation of the 'governmentality literature' and Michel Foucault's lectures (Foucault 1991),[16] is concerned with the practices, techniques and rationalities by which a risk is to be made calculable. François Ewald demonstrated this in his classic study "L'état providence" from the perspective of the Foucault school. He explained the genesis of the category of risk from the social emergence of the insurance system as a calculable probability and a private or state-sponsored promise of security (Ewald, 1993). If risk is seen as a form of calculative rationality, then migrants' technologies of self and migration governance can be defined as particular modes of risk calculation. These are informed by a specific intention and body of knowledge, which might be partial with regard to the outcomes of migration trajectories or migration policies and their implementation.

Niklas Luhmann introduced the distinction between risks and dangers, stating that "the risks that a decision-maker takes and must take can become a danger for those affected" (Luhmann, 1991:117). In terms of relational risk research, Boholm and Corvellec (2011) have set out a cognitive relationship between two different cognitive objects. They define risk objects as things, persons or events that are perceived by individuals as dangerous. In contrast, objects at risk for them are things, persons or events that are valued by individuals and considered to be at risk. From this perspective, risk is defined as relational because it establishes a cognitive link between the object at risk and the risk object perceived to threaten the former. Von Scheve and Lange (2023) build on this approach

[16] Foucault's neologism 'governmentality', a semantic combination of 'govern' and 'mentality', indicates a close relationship between the constitution of technologies of power and technologies of self, an alignment of the modern state and the modern subject.

with the introduction of the concept of "risk entanglement." They define it as "a situation in which a number of actors is, or becomes, related to each other through their construction of risk objects and objects at risk" (von Scheve and Lange, 2023:4).[17] This leads to the conclusion that the dilemma between migrants, who are attracted to megacities in large numbers, and city governments as decision-makers, who seek to ward them off with appropriate decisions in order to protect the vulnerable megacities, their formally resident population and urban infrastructures from being overburdened, constitutes a risk entanglement between migrants' agency and mega-urban migration policy. In a further step, the next section takes up Stephen Castle's call for migration studies to be embedded in the theoretical context of processes of transformation of social structures and institutions and asks whether China, as a society in transition, is also in transition to a risk society or has already developed one.

Urban China – Transformation into a Risk Society?

Ulrich Beck's theory of risk society began with a focus on German society and was published shortly after the Chernobyl nuclear disaster (1986). He later extended his focus to the world risk society (Beck, 1999).[18] According to Ulrich Beck, a risk society results from a dynamic inherent in industrial society. When industrial society maintains an underlying belief in progress, namely, in the ultimate ability of science and technology to solve all problems, which at the same time means equating technical with social progress, it generates the constellations of the risk society and systematically justifies the negative social and environmental consequences of technological progress. It is precisely this feature that distinguishes risk society from industrial society, namely, the impossibility of attributing risks to an external source (Beck, 1986:300f.). "The entry into the risk society occurs at the moment when the hazards that are now decided upon and consequently produced by society undermine and/or cancel the established safe systems of the existing risk calculations of the welfare state.

---

[17] In addition to perceptions and cognitive assessments of risk, the authors also want to use the concept of risk entanglement to include the actor level in order to find out how risk constructions manifest themselves in social relations and risk practices (*ibid.*).

[18] A 2007 published German book of the same title (*Weltrisikogesellschaft,* Frankfurt am Main: Suhrkamp) is not a translation of the 1999 book but an updated study of earlier work.

In contrast to earlier industrial risks, nuclear, chemical, ecological and genetic risks ... cannot be compensated or insured against" (Beck, 1999:76, 77). A risk society can thus also be understood as an outgrowth of the logic of national security, a modernity which, with the welfare state and the insurance system, made the consequences of systemic and individual risks appear controllable.

Previous considerations of the application of Beck's risk theory to Chinese society can be roughly divided into three approaches. Firstly, there are approaches that identify risks as social problems and seek to address them through forms of social governance. They are in the tradition of pragmatic social science that focuses on concrete solutions to problems.[19] Secondly, there are approaches that analyse individual Chinese policy fields from the perspective of a risk society.[20] Thirdly, there are approaches that discuss the question of the transferability of risk theory to China itself (e.g. Gransow, 2003; Xiao, 2012; Chang, 2017). Only the last one will be discussed in more detail here.

The short answer to the question of whether Beck's theory of risk society is applicable to China's current transformation society would be "no." The short answer to the question of whether China's transformation society can be characterised as a risk society would be "yes." China is a fast-developing society (after the COVID-19 pandemic, somewhat out of steam) undergoing multiple transformations: from a planned to a market economy, from an agrarian to an industrial/service/information/digital society, from a rural to an urbanised society and from an isolated to a globalising society, with a logic of sequential and sometimes simultaneous opening and closing. However, this development not only generates (intended) accelerated economic growth but also generates (unintended) accelerated processes that in turn generate new forms of poverty, deeper social inequalities, unemployment, damage to health and the environment, and other forms of negative impacts. Embedded in such a dynamic social environment, the simultaneous occurrence of different types of environmental and social risks creates an extremely complex situation.

Against this background, two points would argue against applying Beck's analysis to Chinese society from the outset. First, in formulating

[19]For example, Wu and Zhou, 2006; Tang and Zhang 2007; Suttmeier, 2008; Mu, 2018, Liu and Chen, 2024.

[20]For example, Yuan, 2021 and Gong, 2020 on the COVID-19 pandemic or Wang, 2018 on urbanisation risks.

his theory, Beck clearly had in mind highly developed Western industrial nations with their corresponding economic, political and legal institutions. Second, Beck describes the risk society as a temporal and qualitative successor of the industrial society (Gransow, 2003:31). Nevertheless, Beck's "risk society" has been translated into Chinese (2004) and has sparked an ongoing debate about China within the world risk society.

Xiao (2012), for example, notes a difference in the nature of individualisation processes in the risk society described by Beck and in the Chinese transition society. Although China's transition to a market economy has brought about a process of individualisation, since this is not accompanied by institutionalised forms of individual freedom and democracy as in Beck's risk society, and since China has not yet created a comprehensive welfare state, this would not correspond to the institution-dependent process of individualisation described by Beck (Beck, 1986:210), but should rather be described as "individualisation with limited institutionalisation" (*bei shanjiande zhiduhua de getihua*),[21] which is oriented towards the particular interests of individuals and small groups. At the same time, this has led to an extensive individualisation of risks (Xiao, 2012:49). Despite this demarcation, Xiao Ying agrees with characterisations of China as a risk society (*ibid.*). In particular, Xiao sees an intrinsic link between the Chinese risk society and the world risk society.

Following his own studies on "compressed modernity" in Korea and China, Chang Kyung-sup analysed Beck's theory of risk and identified both as complex risk societies, with China being even more complex than Korea. Chang defined compressed modernity as "a civilisational condition in which economic, political, social and/or cultural changes take place in an extremely condensed manner in terms of both time and space, and in which the dynamic coexistence of mutually disparate historical and social elements leads to the construction and reconstruction of a highly complex and fluid social system" (Chang, 2017). The rapid economic development in East Asia, which was based on the mobilisation of cheap labour, the exploitation of natural resources (rather than on improved efficiency and safety in production processes) and the pursuit of "faster and faster" efficiency, led to an attitude of "growth first, safety later." The downgrading of safety in favour of "development patriotism" can be attributed to a combination of a lack of experience in public risk management, the immaturity of the market economy and the intervention of the Chinese

[21] 被删减的制度化的个体化.

developmental state, and has slowed down the self-regulating mechanisms of the market.[22] Even the half-hearted reform of the "rule of law" has done little to correct the situation. A lack of safety management (Chang, 2017:9) is reflected in massive environmental hazards, industrial disasters, food contamination, fire and traffic accidents, and serious construction defects due to rapid building. The transition to a "socialist market economy" has led to an accumulation of risks for workers, consumers and citizens in the form of collusion between local government officials (under pressure to demonstrate economic growth successes) and companies (who previously had no reason to fear excessive safety controls on working conditions). The willingness to expose oneself to dangerous working conditions has thus become a decisive factor in market competitiveness. "This is particularly evident," writes Chang, "among 'illegal migrant workers' in the megacities ..." He continues, "It is paradoxical that the Chinese government perceives them as a risk factor at the societal level" (Chang, 2017:13). This observation, which fits well within the theoretical context of China's complex risk society, reflects what has been identified above as the entanglement of migrants' practices with migration and urbanisation policies.

Urban Migration Governance as Risk Prevention

As previously stated, the governance of urban migration can be conceptualised as a distinct mode of risk calculation and risk prevention. The quantifying, qualifying and balancing of sources of danger associated with migration processes should make them manageable as part of urban governance (see Follis, 2021:67). In the context of China's rapid urbanisation, this means in particular making decisions about the exclusion or inclusion of certain migrant groups in the city. It should be noted that urban governance in China is also referred to as entrepreneurial governance. Nevertheless, as Wu Fulong and Zhang Fangzhu have argued, urbanisation in China has not produced an urbanism beyond the control of the state. This is evident, for example, in the current promotion of

[22] Security does not have the status of a public good because (1) the party-state is too closely intertwined with enterprises; (2) social security is much lower for farmers and the self-employed than for urban workers; and (3) there are large differences in the spatial distribution of risk (Chang, 2017:13).

participation at the neighbourhood level, which is organised by the state. The party-state itself pursues a wide range of non-economic goals, particularly those of legitimacy and stability, but at the same time uses entrepreneurial means to achieve its goals. In this way, it has an impact on urban governance (Wu and Zhang, 2025:4,182,183), including the governance of urban migration, which is also characterised by a whole range of economic, political and social stability demands from the party-state.

The management of urban migration can be roughly divided into two categories: mechanisms of exclusion and mechanisms of inclusion of particular groups of migrants. In recent decades, with the gradual relaxation of the *hukou* system and the opening up of ever larger cities to the influx of rural–urban migrants, there has been a gradual trend towards more inclusive migration policies. However, this does not apply to large and very large megacities. Since 2016, these have been subject to specific 'ceilings' on the size of their permanent population. While there is broad agreement that cities cannot indefinitely accommodate the influx of people, and that a city's carrying or management capacity can be seen as a 'red line', it is difficult to come up with a universally convincing number of people that a city can accommodate (Liu, 2023:34,35).[23]

Measures to exclude migrants from urban areas are generally unpopular, especially when they involve violent and coercive interventions such as the demolition of migrants' illegal structures (Yang and Wang, 2023:206).[24] Furthermore, when combined with other forms of exclusion (e.g. the exclusion of migrant children from municipal schools), these measures pose significantly different dangers to municipal decision-makers than those they perceive in the context of inclusion policies. The governance of urban migration through exclusion aims to ward off potential threats, conflicts and costs for the city. However, this approach may have harmful consequences, such as leading to a securitisation of

[23]A draft of Guangzhou's urban development plan (2017–2035), published in 2018 sets a cap of 20 million permanent residents for the year 2035. By then, the city's infrastructure and public services should be able to serve around 25 million people. (广州市城市总体规划 2017–2035. (Master Plan for the City of Guangzhou. Draft Public Notice) http://ghzyj.gz.gov.cn/myzj/doc_1519632992185_0.pdf.

[24]An example that led to a wave of public criticism was the expulsion of migrants from Daxing (Beijing) in November 2017, a form of 'special regulation' intended to highlight the implementation of a policy of 'capping' the size of Beijing's population.

migration governance (Chapter 3) or the stigmatisation of specific migrant groups (Chapter 5).

Conversely, an urban migration policy geared towards inclusion means that problems of social and regional inequality or conflict situations that have led to migration (e.g. in minority areas) may now be transferred to the place of immigration. Moreover, a top-down integration policy is problematic for both the local *hukou* population and urban migrants: for migrants, it leads to considerable uncertainty and the feeling that they cannot take their fate into their own hands, while the local population fears that any benefits granted to the migrant population will be at the expense of their own well-being (Yang and Wang, 2023: 204, 205). In addition, Yang Shangguang and Wang Danyang identify several factors that are important for the success of an inclusive policy, but which have not yet been implemented. These are: (1) an adequate database of urban population trends to enable proper planning of financial and human resources for the provision of public services to the permanent urban population; (2) the establishment of an independent department to deal with the affairs of urban migrants and to undertake long-term reflection on how to limit social exclusion, maintain social justice, and promote social inclusion; (3) access for migrants in megacities to policy knowledge and information in order to exercise their rights and adequately express their demands regarding the implementation of urban migration policies in an appropriate manner; and (4) improvements in the implementation of migration policies at the national, local and grassroots levels, as well as professional support such as feasibility studies on financing or institutional design (Yang and Wang, 2023: 204, 205).

While the Chinese government's long-term thinking tends towards an integrative migration policy – at least with regard to internal migration, integrative measures in urban migration governance were rather rare for the migrant groups covered in the following micro-studies.

(De-)Categorisation of "Migrants" and Chapter Introductions

While in this introductory chapter the terms migrant, rural–urban migrant and migrants in the city have been used in a very general – one might even say undifferentiated – sense, here it is necessary to explain how this broader concept is unpacked into different groups of migrants in megacities that will be the focus of the following chapters.

There are many ways to categorise the increasingly diverse migrant and post-migrant populations in China's megacities. From a theoretical migration perspective (based on positive and negative freedom as manifestations of very different conditions of migration), Hein de Haas (2021:27, Table 2) has suggested four basic categories: precarious migration, improvement migration, distress migration and "free migration." The first two categories would fit the focus of this study. In general, criteria for categorising migration or migrants may include demographic characteristics, generations of migrants, occupations and their changes due to technological innovation, and migration flows, such as short and long distance, from where to where, return migration, urban migrants moving to larger cities and international migration from the Global North or the Global South (Wang *et al.*, 2023:325).

Cinzia Losavio points out that the analytical categories used by researchers are often determined by the legal, political and administrative categories used to describe migrants. Statistical categories, for example, she argues, make migration appear as a controlled and controllable phenomenon (Losavio, 2021:49). Host societies,[25] she elaborates, tend to develop mechanisms of labelling and hierarchical classifications towards migrants. They go hand in hand with mechanisms of inclusion and exclusion, which can correspond to the logic of economic growth or take the form of migration management that follows a logic of public order (Losavio, 2021:56). These two different logics of opening up and closing down to migrants go hand in hand with assessments of labour, skills and talents and are reflected in point systems that serve as filters to pick out the "good migrants" and leave the others to fend for themselves.

The approximately 120 qualitative interviews on which the microstudies presented in this volume are based[26] were conducted between 2009 and 2012 as part of research projects on migrants in the megacities of the PRD, mainly in Guangzhou but also in Shenzhen and Foshan.[27] The original idea of these exploratory interviews, which were initially designed to focus on mega-urban informality and migrant health issues

---

[25] Host societies, it should be added, include national governments and city governments.

[26] With the exception of Chapter 5.

[27] The interviews used here were organised by the author in the context of her research projects within the framework of the Priority Programme "Megacities-Megachallenges. Informal Dynamics of Global Change," (2007–2013). For an overview of the results of the priority programme, see Kraas *et al.* (2019).

was to break through the commonly used and generalising terms such as *liudong renkou* (floating population) and *nongmingong* (peasant workers)[28] used in labelling migrants in the city. Instead, the aim was to make visible the wide range and internal differentiation that these terms conceal, namely, as distinct groups of migrants who are nevertheless all part of the megacity landscape in their own way and represent a wide range of forms of migration. The different target groups of the following micro-studies include mainly intra-Chinese rural–urban migrants but also international migrants from the global South; mainly labour migrants but also migrants for education; mainly legal migrants but also undocumented migrants; and mainly voluntary migrants but also involuntary migrants.

Qualitative social research is an iterative process, and the intensive analysis of the interview material provided, among other things, clues to the interviewees' views and self-perceptions that went beyond the original research framework. Re-reading and re-hearing the interview material, it became increasingly clear that for each of these migrant groups, specific risk situations, risk perceptions, and thoughts and actions about their safety and self-care were central. Thus, risk perceptions (including risk ignorance) are identified as an integral part of the agency and everyday actions of the different migrant groups in creating, transforming or accommodating transient urban spaces.[29]

The following chapters are structured in such a way that their starting point is the agency and self-image of each exemplary focus group. These are analysed from the perspective of relational spatial sociology in order to find out which transient urban spaces are constituted, produced or used by them. The spatial perceptions and spatial constitutions of the various migrant actors then themselves become the starting point for questioning the blind spots of migration and urbanisation policies with regard to the specific focus group of migrants. To this end, each chapter outlines the relevant legal and policy frameworks, poses the question of the compatibility of migrant practices and migration governance, and highlights the entanglement of risks, or at least the gap between them. Specific policy areas, e.g. health, education or labour, are highlighted both for the respective migrant groups and for migration governance. The resulting

[28]流动人口， 农民工.

[29]It is important to note that numerous other significant groups of rural migrants in cities are also in specific risk situations, including those belonging to national minorities and school-aged migrant children (see, e.g. Ampuero Ruiz, 2021; Friedman, 2022).

presentation is intended to make a contribution to a more differentiated sociology of migration and the city, which has so far been accused of lacking agency analyses of migrants in the city and socio-theoretical underpinning.

The chapters present micro-studies of a variety of six migrant groups living in the megacities of the PRD. They perceive their urban environment and individual or collective risks differently and constitute specific transient urban spaces in different ways. What they have in common is that more or less none of them want to be labelled as "migrants," at least this was the experience of our interviews. The spatial and social positioning of each of these migrant groups adds a small piece to and within the societal mosaic of the PRD's expanding and intensifying mega-urban area.

The focus of Chapter 2 is on injured rural–urban migrant workers, who in China are not expected to stay in the city. With less than a third of migrant workers covered by injury insurance (2021), it is generally assumed that migrants who are injured and unable to work will return to the countryside. Based on 22 interviews with migrant workers who suffered work-related accidents in Guangzhou's manufacturing sector in 2009/2010, the chapter asks why they did not return to the countryside and instead stayed in Guangzhou city. Five main reasons are identified, including the decision to sue the employer. It is argued that the body as a "disruptive factor" forms the basis of altered spatial experiences and behaviours, leading to the perception of spaces of vulnerability and the production of spaces of contestation. The analysis is embedded in an introduction to the evolution of occupational health and safety (OHS) in China and its legal and institutional framework (up to the early 2020s). It argues that a "growth first, safety later" attitude, as part of the collusion between local governments and enterprises, shifts work-related health risks to the individual migrant worker.

Chapter 3 focuses on migrant workers' NGOs (mainly in Shenzhen and Guangzhou) and their capacity to create spaces of care for (and with) migrant workers. To this end, it also examines the spatiality of state power and how it restricts the activities of such organisations. Based on eleven interviews conducted in 2011/2012 with eight migrant-worker NGOs in the PRD, it is argued that the reciprocal relationship that developed between migrant NGOs and the "care recipients turned volunteers" was one of trust and an important component of migrants' self-incorporation into the city. Neil Brenner's reflections on the spatiality of state power provide an analytical tool for discovering the production of Chinese party-state space in its three dimensions: state intervention targeting migrant-worker NGOs; state imaginaries of a welfare-focused nonprofit sector; and state perceptions of foreign funding of migrant-worker NGOs as a non-traditional security threat to the Chinese nation. It concludes that the contradictory dynamics of state and non-state actors can also be identified as an example of "risk entanglement."

Chapter 4 focuses on migrant women in the entertainment and sex industry in Shenzhen. Officially, the provision of commercial sex services in China is illegal, morally condemned and socially discriminated against. The chapter consists of two parts: The first part is based on thirty in-depth interviews conducted in Shenzhen in September and October 2009. It takes the interviewees' self-understanding as urban *xiaojie* (Miss) as a starting point to explore what "becoming urban" means for this group of migrants, for whom there is no blueprint for integration into urban society. The second section discusses the urban, legal and political environment in which rural migrant girls and women become urban *xiaojies*, including the underground rules of the sex industry (*jianghu* spaces); the legal framework and enforcement policies on prostitution in China; and the public discourse on the pros and cons of legalising prostitution.

Chapter 5 focuses on African traders who discovered the potential and opportunities of Guangzhou, with its long tradition of international trade. It focuses on two questions: What kinds of urban spaces have African traders produced in an uncomfortable social environment characterised by many instances of everyday discrimination, racism and exclusion? And what impact have local and national immigration policies and legislation had on African traders in Guangzhou? Three types of transnational spaces produced or co-produced by African traders are identified: business spaces, spaces of care created by a variety of different African organisations and spaces of intersection between transnational African migrants and internal Chinese migrants. The second part of the chapter analyses local and national immigration policies, including the construction and targeting of the so-called "triple-illegal" population of foreigners in Guangzhou. One of the main effects of the intense pressure on African traders in Guangzhou has been the emergence of a dispersed pattern of African residence in the PRD.

Chapter 6 focuses on a highly educated group of China's internal migrants, namely college graduates from rural areas who have made it to Guangzhou. While young graduates are expected to return to their region of origin, or at least move to a second- or third-tier city, most prefer to stay in the bustling megacity after graduation. Key questions include the following: What kind of urban spaces have been produced by the agency and individual perspectives of these graduates? Will the educational and migration biographies that have taken them from villages to megacities translate into upward social mobility that will enable them to join the urban middle class? Why are they unwilling to move to smaller towns and instead cling to first-tier cities despite the tense employment conditions there? The chapter is based on thirty in-depth interviews conducted in the second half of 2011 with highly educated rural-to-urban migrants. Their educational biographies are intertwined with their paths up the administrative hierarchy from towns to big cities, where higher education institutions are concentrated. Like other migrants in the city, rural graduates with small budgets often live in one of Guangzhou's many urban villages, but unlike other migrant groups, they prefer to live in a village close to a university campus. Another finding is that the self-positioning of the interviewees in society uses more rigid standards than professional sociological studies to determine the threshold at which one is considered to belong to the middle class. The reasons given for not wanting to move to smaller towns were the lack of social networks, fewer job opportunities and lower social status.

Chapter 7 examines how a group of resettlers from the Three Gorges Dam (TGD) area, who became "resettlement villagers" in Foshan in the early 2000s, appropriated their resettlement space over a period of more than ten years. The chapter is based on twenty-six in-depth interviews conducted in December 2012 with members of the resettlement village in Foshan. Building on the idea of the "deserving" and "undeserving" as applied by Charles Watters (2013) to the field of forced migrants, it argues that the contestation over the resettlement space has arisen from the different perceptions and contextualisations of this space by the local governments involved, the displaced families and the administrative host village. Taken together, this has created a transient urban space in a state of arrested development, without decay but without a clear development perspective.

As a conclusion, Chapter 8 considers the PRD itself as a spatio-temporal transient urban space. This includes the economic upgrading of the region, the growth and competition between the nine cities of Guangdong province, and the ambitious state-led spatial transformation of the PRD into a Greater Bay Area (GBA) in cooperation with Hong Kong and Macau, with the aim of making the GBA a world-class mega-urban region. This development is being driven by processes of population concentration within the PRD, particularly in the four major megacities of Shenzhen, Guangzhou, Dongguan and Foshan. However, it is argued that more needs to be done to facilitate the settlement intentions of younger generations of migrants. Against this background of the enduring promise of the megacity, the empirical-methodological and theoretical contributions of this study are discussed.

References

Albrow, M. (1997). Travelling beyond local cultures: Socioscapes in a global city, in Eade, J. (ed.), *Living the Global City. Globalization as Local Process*, London and New York: Routledge, pp. 37–55.

Ampuero-Ruiz, P. (2021). *'They Must be Represented'. The (Re)production of Social Hierarchies among Migrant Workers in Southern China*, Dissertation (Dr. phil.), Martin-Luther-Universität Halle-Wittenberg.

Beck, U. (1986). *Risikogesellschaft. Auf dem Weg in eine andere Moderne*, Frankfurt am Main: Suhrkamp.

Beck, U. (1999). *World Risk Society*, Cambridge: Polity Press.

Berking, H. and Löw, M. (2008). *Die Eigenlogik der Städte: Neue Wege für die Stadtforschung*, Frankfurt am Main: Campus Verlag.

Boholm, A. and Corvellec, H. (2011). A relational theory of risk, *Journal of Risk Research* 14(2), 175–190.

Bork-Hüffer, T. (2012). *Migrants' Health Seeking Actions in Guangzhou, China. Individual Action, Structure and Agency: Linkages and Change*, Stuttgart: Steiner-Verlag.

Bork-Hüffer, T., Etzold, B., Gransow, B., Tomba, L., Sterly, H., Suda, K., Kraas, F., and Flock, R. (2016). Agency and the making of transient urban spaces: Examples of migrants in the City in the Pearl River Delta, China, and Dhaka, Bangladesh. *Population, Space and Place* 22, 128–145.

Castles, S. (2010). Understanding global migration: A social transformation perspective, *Journal of Ethnic and Migration Studies*, 36(10), 1565–1586.

Chan, K. W. (2021). *Internal Migration in China: Integrating Migration with Urbanization Policies and Hukou Reform. Global Knowledge Partnership on Migration and Development (KNOMAD)*, Policy Note 16 (November), pp. 1–9.

Chang, K.-S. (2017). China as a complex risk society. Risk components of post-socialist compressed modernity, *Temporalités* 26, https://doi.org/10.4000/temporalites.3810.

Chu, Y.-W. (2020). China's new urbanization plan, *Cities* 103, 1–10.

De Haas, H. (2021). A theory of migration: The aspirations-capabilities framework, *Comparative Migration Studies* 9(8), 1–35, https://doi.org/10.1186/s40878-020-00210-4.

Dean, M. (1998). Risk, calculable and incalculable, *Soziale Welt* 49, 25–42.

Ewald, F. (1993). *Der Vorsorgestaat*, Frankfurt am Main: Edition Suhrkamp.

Follis, K. (2021). The politics of conceptualizing border/security, in Carmel, E., Lenner, K., and Paul, R. (eds.), *Handbook on the Governance and Politics of Migration*, Cheltenham: Edward Elgar, pp. 60–72.

Friedman, E. (2022). *The Urbanization of People: The Politics of Development, Labor Markets, and Schooling in the Chinese City*, New York: Columbia University Press.

Gao, X. (2021). *Thinking of Space Relationally. Critical Realism beyond Relativism – A Manifold Study of the Artworld in Beijing*, Bielefeld: Transcript.

Glick Schiller, N. and Caglar, A. (eds.) (2011). Downscaled cities and migrant pathways: Locality and agency without an ethnic lens, in *Locating Migration. Rescaling Cities and Migrants*, Ithaca: Cornell University Press, pp. 190–212.

Gong, W. 龚维斌 (2020). 当代中国社会风险的特点 – 以新冠肺炎疫情及其抗击为例 Dangdai Zhongguo shehui fengxian de tedian – yi xinguan feiyan yiqing jiqi kangji wei li (Characteristics of social risks in contemporary China – The example of the COVID-19 epidemic and its control), 社会学评论 (*Sociological Review*) 8(2), 21–27.

Gransow, B. (2003). Social assessment in China – Action learning for the risk society? *Berliner China-Hefte* 25(Oktober), 30–43.

Gransow, B. (2011). Migrant communities and social change in Chinese megacities: Slum formation or urban innovation? in Bade, K., Lorentz, B., and Pries, L. (eds.), *Migration and Integration. Reflections on Our Common Future*, Leipzig: CEP Europäische Verlagsanstalt, pp. 65–97.

Gransow, B. (2012). Contested urbanization in China: Exploring informal spaces of migrants-in-the-city, *Harvard Asia Quarterly* XIV(1&2), 12–24.

Guojia xinxing chengzhenhua guihua 国家新型城镇化规划 [National new-type urbanization plan (NUP)]. (2014–2020). https://www.gov.cn/zhengce/2014-03/16/content_2640075.htm.

Häußermann, H. (1997). The city and urban sociology: Urban ways of living and the integration of the stranger, in Paetzold, H. (ed.), *City Life: Essays on Urban Culture*, Maastricht: Jan van Eyck Akademie, pp. 136–146.

He, S. and Qian, J. (2017). From an emerging market to a multifaceted urban society: Urban China studies, *Urban Studies* 54(4), 827–846.

Kraas, F., Hackenbroch, K., Sterly, H., Heintzenberg, J., Herrle, P., and Kreibich, V. (eds.) (2019). *Mega Cities. Mega Challenge. Informal Dynamics of Global Change. Insights from Dhaka, Bangladesh and Pearl River Delta, China*, Stuttgart: Borntraeger Science Publishers.

Lefebvre, H. (1968/2016). *Das Recht auf Stadt*, Hamburg: Nautilus.

Lefebvre, H. (1991). *The Production of Space*, Oxford: Blackwell Publishing.

Li, P. (2020). *Urban Village Renovation. The Stories of Yangcheng Village*, Singapore: Springer.

Liu, X. (2023). *Risk Prevention and Control System of Urban Public Security*, Singapore: Springer Nature.

Liu, Y. 刘衍峰 and Chen, J. 陈静漩 (2024). 风险社会视角下中国式现代化的挑战及应对, Fengxian shehui shijiao xia Zhongguoshi xiandaihua de tiaozhan ji yingdui (Challenges and responses to Chinese modernization from the perspective of risk society), 天水行政学院学报 (*Journal of Tianshui Institute for Administration*) 145(1), 44–50.

Liu,Y., Li, Z., Liu, Yu., and Chen, H. (2015). Growth of rural migrant enclaves in Guangzhou, China: Agency, everyday practise and social mobility, *Urban Studies* 52(16), 3086–3105.

Losavio, C. (2021). China's internal migrants: Processes of categorisation and analytical issues, *China Perspectives* 2, 49–60.

Löw, M. (2001). *Raumsoziologie*, Frankfurt am Main: Suhrkamp.

Löw, M. (2008). The constitution of space: The structuration of spaces through the simultaneity of effect and perception, *European Journal of Social Theory* 11(1), 25–49.

Luhmann, N. (1991). *Soziologie des Risikos*, Berlin, New York: de Gruyter.

Lü, X. and Perry, E. (eds.) (1997). *The Danwei – Changing Chinese Workplace in Historical and Comparative Perspective*, New York: M.E. Sharpe.

Mau, S. (2021). *Sortiermaschinen. Die Neuerfindung der Grenze im 21*, Jahrhundert, München: C.H. Beck.

Meyer-Clement, E. (2016). The great urban leap? On the local political economy of rural urbanisation in China, *Journal of Current Chinese Affairs* 45(1), 109–139.

Mu, Y. 木永跃 (2018). 超大城市流动人口社会风险及其治理, Chaoda chengshi liudong renkou shehui fengxian jiqi zhili (Social risks and governance of floating population in megacities), 新视野, *Xin Shiye* (*Expanding Horizon*) 6, 103–109.

Park, R. E. (1915). The city: Suggestions for the investigation of human behavior in the city environment, *The American Journal of Sociology* XX(5), 577–612.

Petersen, W. (1958). A general typology of migration, *American Sociological Review* 23(3), 256–266.

Siebel, W. (1997). Die Stadt und die Zuwanderer, in Häußermann, H. and Oswald, I. (eds.), *Zuwanderung und Stadtentwicklung*, Leviathan Special Issue 17, Opladen/Wiesbaden: Westdeutscher Verlag, pp. 30–41.

Simmel, G. (1903/1998). Die Großstädte und das Geistesleben, in Klaus Lichtblau (ed.), *Soziologische Ästhetik*, Bodenheim: Philo, pp. 119–133.

Suttmeier, R. (2008). The "sixth modernization?" China, safety and the management of risks, *Asia Policy* 6, 129–146.

Tong, X. 童星 and Zhang, H. 张海波 (2007). 中国转型期的社会风险及识别-理论探讨与经验研究 Zhongguo zhuanxingqi de shehui fengxian ji shibie – lilun tantao yu jingyan yanjiu (*Social Risks and Their Identification in China's Transitional Period: Theoretical Discussion and Empirical Research*) Nanjing: Nanjing University Press.

Von Scheve, C. and Lange, M. (2023). Risk entanglement and the social relationality of risk, *Humanities and Social Sciences Communications* 10(170), 1–10.

Wang, C. 王春光 (1995). 社会流动和社会重构 – 京城浙江村研究 Shehui liudong he shehui zhonggou - jingcheng Zhejiangcun yanjiu (*Social Mobility and Social Structure – Research on Beijing's Zhejiang Village*), Hangzhou: Zhejiang People's Press.

Wang, L. 王立志 (2018). 多种背景下中国城镇化风险议题研究评述, Duozhong beijing xia Zhongguo chengzhenhua fengxian yiti yanjiu pingshu (Review of research on urbanisation risk issues from different backgrounds), 重庆三峡学院学报 (*Journal of Chongqing Three Gorges University*) 34(177), 44–52.

Wang, Z., Lin, L., Tang, S., and Xiao, Y. (2023). Migration and migrants in Chinese cities: New trends, challenges and opportunities to theorise with urban China, *Transactions in Planning* 2(4), 317–331.

Williams, A. and Balaz, V. (2012). Migration, risk and uncertainty: Theoretical perspectives, *Population, Space and Place* 18, 167–180.

Wu, F. (2022). *Creating Chinese Urbanism. Urban Revolution and Governance Changes*, London: UCL Press.

Wu, F. and Zhang, F. (2025), *Governing Urban Development in China*, London: Routledge.

Wu, X. 吴雪明 and Zhou, J. 周建明 (2006). 中国转型期的社会风险分布与抗风险机制, Zhongguo zhuanxingqi de shehui fengxian fenbu yu kangfenxian jizhi (The distribution of social risks and anti-risk mechanisms in China's transformation period), 社会学 Shehuixue (*Sociology*) 9, 61–68.

Xiang, B. (2005). *Transcending Boundaries. Zhejiangcun: The Story of a Migrant Village in Beijing*, Leiden–Boston: Brill.

Xiao, Y. 肖瑛 (2012). 风险社会与中国 Fengxian shehui yu Zhongguo (Risk society and China), 探索与争鸣 (*Tansuo yu zhengming, Explore and Argue*) 4, 46–51.

Yang, S. and Wang, D. (2023). *Urban Migration and Public Governance in China. A Case Study of Shanghai*, Singapore: Springer Nature.

Yang, X. and Chan, K. W. (2023). Forever young: China's migration regime and age patterns, *Eurasian Geography and Economics*, 1–28, https://doi.org/10.1080/15387216.2023.2279545.

Yuan, E. (2021). Governing risk society: The socio-technological experiences of China and South Korea in the COVID-19 pandemic, *Asian Journal of Communication* 31(5), 322–336.

Zhang, L. (2001). *Strangers in the City. Reconfigurations of Space, Power, and Social Networks within China's Floating Population*, Stanford: Stanford University Press.

Chapter 2

Spaces of Unprotectedness and Contestation: Injured Migrant Workers in Guangzhou's Manufacturing Industry

"A lot of the things we do on the job are very dangerous, but no one buys insurance."

"I only know that after my injury, the company has to pay.... I'm filing a suit, it's public."

Introduction

Studies of international and internal migration have generated debates about the "healthy migrant phenomenon," which refers to younger, stronger and healthier members of rural communities migrating to cities for work while elderly, weak or sick people remain in their home villages (e.g. Elshahat *et al.*, 2022; Gao *et al.*, 2021; Chen *et al.*, 2014). In China, where rural migrants have been more or less excluded from urban social security systems for decades, another dimension of the "healthy migrant phenomenon" can be seen in the reverse process of those who suffer severe work-related accidents or illnesses and return home to their villages for care and support from their families and communities. As Chen Chuanbo put it in his convincing documentation of such cases, "The countryside exports good health while importing ill health" (Chen *et al.*, 2014:1). But in fact, some migrants who have had severe work-related accidents nevertheless remain in the city instead of returning home to the countryside. This group of migrants is the subject of this chapter.

Injured migrants who are temporarily or permanently removed from work processes because they can no longer function physically become "unavailable" bodies (Gugutzer, 2022:163). These "dysfunctional" bodies of migrant workers therefore often tend to disappear from the radar screens of migration or urban studies. Severe work-related accidents represent a major break in the lives of migrants, especially those of the first generation whose families live in the countryside and who generally do not have social insurance. Such accidents then represent a second rupture in their (working) lives, following the migration itself. Accidents mean physical pain and considerable mental pressure due to the resulting limitations or even loss of working capacity, loss of income and potentially exorbitant costs of medical treatment and hospital stays. In many cases, it is unclear whether (or to what extent) these costs can be assumed by employers and/or accident or health insurance.

Viewed from the perspective of the relational sociology of space,[1] work-related accidents change the positioning of the suffering subject in relation to objects, other persons and the subject's perception thereof. At the same time, the injured migrant worker reveals the limits of the sociology of space because the latter tends not to focus on the physicality as such of the subjects it describes. A serious work injury also confounds the fabric of relations between the now disabled body and its environment, leaving the positioning as a "migrant in the city" not uncontested for that individual and others. The disabled body represents a provocation in the context of work migration. It unsettles both the self-image of the migrant and the relations to that person's environment. This chapter will therefore incorporate various perspectives from the sociology of the body.

The goals of this chapter are to find out why migrants remain in the city following work-related accidents, how they manage these crisis situations, what kind of knowledge they generate from the bodily experience of being injured and what kind of social spaces might emerge from these experiences as "migrants in the city." The chapter is based on 22 in-depth interviews with injured migrant workers conducted in 2009 and 2010.[2]

---

[1] See Chapter 1, section on "Sociology of space: Producing transient urban spaces".

[2] See interview list at the end of the chapter. Parts of the interview material have been used in Gransow *et al.* (2014).

They all had suffered work-related accidents in Guangzhou's manufacturing industry.

This chapter is structured as follows: After this brief introduction, the second section outlines the sociology of the (injured) body, which (as patient and agent) may become the source of "implicit" knowledge about its unprotectedness and vulnerability. The third section provides general background data on migrants' work-related accidents and their participation in accident insurance systems in China. The fourth section presents several interviews with migrant workers who decided to stay in the city after severe work-related accidents and discusses their motives and reasons versus those of injured workers who returned to their home villages. The fifth section sketches the legal and institutional framework of occupational health and safety for migrant workers from the 1990s to the early 2020s, addressing the question of whether the problems highlighted by the interviewees a decade earlier have since been solved or remain an issue.

It is argued that while the Pearl River Delta (PRD) has seen a decade-long process of economic restructuring with sectors such as e-commerce and the gig economy assuming prominent roles, structural problems such as disputes between employers and injured migrant workers over compensation or classifying accidents as work-related remain notorious – recently involving an even higher number of traffic accidents affecting delivery drivers. Many migrants are still left to their own devices when handling the exceptional and threatening situation of a work-related accident. In light of these and other considerations, the chapter concludes that not much has changed over the past decade.

The Body as a Disruptive Factor

Migrant workers and their routines in the manufacturing sector are embedded in global supply chains and in broader historical contexts of industrialisation and urbanisation in the PRD. More specifically, their workplaces are part of a regime of industrial labour that – with its divisions of labour and rationalised activities – disciplines the workers' bodies (Taylorism). Physical sensitivities, needs and bodily manifestations are to be subordinated to the work processes. As an economic resource, the body has to be kept fit and healthy. Of crucial importance for the logic of industrial production is a body that is both functioning and controlled at the workplace (Lengersdorf, 2022:39).

The spatial order of industrial work relations is reflected in the lived experience at workplaces (Löw, 2005: 247). The regularity of interactive procedures and the coordination of bodies within these work processes result in the formation of collective processes and placements of machines, materials and living bodies, which together constitute and generate the work space in relational configurations (Lengersdorf, 2022:42). Not envisaged in these processes, work-related accidents represent disturbances, and the bodies in question become disruptive factors (Schroer, 2005:15).

The high incidence of accidents in sectors that employ large numbers of migrant workers is inversely related to the low risk awareness of many of these workers. In the manufacturing sector, for example, accidents are enabled by an absence of occupational safety mechanisms, a lack of safety features on machinery and insufficient personal protective equipment such as goggles, gloves, shoes and clothing. In addition, there is insufficient education about workplace hazards. This is particularly the case for smaller privately owned factories with low profit margins where many of the migrant workers find informal employment. Although migrant workers face high occupational health and safety risks, they express only low levels of risk consciousness and tend to individualise these risks in their own accounts. Young male migrant workers in particular tend to emphasise the strength of their bodies, and this somewhat exaggerated self-image of strong bodies might also contribute to the healthy migrant phenomenon. The body seems to serve as magic armour that can prevent injuries – or alternatively, it is assumed that injuries only happen to others (Wu, 2007:61, 63; Gransow, 2010).

If an accident disturbs a work process which can cause financial losses for an enterprise, it can trigger a veritable financial crisis for the injured individual. In addition to pain and potentially permanent physical impairment, "injuries may result in practical doubts which invade every element of the individual's previously taken-for-granted routines and identities… The crisis here challenges an individual's identity by destroying their confidence in their bodies and their world" (Shilling, 2008:17).[3]

Following an accident at a workplace, the migrant worker is usually taken to a hospital and becomes a patient. Tests, treatments, supervision, meals and other routines subject the worker to the spatial constitution of

[3] Shilling (2008) analysed the conditions and consequences of accidents, using the example of outstanding athletes.

the hospital, but, as the term "patient" already implies, from a passive, enduring and suffering perspective. As social institutions that make use of modern technologies and are measured by the generation of profit, factories and hospitals are eminently comparable. As social spaces, however, factories and hospitals serve different social functions. As a patient in a hospital, the "migrant worker turned accident victim" now participates differently in the production of urban spaces than previously as a factory worker – formerly as a healthy body contributing to a production process and now as an injured body or patient who becomes the "product" of the hospital's services. In both cases, however, the (more or less) living body fulfils the material conditions of acting as a subject and of perceiving or altering spaces, while also fulfilling the conditions of an object serving the spatial perception and spatial production of other persons. Here, it should be noted that the body, with its own not-always-controllable expressions (such as pain, sweat, reddening, freezing, laughing, weeping, desire, etc.), is not simply a performing body. This becomes clearer when we consider the ways knowledge is produced in connection with a work-related accident.

An accident is something that befalls a person, i.e. is not sought out. The experience of this type of drastic event, and the knowledge thereby gained, generally defies intersubjective communication (Manzei-Gorsky, 2022:74, 76). Regarding the sociology of the body and its praxeological approaches in particular, physical experiences yield a form of unarticulated knowledge that the philosopher of science Michael Polanyi has termed "tacit knowing" (Polanyi, 1985). In contrast to explicit formal knowledge, this implicit knowledge consists of capabilities, ideas or experiences that people can have but are not readily conveyable. The difference between explicit and implicit knowledge lies not only in the content but also in the structure and genesis: "*Tacit knowing* is far more a matter of bodily interaction with the environment and refers to complex processes as well as situational perception and comprehension of different concrete situations …" (Böhle, 2022:177). Expanding the understanding of knowledge and its generation has implications for the conception of meaningful or intentional action, whereby the body can both carry out and initiate meaningful action.

The implicit knowledge gained from bodily experience can become a catalyst for creative ideas and actions. As Chapter 3 of this book will show, some migrant workers in China who suffered occupational injuries later founded NGOs that support other migrants facing similar circumstances, whom they could help thanks to the implicit knowledge and lessons they had gained from their own accident experiences. At the same time, their work for the NGOs offered an alternative source of income – at least until 2013 when new legal developments rendered the existence of these migrant-worker NGOs essentially impossible.

High Numbers of Work Injuries and Low Rates of Injury Insurance

During the early 2000s, labour and health policies in China were reoriented towards a more pro-migrant approach. On the one hand, the problem of migrants' work injuries was acknowledged by the political leadership. But, on the other, it is difficult to obtain accurate data on the occurrence of these occupational injuries. An important indicator of China's occupational safety record is the number of work-related fatalities. After a record high of 138,965 fatalities in 2002, the number steadily decreased to 83,196 in 2009 (Chan and Gao, 2012:364), and then decreased further to 37,852 in 2017 and 20,963 in 2022 (National Bureau of Statistics of China, 2018, 2023). A similar declining tendency has been observed for work-related accidents in general in China (Ye *et al.*, 2016:7, for the years 2003–2012; Wang *et al.*, 2018:3, for the years 2002–2015). However, the data on accidents are fragmented (according to severity, sector, region, etc.) and difficult to combine or compare, resulting in a lack of transparency. According to the China Labor Statistics Yearbook, in 2010, there were 1.12 million certified worker accidents nationwide (2021:1.27 million), including 214,002 injured workers in Guangdong province (2021:155,592) (National Bureau of Statistics of China, 2011:406, 407, 2022:394, 395). The data do not specify whether they involve migrant workers.

According to Wang *et al.* (2018:2), a work-related accident in China is defined as an unexpected and untoward event that "causes casualties or economic losses in production and business operation activities." The different categories of accidents include especially serious accidents, major accidents, serious accidents and ordinary accidents.[4] But below the category of "ordinary" accidents, there are also many "minor" incidents that usually involve "a handful of people at most" (CLB, 2020). In 2014,

[4]An "ordinary accident" means fewer than three deaths, fewer than ten serious injuries or direct economic losses of under 10 million RMB.

the China Labour Bulletin (Hong Kong) launched its Work Accident Map[5] to track and categorise workplace accidents reported in the Chinese media using a baseline of at least one worker's death or an adverse effect on three or more workers. Given the map's reliance on official media and to some extent social media, its information is also skewed because, e.g. "smaller incidents in factories ... are probably underreported" (CLB, 2020).

Coal mining, construction, transportation and manufacturing have particularly high accident risks and all of these industries primarily employ migrant workers. The frequency of work-related injuries and diseases[6] differs by the type of enterprise ownership. The situation is much more severe at domestic privately owned enterprises than state-owned enterprises, which generally have better occupational health and safety systems and employees with an urban *hukou* (Chen and Chan, 2010). In addition, migrant workers are especially subject to occupational injuries for reasons including excessively long working hours, lack of on-the-job training, high mental stress at work and possibly past histories of work injuries (Zhang, 2007:196; Yu *et al.*, 2012:458; Gong *et al.*, 2012:848). The literature on migrants' occupational health and safety in China has grown considerably (Fitzgerald *et al.*, 2013; Ling *et al.*, 2014) but is still scattered, and official data on occupational injuries are usually not disaggregated by social group, such as local urban workers versus migrant workers, employment status or gender.

In 2004, China instituted the "Work-Related Injury Insurance Regulation" which covers work-related injuries, disability, death and occupational diseases (Brown, 2010). A revised version (2010) became part of the "Social Insurance Law" which came into effect in 2011. The law includes a chapter on workers' compensation. Despite the high risk of work-related injuries (and diseases), participation by migrant workers

---

[5] https://maps.clb.org.hk/?i18n_language=en_US&map=2&startDate=2022-11&endDate=2023-05&eventId=&keyword=&addressId=&parentAddressId=&address=&parentAddress=&industry=&parentIndustry=&industryName=.

[6] Based on the interview material, this chapter focuses solely on work-related accidents, although in fact migrant workers suffer no less from work-related diseases, especially pneumoconiosis caused by the production of dust, e.g. in coal mining. Victims of work-related diseases might find it even harder to demonstrate the source of their condition than victims of accidents. For more on work-related diseases, see Ho (2017).

Table 1. Migrant workers (农民工) in occupational injury insurance schemes (2010–2021, selected years).

Year	Total number of migrant workers (million)	Participation in occupational injury insurance (%)
2010	242.23	24.1
2011	252.78	23.6
2017	286.52	27.2
2018	288.36	27.8
2019	290.77	29.6
2020	285.60	31.3
2021	292.51	31.0

Source: http://www.stats.gov.cn/tjsj/zxfb, MoHRSS (2019), Ten Brink *et al.* (2022), and Tian *et al.* (2021).

increased but remained low. By 2021, it had not exceeded 32% (see Table 1).

Nevertheless, migrant workers' participation in injury insurance has clearly been higher than that in all other types of insurance (Tian *et al.*, 2021:2).[7] Their participation in pension and medical insurance has remained at around 20%, and only 15% in unemployment insurance. Regional variations in injury insurance participation have also been evident. For example, in 2011, when the average overall rate was 23.6%, it was 27% for the eastern region, 14.8% for the central region and 17% for the western region (Guojia, 2012).

Following Tian *et al.*, three main causes for the low participation by migrant workers in the social insurance system can be summarised: (1) the fragmentation and poor transferability of the social insurance system plus institutional discrimination against migrant workers in the urban labour market; (2) underestimation of migrants' risk of illness plus low income levels, which lead them to avoid social insurance costs; and (3) the high prevalence of labour-intensive firms with low profit margins that employ migrant workers and choose not to provide insurance for their employees (Tian *et al.*, 2021:2). While OHS legislation and administration have improved for migrant workers over the years,[8] the informal work that

[7] Tian's data are for the years 2008 to 2017.

[8] See fifth section of this chapter.

migrants often do has made it difficult to prove employer–employee relationships in the event of work-related accidents.

In addition, while the Industrial Injury Insurance Fund established in 2004 can be used for rehabilitation services which might be crucial to full recovery, only few migrant workers take up this offer. Lack of information about injury insurance legislation is only one reason for their reluctance to participate in such programmes despite their eligibility. More importantly, injured workers often fear that using rehabilitation services could prolong the period they need to refrain from work or negatively influence the process of getting compensation from their employers (Li, 2011; see also Hu *et al.*, 2020:4).

Injured Migrant Workers Staying in the City: Five Cases

To understand in greater detail the reasons and motives behind injured migrant workers' decisions to stay in the city, this section presents the reasons given by victims of work-related accidents in the manufacturing sector of Guangzhou. The five cases were selected for the evidence they provide regarding decisions to remain in the city after accidents. At the time of the interviews, the workers had already recovered from their injuries (affecting their hands in most cases but also the head, torso and foot).

A composite method of semi-structured and in-depth approaches was used to conduct the interviews. It focused on migration background, socioeconomic conditions before and after the accident, working conditions, injury conditions, health conditions and strategies, and conflicts with employers. The primary information sought was the following: What are the working conditions and motives of migrants in the city who decide to stay on after the traumatic experience of a serious work injury? What happened before, during and after the accident? How did these migrant workers manage their individual and potentially also family crisis situations? What kind of experience/knowledge did the migrants generate from the injured body? What kind of transient urban spaces could emerge from the migrants' agency and imagination? The in-depth interview method provided room for the interviewees to expand on the complex dynamics of their experience of work-related injuries, the causes and the traumatic effects on their lives.

From the perspective of body studies, I draw on Chris Shilling's (2008) three phases of habit, crisis and creativity to analyse the work routines, accidents and consequences drawn by these interviewees. A process-oriented approach is employed to trace how the accidents are described, whether and how the existence or absence of preventive measures at the workplace is mentioned, how the circumstances of the individual accidents are perceived by the injured persons themselves, whether and how they evaluate first aid measures and the extent and quality of medical treatment, how they dealt with the associated costs, and finally the healthcare services, health insurance situation and the matter of compensation.

1. "A lot of the things we do on the job are very dangerous, but no one buys insurance."
   – Mr. Gao (PW 20, from Sichuan, working in an electric appliance factory, 26 years old, hand injury).

Mr. Gao,[9] a machinery repair technician, injured his right hand during a night shift. While acknowledging that he was overtired, Mr. Gao sees the real reason for his injury mainly as a technical problem with the machinery:

> "The fact that I wasn't rested enough was part of the reason for the injury, but mainly the machine had a problem because the power supply was cut off. There's a moulding tool mounted on the machine, and there's a control unit to start and stop it. It had to be started by hand at first, but because of the short circuit it started up on its own."

In the beginning, the treatment costs were borne by the factory, but Mr. Gao's demand for compensation led to a dispute with his boss, and finally he left the factory. "When I sent a request to the labour authorities back then and they did an inspection at the factory, the boss knew about that of course, and it wasn't good for me to stay there longer. We didn't speak with each other, but although he didn't give me hell it wasn't good for me to stay."

Mr. Gao laments the lack of workplace safety as well as the lack of proper insurance at the factory: "A lot of the things we do on the job are very dangerous, but no one buys insurance."

---

[9] The names in this section are not the real names of the interviewees.

Since 2004, all employers have been required to have work-related injury insurance for their employees and to pay the relevant premiums, while their workers, including migrants with de facto employment relations, are entitled to benefits from such insurance. The injury insurance is therefore financed solely by the enterprises. However, migrants have to prove that they have an actual employment relationship with the enterprise (see Cheng and Darimont, 2005:87f.; Gransow, 2010:19). Some employers at small firms with only a few workers try to make deals by buying certain types of insurance. This is described by a representative of an NGO (that advocates for migrants' rights and interests) as follows:

> "Cheating the insurance company is something you can observe frequently in Guangdong province. Many factories only buy insurance for a few people, not for the majority; if something happens they write the name of a person for whom they bought the insurance.... If an accident occurs, the firm sends the victim to the hospital under the name of an insured person, and then cheats by asking the insurance company to pay. After the firm receives the money, it doesn't give it to the worker, because first it has to pay for the hospital, and then it wants to make a bit of money for itself" (in Gransow, 2010:19).

Disputes over responsibility for the medical bills or for compensation costs – as in Mr. Gao's case – following the injury can not only lead to exclusion and isolation of the injured worker but also force them to leave the factory and find a new job. This might be more difficult than before the injury, and the next workplace might therefore have even higher levels of risk than the previous one.[10]

2. "Back home, I imagine, they would just have amputated my hand!" – Mr. Sun (PW 9, from Jiangxi, working in a printing factory, in his early twenties, hand injury).

Working in a printery, Mr. Sun injured his hand while operating a machine tool used to place items inside the system and press them. "Originally, my machine had a safety feature, an infrared sensor that

[10] See also the third case, interview with Ms. Wu (PW 12), who became increasingly isolated in her firm after filing a complaint against the company.

prevented the door from closing if something was in the way. But the foreman said he removed it when he bought it." A number of factors appear to have played a role here: the missing shield on the machine, the lack of responsibility shown by the foreman and finally the lack of knowledge about safety measures and legal issues on the part of the injured worker. "When that happened to my hand," Sun continued, "I didn't know whether I should blame the foreman ... things like that aren't really covered by the laws."

For Mr. Sun, the main argument for not going back home after being injured is the more advanced medical treatment in Guangzhou city. "[I didn't think of going back home when I had the hand injury], because down there, we don't have the technique there; I try to survive here in Guangzhou city. Back home, I imagine, they would just have amputated my hand!"

Mr. Sun's fear of inferior treatment in his rural hometown that might have cost him his hand is backed by statements of migrants with work-related injuries who did not receive proper treatment back home. Chen *et al.* (2014:6, 7) describe the situation of returned migrants whose economic difficulties effectively restrict their choice of medical providers. As such, they would commonly go to unregistered clinics (recommended by neighbours or others) or even turn to superstitious methods of treatment (such as fortune tellers) for consultation or to buy medicine at lower prices. By following such recommendations from others, however, their health situations often worsened and they were compelled to seek higher-level health providers, resulting in longer-lasting treatment and unnecessary costs.

3. "… After all, the trade union at the site was then disbanded."
   – Ms. Wu (PW 12, from Guizhou, working in a hat factory, 27 years old, hand injury).

Ms. Wu normally does needlework in a textile factory making caps and hats. She complains that she got her injury on the thumb of her left hand because she was instructed to take over the operation of a clinching machine from a male worker who was injured at that machine earlier. "Our factory, it makes these caps, actually I had always done sewing, but then the guy who operated the clinching machine for the sewing work got injured here. And then he didn't work here anymore. But the company didn't want to hire any new people, so someone from the existing staff had to take that on." The job fell to Ms. Wu, who was then injured at the clinching machine just like her predecessor (and it is not inconceivable that her successor will suffer a similar fate).

Because of permanent damage to her hand, Ms. Wu cannot resume her previous work as a seamstress. "The sewing I used to do with this hand, that's all not possible anymore, because even with the slightest pressure it can hurt inside here. That's just the way it is, there's nothing that can be done about it. I don't have any feeling here anymore, it's like a piece of wood! But if I try to do something that requires strength, then it hurts like mad! That's why I also can't do the clinching work that I did before, and why I can't do sewing at all! That's why I want to take care of this thing here as soon as possible (Ms. Wu filed a complaint against the company), and leave here; all the Guangdong people here are laughing their heads off at me! They really are, many people here at the factory come from the same place as the boss, so of course they're loyal to him. So what it comes down to is that it makes absolutely no sense anymore to keep working here."

Turning to the trade unions was not an option for Ms. Wu. She says, "There probably were trade unions before I came here. But [no longer] since around 2008, I've heard, because other people got injured before I did, who then went to the trade unions for advice, but that brought a lot of trouble – after all, the trade union at the site was then disbanded." Injured migrant workers such as Ms. Wu were more apt to receive support from migrant-labour NGOs, 20 or 30 of which had arisen in the PRD since the mid-1990s.[11] Some of them were founded by migrant workers who themselves had suffered an occupational injury or illness.

4. "The medical treatment cost 50,000 yuan, all of which I borrowed from the village, …
   I don't dare to return!"
   – Ms. Li (PW 6, from Jiangxi, working in a metal fitting and plastic factory, in her fifties, torso injury).

[11] The exact number of migrant-labour NGOs in the PRD is difficult to determine because of their sometimes disguised or absent registration. The number also depends on whether the different offices of one NGO are counted as one organisation or several. Because these organisations find it difficult to grow for a number of reasons, some adopted a strategy of opening more small offices in different locations. See also Chapter 3.

Only one month after she started working as a cleaner in a plastic factory, Ms. Li was injured by goods falling on her in a warehouse in Panyu/Guangzhou. She reports, "When I was in the hospital, and woke up after losing consciousness, they called my family at first and my relatives came. Then, and I don't know exactly what was going on, they called the company … who probably then said it's nothing and I should leave the hospital. We didn't understand that either ... The other patients could see that I couldn't get up from a sitting position ... Around evening someone from the company came who is responsible for paying the wages, not the boss, but someone else in charge. He said if you're supposed to leave the hospital but aren't going ... then you'll have to pay for it yourself. But I said I can't stand up, I can't walk, how am I supposed to leave the hospital? ... That day they [the company] brought me home, and afterwards didn't concern themselves with me anymore." Ms. Li's boss denied responsibility afterwards. So, she had X-rays taken of her injuries at her own cost, but this did not soften the company's stance either. Ms. Li and her family borrowed money to pay for her treatment. The company, with which she did not have a contract, then denied knowing her. With the help of an NGO that acts on behalf of migrant workers, Ms. Li was able to gather the necessary paperwork and sue her boss to pay for her treatment. He was finally ordered to pay 50,000 yuan, which Ms. Li otherwise had to pay herself. But despite this decision, the boss has not paid. "He absolutely refuses to admit that I worked at his company, and thinks he can get out of it this way. So I then called the arbitration committee (*zhongcai*)[12] at the labour agency – I tell you, it's been going on like this for years." Chen *et al.* report on cases where the boss did not send the accident victims to a proper hospital or sent them to a less qualified health centre in order to save money.[13]

[12]仲裁.

[13]"I was sent to the county hospital and asked to pay 10,000 yuan in advance for in-patient treatment. The boss thought that was too expensive and transferred me to another hospital in the city but again refused to pay the same amount in advance for the in-patient stay. We then went to a smaller township hospital, and once again the boss refused to pay the same amount for in-patient treatment. We finally went to a county Chinese medical hospital and stayed there because it only asked my boss to pay 2,000 yuan in advance. By going through this process, two more hours passed, and with less qualified doctors at the Chinese medical hospital, my leg was badly treated, and I nearly died from the treatment" (Chen *et al.*, 2014:6).

Ms. Li's employer was ordered by a court to pay the hospital costs, but has yet to accept the decision. "The medical treatment cost 50,000 yuan, all of which I borrowed from [people in] the village, and under these circumstances I don't dare to return! Of course, they expect me to pay back the money!" As long as she is unable to pay back the money she borrowed to cover the treatment costs, Ms. Li is reluctant to return to her village.

Comparable to the case of Ms. Li is the one of Ms. Bao (PW 17) from Chongqing, who worked in a shoe factory in Guangzhou where her hand was injured. Ms. Bao feels ashamed to return to her hometown without money and gifts, where her parents look after her daughter. "After I hurt my hand, I could not earn any money. Every fen my husband earned over the last half year had to be spent for this (medical treatment). Now we don't have one fen left – how should we go home? How could we visit the elderly (and ask them for support)?" For her, the financial difficulties caused by her accident at work are the reason for not returning home, for fear of losing face on appearing empty-handed at her family home.

According to China's "Work-Related Injury Insurance Regulation," employers are required to pay not only the medical expenses of employees with work-related injuries but also a disability allowance based on the seriousness of the injury (Brown, 2010:115/116). But when employers do not act in accordance with the law, it becomes quite difficult for the injured workers to claim the medical expenses and compensation.

5. "I only know that after my injury, the company has to pay.... I'm filing a suit, it's public."
   – Mr. Zhang (PW 1, from Jiangxi, working in a furniture factory, 36 years old, hand injury).

Mr. Zhang injured his right hand while working in a furniture factory producing billiard tables and accessories. He reported that the accident was not a result of operating a machine as such, but because the wooden material he had to push through the machine was rotten. "Using my hand to push the wooden material into the machinery, the material fell apart and my hand was pulled into the machinery."

Regarding the insurance situation, Mr. Zhang described his situation as follows: "First they [the company] also paid for insurance. But it had expired by the time of my injury, and hadn't been renewed. They said that we had all come to the company via relatives, all from the same village, and all with very similar names just with different last characters. So some names got mixed up, and mine was overlooked. I don't know whether it was a collective or individual insurance policy. We've never seen the documents for it. I assume they bought accident insurance, and not retirement insurance."

Without help from law firms or NGOs, migrant workers do not know how to handle all this. Mr. Zhang says, "Most of them have no idea [of compensation], myself included, I don't understand it either. I only know that after my injury, the company has to pay. There were six or seven people before me, they didn't even try. One was about to, he had lost four whole fingers, he didn't see a single fen, and then he left. What should he have done? The company gave him nothing. People don't talk about these things openly. I heard that the company supposedly gave him 10,000 yuan, others say that he got nothing. Those are internal secrets, we can't really know them. At any rate, whatever he got was for the medical costs, not like me; I'm filing a suit, it's public, whereas he did it in private."

As more regulations target employment conditions, accidents and occupational illnesses, migrants are becoming more aware of their rights – even if they are not always sure of the details. Chang Kai, a professor of labour relations at Renmin University Beijing, has been quoted as saying that many workers who get sick or injured do not know which government agency they should turn to (Chen and Yan, 2011:4). In addition, only a few institutions have thus far been certified to determine the extent to which accidents impact the ability to work. Employee compensation claims can only be submitted after the degree of disability is officially assessed and certified by the local government's appraisal committee (Brown, 2010:120). This contributes to prolonging the process. A study by the Yilian Legal Aid and Labor Study Center on migrant workers who suffered injuries on the job (2008–2010) concluded that the workers had to wait an average of two years for compensation (Cao, 2011).

Reasons for staying in the city

The interviewees are in the special position of having experienced the unprotectedness of their bodies but also their strength in fighting for their labour rights. Overall, from the above-mentioned cases, we can identify the following reasons why these migrant workers have stayed in the city after a work-related accident instead of returning to their rural homes:

- Having family members in the city who can take care of them;
- Receiving more advanced medical treatment at urban hospitals;
- Having retained/regained their work ability (even at a decreased level) and being under economic pressure to restart work or find a new job (if the employer disputes responsibility for the accident);
- Having filed a case against the employer and fought for reimbursement of medical costs and/or compensation;
- Having borrowed money in their home village for medical costs and being unable to pay the debts back home;
- Feeling ashamed to return home to the family without any gifts or money after all income has been spent on medical treatment.

Viewed from a pull-versus-push perspective, the first four factors can be seen as pull factors in migrants' decisions to stay in the city.[14] The two last factors represent a type of "reversed push" or "stop" factor that discourages migrants from returning home. Those migrants remain in the city because they feel they cannot go home. In any event, the respondents' arguments shatter the oversimplified myth of the "healthy migrant phenomenon" or at least its assumption that "the injured or ill migrant workers will return home." However, this finding in no way diminishes the importance of the phenomenon of injured or ill migrants returning home.

Reasons for returning home

The study by Chen Chuanbo *et al.* (2014:5) on migrants who returned to their home villages in Hubei and Sichuan provinces following

---

[14]In addition, it has been argued that migrant workers' intentions to remain in cities (independent of their health status) is stronger in cities with higher GDP per capita (such as Guangzhou, Shenzhen and Zhuhai in the PRD) (Li and Chunyu, 2016:83). This might also have influenced the injured workers' decisions. But the same authors also found that insurance and medical treatment had a positive effect on migrants' intentions to stay in the city while the violation of rights and interests at work did not show analogous effects. More research seems needed on the reasons for different groups of migrants' intentions to stay in the city.

work-related accidents in cities explicates the main reasons for returning home:

- Family members could care for the injured migrants more easily at their homes;
- Hospital doctors back home were seen as more reliable than those in the city;
- Considerable or even complete loss of the ability to work (including not only physical injuries or diseases but also mental conditions);
- Long-term effects of occupational injuries or diseases;
- Loss of ability to afford living and treatment expenses in cities;
- Reimbursement for medical treatment only possible from hometown hospitals (because of the New Cooperate Medical Scheme NCMS).[15]

Treatment at home means a heavy burden of financial and care obligations for the family as well. Other family members might also leave to work as migrants (albeit to different cities), which exacerbates the difficulty of providing care at home. Injured workers who have to borrow money from family members may easily run up debts and even fall into abject poverty. Regarding the financial risks faced by victims of work-related accidents, the NCMS provides only very limited support. An especially high-risk group of injured migrants consists of those who lose all ability to work, return home and need to be cared for by elderly parents. In general, it seems that injured workers stay at home only until they recover and regain their ability to work (normally a couple of months or so) and then leave to work again. It also happens (mainly among the younger generations) that accident victims return home but then go back to the city because of discrimination as disabled persons and/or because they had previously adjusted to city life (Chen *et al.*, 2014:6, 7).

Comparison of reasons

A comparison of reasons given by injured rural-to-urban migrant workers for staying in the city versus those for returning home does

[15]The New Rural Cooperative Medical Scheme (NCMS) was established in 2003. It is a voluntary community-based rural health insurance programme to reduce the risk of catastrophic health spending for rural residents in China. By the end of 2014, nearly all rural residents in China had joined the NCMS but the coverage is relatively low.

not provide a clear picture in terms of push-and-pull factors. But the following factors seem crucial from the perspective of decision-making processes:

The degree of work ability and economic pressure: Depending on the degree of regained work ability following an injury and the pressure to earn money, migrant workers might stay on in the city or go back to their home villages and then return to the city as soon as possible.

Preferences in medical treatment: An injured migrant worker might prefer medical treatment in the city because of trust in advanced medical techniques or might prefer treatment back in the countryside if hospital doctors at home are considered more reliable than those in the city – or if reimbursement can only be received from the hometown hospital.

Family care situation: Whether injured migrant workers stay in the city or return home may depend on whether they have family members in the city who can care for them or whether their family back home has sufficient available members and resources.

Financial risks: Injured migrant workers who borrowed money from villagers back home and/or used all their savings for their medical bills seem reluctant to return to their home villages without being able to pay back their debts. This means they do not stay in the city because they want to, but because their personal moral economy dictates that they have to. Moreover, severely injured migrant workers who return to their home villages might generate financial burdens of a magnitude that threatens their entire family with abject poverty.

Rights consciousness: Those injured migrant workers who stay on in the city express a higher degree of awareness and determination to use legal means to fight for compensation and/or reimbursement of medical bills.

Both groups of migrant workers, i.e. those who returned home and those who stayed in the city, had become victims of work-related accidents and as such found themselves in positions of extreme unprotectedness. But only those who remained in the city were able to expand their agency to use legal means to defend their contested labour rights.

Occupational Health and Safety Situation of Migrant Workers: Legal and Institutional Framework

As discussed earlier, China's economic rise has been accompanied by a huge number of work-related fatalities, accidents and diseases. Around the turn of the 21st century, the Chinese government therefore started to establish a comprehensive legal and administrative occupational health and safety (OHS) framework. While the OHS legal framework is becoming ever more consistent, it is still plagued by loopholes, lack of enforcement, unclear responsibilities and insufficient exchange of information among relevant administrative bodies. As a result, government action to improve the safety of workers tends to be taken after serious accidents (such as the Tianjin port explosions in 2015 or recurrent serious mine explosions) rather than on an ongoing basis.

Legal framework

As promised back in the 1994 "Labour Law," China initiated comprehensive protective legislation for OHS (see Table 2). In 2001, the government passed an "Occupational Diseases Prevention and Control Act." It called for preventive medical procedures and the replacement of dangerous technology and materials. In addition, the 2002 "Work Safety Law" required pre-job education and training and the provision of proper protective equipment. Employers are responsible for work safety and have to undertake safety management by appointing relevant personnel committees, establishing safety rules and following reporting requirements. Unions or other employee organisations have the right to supervise safety matters. According to the "Labour Contract Law" (2008), work safety provisions and measures to prevent occupational hazards have to be included in the labour contract (Brown, 2010:105, 109).

In 2004, China instituted the "Work-Related Injury Insurance Regulation," which covers work-related injuries, disability, death and occupational diseases (Brown, 2010:115). The country's first comprehensive "Social Insurance Law" went into effect in 2011. It unifies local rules and regulations on social insurance matters and covers pension, medical, unemployment, work-related injury and maternity insurance. Chapter 4 (articles 33–43) of the "Social Insurance Law" deals with work-related injury insurance. According to Article 33, work-related injury insurance

Table 2. Occupational health and safety laws and regulations (1994–2021).*

Year	Document (came into effect)	Main points
1995	Labour Law of the PRC	Regulates • labour contracts and collective contracts • work and leisure time • wages • work safety and health • protection of female and young employees • social insurance and social benefits • labour conflicts
2002	Occupational Diseases Prevention and Control Act	Establishes • occupational hygiene standards and technical specification systems • supervision and law-enforcement strength of occupational disease prevention and control • supervision of occupational hazards in construction projects and monitoring of occupational diseases • supervision of occupational health agencies • basic occupational health service (BOHS) pilot activity
2002	Regulations on Labour Protection in Workplaces Where Toxic Substances Are Used	• Applies to occupational poisoning hazards • Stipulates that employing units shall take effective measures to prevent occupational poisoning accidents
2002	Work Safety Law	Requires • employers to meet safety standards and to undertake safety management • establishment of safety rules
2004	Work-Related Injury Insurance Regulation	Covers • work-related injuries • disability • death • occupational diseases • Industrial Injury Insurance Fund Recommends • rehabilitation services

(*Continued*)

Table 2. (*Continued*)

Year	Document (came into effect)	Main points
2008	Labour Contract Law	Regulates • labour contracts (normally written and permanent) • minimum wages • penalties if wages are withheld or below the minimum wage • dispatched labour, part-time work and subcontracting
2011	Social Insurance Law	Unifies • local rules and regulations on social insurance matters Includes • pension, medical, unemployment, work-related injury and maternity insurance with a chapter on workers' compensation benefits
2011	Revised Work-Related Injury Insurance Regulation	Earmarked • part of workers' compensation fund for prevention purposes
2012	Regulation on Special Protection of Women Workers (replaced 1988 Regulations)	Includes • employers' obligation to prevent sexual harassment against women
2018	Amendment to the Law on Occupational Diseases Prevention and Control Act (updated 2011, 2016, 2017, 2018)	Facilitates • access to the diagnosis of occupational diseases
2021	Revised Work-Related Injury Insurance Regulations (updated 2011, 2021)	Expanded • the scope of coverage by including employees in the informal sector
2021	Revised Work Safety Law (updated 2009, 2014, 2021)	Provides • protection for temporary agency workers (mainly migrant workers)

Note: *For a more comprehensive list of OHS laws and regulations, see Wang *et al.* (2018:10, 11).
Source: Braun (2011), Brown (2010), Schnack and Yuan (2010), ILO, (2012), Wang and Tao (2012), Li (2017) and MoHRSS (2022). Updated version of Table 1 in Gransow *et al.* (2014:4).

premiums shall be paid in full by the employing entities rather than by workers. If employers do not pay the insurance premium, they should pay the work-related injury insurance benefit. If they refuse to pay, the insurance authority provides advance payment (article 41) (Gransow *et al.*, 2014:3).

After several rounds of amending the "Work Safety Law," the revised law (with 119 articles in total) came into effect on 1 September 2021. It aims to enhance work safety and prevent or reduce work-related accidents. Its amendments seek to improve the monitoring and prevention of workplace hazards, clarify the responsibilities of relevant authorities and strengthen legal responsibility for violations of the law. Also included is a provision to protect employees in the platform economy.[16] Trade unions shall supervise enterprises' work safety and participate in the investigation of accidents in accordance with the law (CLB, 2020).

From the perspective of labour legislation in general and the amended regulations on work safety and injury insurance in particular, the OHS situation has shown considerable improvement. But in practice, the procedures require specific knowledge, comprehensive paperwork and years on average to accomplish. "The legal process to deal with work-related injury takes so long in China, because of the time-consuming task of applying for evidence. At least 10 items are needed, including an official diagnosis, the work-related injury identification letter, an assessment of the ability to work and a lawsuit" (Wang, 2011:20). Overall, implementing and enforcing the law have remained very difficult.

Institutional framework

When the Hu/Wen administration took office in the early 2000s, the previous tradition of solving OHS problems under a coordinated strategy of labour protection came to an end. With the enactment of the "Occupational Diseases Prevention and Control Act" (2001), occupational health administration fell under the jurisdiction of health departments now responsible

[16]The work-related injury insurance does not fit the situation of gig workers (零工 *linggong*) in terms of contributions, recognition of work-related accidents or compensation. With gig workers exposed to high occupational injury risks, finding adequate solutions is a very urgent matter. Experiments are underway with commercial insurance funded by platforms, separate injury insurance established and subsidised by the government and paid by individuals, and adjustments to the existing injury insurance scheme (Ran and Zhao, 2023).

for diagnosing occupational diseases as a prerequisite for workers to obtain compensation (Li, 2017:60).

Chinese leaders have attempted to improve work safety not only by new laws and regulations but also by restructuring the institutional framework of occupational health and safety. In 2003, the Work Safety Commission (WSC) under the State Council was established. To enforce its policies and regulations, work safety bureaus were set up nationwide at the local level (Chan and Gao, 2012:361). Two years later, the former State Bureau of Work Safety (at vice-ministerial level) was renamed the State Administration of Work Safety (SAWS) and upgraded to ministerial level (Chan and Gao, 2012:361, 62; Li, 2017:60; Gransow *et al.*, 2014:5). While the Work Safety Commission is in charge of directing and coordinating national work safety management and advancing major policies and principles, the SAWS (including the State Administration of Coal Mine Safety) is responsible for administering and enforcing general work safety laws and regulations. The SAWS initially had a broad enforcement mandate covering occupational safety inspection as well as occupational health inspection. But after it was upgraded, the labour departments were once again stripped of OHS responsibilities (Li, 2017:61). What remained under the purview of the labour administration was China's workers' compensation system, which was formalised and institutionalised as a type of public social insurance designed to prevent work accidents and occupational diseases. Labour departments were also mandated to enforce the "Regulation on Special Protection for Women Workers."

On the basis of this institutional reorganisation, the Chinese leadership tried to overcome the segmented regulatory system that had limited state capacity to monitor safety performance and enforce policies (see Chan and Gao, 2012:359). But even with this new structure of the country's occupational safety and health agencies, numerous ministries and agencies were still involved in managing the work safety system. For example, the SAWS was responsible for on-site health inspections, the Ministry of Human Resources and Social Security for work injury insurance and the Ministry of Health for occupational health examinations and occupational disease diagnoses (ILO, 2012:18). In addition, because work safety is managed on a locality basis, work safety officials may face the dilemma of pursuing their responsibilities while local leaderships express (or demand) loyalty towards local entrepreneurs (see Chan and Gao, 2012:360, 361).

In 2018, the SAWS was dissolved and became part of the newly created Super Ministry of Emergency Management (MEM) under the

State Council.[17] Due to a State Council reform in 2018, the MEM was established to oversee preparation and response for a wide range of natural and man-made disasters.[18] It is responsible for emergency management, workplace safety and emergency rescue. Under its purview, local government officials are responsible for ensuring that all workplaces comply with work safety regulations. But in practice, local government offices responsible for work safety are often understaffed and have little incentive to conduct regular workplace inspections. It is mainly in the aftermath of accidents in their jurisdictions that they have taken action to determine the causes, penalise the guilty parties and write reports (CLB, 2020).

In 2022, the MEM reported on nationwide workplace safety checks and on establishing a long-term mechanism for regular and strict management of workplace safety. It issued regulations on workplace safety accountability for local party and government leaders and implemented fifteen measures for workplace safety.[19] Despite the institutional rearrangement of work safety under the MEM, fatal chemical plant explosions continued to happen (in Jiangsu province in 2019 and Liaoning province in early 2023). A statement from the Work Safety Committee noted that

---

[17]Together with the National Mine Safety Administration.

[18]The MEM merged emergency management departments from various ministries and took over the former paramilitary Firefighting Corps of the People's Armed Police (now Firefighting Service of the MEM).

[19]The fifteen measures are the following: (1) ensure that local Party committees are responsible for workplace safety; (2) ensure that local governments are responsible for workplace safety; (3) ensure that the departments with relevant expertise are responsible for safety supervision; (4) call leaders and supervisors to account for any violations of safety regulations; (5) ensure that leaders of enterprises assume the principal responsibilities for workplace safety; (6) immediately launch nationwide work safety inspections; (7) in the project approval process, strictly adhere to the safety red line; (8) crack down on illegal subcontracting and license renting; (9) strengthen safety management regarding labour dispatch and flexible employment; (10) strike hard at illegal production and business operations; (11) address lax and weak law enforcement and inspection; (12) strengthen safety supervision law enforcement contingents; (13) reward those who report hidden risks in workplace safety; (14) punish those who cover up, misreport, underreport or report accidents in a tardy manner; and (15) coordinate efforts to promote economic development, respond to COVID-19 and ensure workplace safety. https://conventuslaw:com/report/china-fifteen-measures-for-work-safety-and-upcoming-nationwide-work-safety-inspection.

an initial investigation had exposed significant flaws in the safety management of the plant's high-risk operations.[20]

Conclusion and Outlook

The picture emerging from official statistics of work accidents and fatalities, and from the laws and regulations that have been promulgated, suggests that since the beginning of the 21st century, China has become a safer place to work, including for migrant workers. The number of work-related accidents and fatalities has decreased considerably. After several rounds of revision of the Work Safety Law (2021), the legal framework for work safety has improved, monitoring and prevention of workplace hazards have been strengthened, and the safety-related responsibilities of production and business entities, State Councils and local governments have been addressed. The administrative restructuring of the SAWS as part of the Ministry of Emergency Management established in 2018 paved the way for better supervision of work safety and long-term plans for improving it through projects such as "integrating industrial Internet plus work safety."[21]

However, statistical data and legal documents can provide only limited information on the implementation and reception of safety issues on the ground. For example, statistical data do not include the work-related accidents that happen in small factories with only a few victims. The still relatively low percentage of migrant workers covered by accident insurance and the changing institutional settings and responsibilities in the field of OHS indicate that implementation still faces a number of obstacles, such as informal arrangements among key actors, including enterprises/employers, migrant workers, local governments and big insurance companies that provide particular actors with some income/profit advantages in the short run but undermine the idea of a rights-based labour system as well as efforts to establish an injury insurance system with a high degree of migrant worker participation in the long run (Zhang, 2021; Zhu *et al.*, 2014).

Challenges and problems described by the interviewees still seem to exist. These include a lack of work safety devices and equipment, long working hours, post-injury conflicts with employers over payment for

[20]https://english.news.cn/20230127/fd71ed003825499190aed7a205876249/c.html.

[21]National Emergency Management System Plan during the 14th Five-Year Plan Period, 2021–2025. https://www.mem.gov.cn/zl/202208/P020220823583813558584.pdf.

medical treatment and compensation, lack of support from trade unions, lack of information about their insurance situation, and long and complicated certification procedures to address work-related accidents, to name just a few. It is doubtful that injured migrant workers find it easier to tackle the complex aftermath of a work accident today, including the associated health complications and financial risks. The situation might now even be worse because the migrant-worker NGOs which interviewees had previously approached for help no longer exist. The vacuum left has not been filled by the trade unions or other workers' associations. The work safety situation on the ground has thus far appeared to remain weak in terms of law enforcement, work safety inspection, work contracts and the negotiating power of injured and other migrant workers *vis-à-vis* their employers.

In retrospect, migrant production workers who suffered work-related injuries saw their self-image as "healthy migrant workers" with "bodies like armour" shattered. Instead, they learned the hard way about the vulnerability of their own bodies and the lack of social protection when suddenly faced with the high costs of hospitalisation and medical treatment. One of the reasons why migrants stayed in the city after an accident at work, rather than returning to the countryside, was that they were aware of their right to sue their former employer if the latter was unwilling to pay for their medical treatment and/or compensation. In 2010, those interviewees who were courageous enough to do so were still supported by migrant workers' organisations, which provided them with the necessary information, help with the formalities and emotional support.

Looking ahead, migrant workers in the PRD in the early 2020s faced the dual impact of economic restructuring and the COVID-19 pandemic on their working and living conditions. An analysis of recent coping strategies of migrant workers in the PRD, especially in the manufacturing sector, suggests various socio-spatial impacts of economic restructuring on their working and living conditions, including a diversification of migration patterns in terms of destinations, distances and responses of older and younger generations (Wang *et al.*, 2021). Although the vulnerability to occupational accidents may change in terms of locations and industries, it remains high under the conditions of widespread informal labour relations and a "growth before security" attitude, shifting the associated risk to workers. Without collective rights, including the right to form migrant-worker organisations, filing an individual claim remains one of the few legal ways for vulnerable migrant workers to defend their rights in the city.

Appendix

List of interviews with migrant workers in manufacturing firms in Guangzhou (December 2009–April 2010)

Production worker interview number	Work site	M/F	Age	Education	Work-related injury/ problem	Place of origin
PW 1	Billiard accessories factory	M	36	Junior middle school (finished)	Hand injury	Jiangxi
PW 2	Plastic film factory	M	35	Junior middle school (unfinished)	Hand injury	Hunan
PW 3	Furniture factory	M/F	~45–50	u.k.	Payment dispute	Jiangxi
PW 4	Metal fitting factory	M	u.k.	u.k.	Head injury	Yunnan
PW 5	Metal fitting factory	M	37/38	u.k.	Hand injury	Guangdong
PW 6	Metal fitting and plastic factory	F	~ 50	u.k.	Waist injury	Jiangxi
PW 7	Concrete factory	M	28	Senior middle school (unfinished)	Waist injury	Sichuan
PW 8	Printing factory	M	25	Technical secondary school (finished)	Payment dispute	Sichuan
PW 9	Printing factory	M	u.k.	Technical secondary school (finished)	Hand injury	Jiangxi
PW 10	Printing factory	M	20	Technical secondary school (unfinished)	Hand injury	Guangdong

PW 11	Furniture factory	M	45	u.k.	Hand injury	Hunan
PW 12	Hat factory	F	27	u.k.	Hand injury	Guizhou
PW 13	Luggage factory	M	u.k.	Technical secondary school	Hand injury	Guangdong
PW 14	Garment factory	M	37	Senior middle school (unfinished)	Payment dispute	Fujian
PW 15	Machinery production	M	43	Junior middle school (finished)	Foot injury	Yunnan
PW 16	Car repair station	M	40	u.k.	Head injury	Hunan
PW 17	Shoe factory	F	u.k.	u.k.	Hand injury	Chongqing
PW 18	Metal fitting factory	M	23	u.k.	Hand injury	Hubei
PW 19	Kitchen unit factory	M	19	Technical secondary school (finished)	Hand injury	Guangdong
PW 20	Electric appliance factory	M	26	Junior middle school	Hand injury	Sichuan
PW 21	Pipe factory	M	29	u.k.	Payment dispute	Sichuan
PW 22	Leather product factory	M	20	Technical secondary school (finished)	Payment dispute	Jiangxi

Note: *u.k.= unknown.

References

Böhle, F. (2022). Wissen, in Gugutzer, R., Klein, G., and Meuser, M. (eds.), *Handbuch Körpersoziologie 1*, Wiesbaden: Springer Nature, pp. 175–179.

Braun, A. (2011). *Das Ende der billigen Arbeit in China.* Arbeitsrechte, Sozialschutz und Unternehmensförderung für informell Beschäftigte, Wiesbaden: VS Verlag.

Brown, R. (2010). *Understanding Labor and Employment Law in China*, New York: Cambridge University Press.

Cao, Y. (May 18, 2011). Injured workers wait two years for compensation, *China Daily*.

Chan, H. and Gao, J. (June 2012). Death versus GDP! Decoding the fatality indicators in work safety regulation in Post-Deng China, *China Quarterly* 210, 355–377.

Chen, C., Ding, S., Cook, S., and Pong, M. (2014). Coming home. The return of migrant workers with illness or work-related injuries in China's Hubei and Sichuan provinces, UNRISD Working Paper 2014–5.

Chen, J., Chen, S., Landry, P., and Davis, D. S. (2014). How Dynamics of Urbanization Affect Physical and Mental Health in Urban China, *The China Quarterly* 220 (December): 988–1011.

Chen, M. and Chan, A. (2010). Occupational health and safety in China: The case of state-managed enterprises, *International Journal of Health Services* 40(1), 43–60.

Chen, X. and Yan, J. (August 19, 2011). Records to be kept for workers in risky jobs. *China Daily*.

Cheng, Y. and Darimont, B. (January 2005). Occupational accident insurance reform and legislation in China. *International Social Security Review* 58(1), 85–97.

CLB (China Labor Bulletin). (2020). Work safety. https://clb.org.hk/content/work-safety (accessed April 13, 2023).

Elshahat, S., Moffat, T., and Newbold, B. (2022). Understanding the healthy immigrant effect in the context of mental health challenges, *Journal of Immigrant and Minority Health* 24, 1564–1579.

Fitzgerald, S., Chen, X., Qu, H., and Sheff, M. G. (2013). Occupational injury among migrant workers in China: A systematic review, *Injury Prevention* 19, 348–354.

Gao, L., Penning, M., Wu, Z., Sterrett, S.J., and Li, S. (2021). Internal migration and the health of middle-aged and older persons in China: The healthy migrant effect reconsidered, *Research on Aging* 43(9–10), 345–357.

Gong, P., Liang, S., Carlton, E., Jiang, Q., Wu, J., Wang, L., and Remais, J. V. (March 3, 2012). Urbanisation and health in China, *The Lancet* 379, 843–852.

Gransow, B. (2010). Body as armor. Health risks and health consciousness among rural migrants in urban China, in Gransow, B. and Zhou, D. (eds.) *Special Issue: Migrants and Health in Urban China,* Berliner China-Hefte, Vol. 38, Münster: Lit Verlag, pp. 9–27.

Gransow, B., Zheng, G., Leong, A., and Ling, L. (2014). Chinese migrant workers and occupational injuries. A case study of the manufacturing industry in the Pearl River Delta, UNRISD Working Paper 2014–1. https://www.econstor.eu/bitstream/10419/148764/1/861317688.pdf.

Gugutzer, R. (2022). *Soziologie des Körpers*, Bielefeld: Transcript.

Guojia tongjiju (国家统计局 National Bureau of Statistics of China). (2012). 2011年我国农民工调查监测报告 2011 nian woguo nongmingong diaocha jiance baogao (2011 China Migrant Workers' Survey and Monitoring Report), Published April 27.

Ho, W. (2017). *Occupational Health and Social Estrangement in China*, Manchester: Manchester University Press.

Hu, R., Hu, N., Liu, R. *et al*. (2020). Association between occupational health and safety knowledge and behaviours among migrant workers: Results from a cross-sectional study in China, *BMJ Open*. DOI: 101136/bmjopen-2020-040143.

ILO (International Labour Organization). (2012). National Profile Report on Occupational Safety and Health in China. https://pdf4pro.com/amp/view/national-profile-report-on-occupational-safety-and-health-4f8c2f.html (accessed April 12, 2023).

Lengersdorf, D. (2022). Arbeit, in Gugutzer, R., Klein, G., and Meuser, M. (eds.) *Handbuch Körpersoziologie 2*, Wiesbaden: Springer Nature, pp. 33–44.

Li, A. and Chunyu, M. D. (2016). Rural migrant workers' intention to stay in the city. A case study of the Pearl River Delta, China, in Liang, Z., Messner, S., Huang, Y., and Chen, C. (eds.), *Confronting the Challenges of Urbanization in China*, Insights from Social Science Perspectives, New York: Routledge, pp. 73–93.

Li, L. (January 25, 2011). Injured laborers unaware of free rehab amid compensation fears, *China Daily*.

Li, M. (2017). Protection for migrant workers under evolving occupational health and safety regimes in China, *Relations Industrielles/Industrial Relations* 72(1), 55–76.

Ling, L., Rani, M., Sang, Y., Lv, G., and Barber, S. (2014). Two decades of research on migrant health in China: A systematic review. Lessons for future inquiry, United Nations Research Institute for Social Development (UNRISD) and Sun Yat-sen Center for Migrant Health Policy Working Paper 2014–8.

Löw, M. (2005). Die Rache des Körpers über den Raum? Über Henri Lefebvres Utopie und Geschlechterverhältnisse am Strand (The body's revenge over space? On Henri Lefebvre's utopia and gender relations on the beach), in Schroer, M. (ed.) *Soziologie des Körpers* (Sociology of the body), Frankfurt am Main: Suhrkamp, pp. 241–270.

Manzei-Gorsky, A. (2022). Krankheit und Gesundheit, in Gugutzer, R., Klein, G., and Meuser, M. (eds.) *Handbuch Körpersoziologie 1*, Wiesbaden: Springer Nature, pp. 71–76.

MoHRSS (Ministry of Human Resources and Social Security). (2019). 全国工伤保险参保人数大2.39 亿人 Quanguo gongshang baoxian canbao renshu da 2.39 yi ren (239 million people are participating in China's injury insurance). http://www.gov.cn/zhengce/2019-05/13/content_5391241.htm (accessed April 10, 2023).

MoHRSS (Ministry of Human Resources and Social Security). (2022). 中华人民共和国安全生产法 Zhonghua renmin gongheguo anquan shengchan fa (Work safety law of the People's Republic of China), Published 13 May, 2022. http://www.mohrss.gov.cn/SYrlzyhshbzb/dongtaixinwen/shizhengyaowen/202205/t20220513_448176.html.

National Bureau of Statistics of China. (2011). 中国劳动统计年鉴 (*China Labor Statistics Yearbook*), Beijing: China Statistics Press.

National Bureau of Statistics of China. (February 28, 2018). Statistical Communiqué of the People's Republic of China on the 2017 National Economic and Social Development. http://www.stats.gov.cn/english/press release/201802/t20180228_1585666.html (accessed April 15, 2023).

National Bureau of Statistics of China. (2022). 中国劳动统计年鉴 Zhongguo laodong tongji nianjian (*China Labor Statistics Yearbook*), Beijing: China Statistics Press.

National Bureau of Statistics of China. (February 28, 2023). Statistical Communiqué of the People's Republic of China on the 2022 National Economic and Social Development. https://www.stats.gov.cn/english/PressRelease/202402/t20240228_1947918.html (accessed April 12, 2025).

Polanyi, M. (1985). *Implizites Wissen*, Frankfurt am Main: Suhrkamp.

Ran, X. and Zhao, Y. (2023). Behind the flexibility: Insufficient occupational injury protection of gig workers in China, *Frontiers in Public Health*. DOI: 10.3389/fpubh.2023.1117180.

Schnack, H.-C. and Yuan, Y. (2010). Regulating migration in China. A selection of recent policy documents, in Gransow, B. and Zhou Daming (eds.) *Migrants and Health in Urban China, History and Society*, Berliner China-Hefte, Vol. 38, Münster: Lit Press, pp. 124–150.

Schroer, M. (2005). Zur Soziologie des Körpers, in Schroer, M. (ed.) *Soziologie des Körpers*, Frankfurt am Main: Suhrkamp, pp. 7–47.

Shilling, C. (2008). *Changing Bodies. Habit, Crisis and Creativity*, London: Sage Publications.

Ten Brink, T., Müller, A., and Liu, T. (2022). The introduction of pension, accident, and health insurance in urban China, in Kuhlmann, J. and Nullmeier, F. (eds.) *Causal Mechanisms in the Global Development of Social Policies*, Cham: Palgrave Macmillan, pp. 33–66.

Tian, Y., Chen, Y., Zhou, M., and Zhao, S. (October 2021). Institutional design and incentives for migrant workers to participate in social insurance in China: Evidence from a policy experiment in Chengdu City, *Frontiers in Public Health* 9, 1–10.

Wang, B., Wu, C., Kang, L., Reniers, G., and Huang, L. (2018). Work safety in China's thirteenth Five-Year Plan (2016–2020): Current status, new challenges and future tasks, *Safety Science* 104, 164–178. https://doi.org/10.1016/J.SSCI.2018.01.012.

Wang, H. and Tao, L. (2012). Current situations and challenges of occupational disease prevention and control in China, *Industrial Health* 50, 73–79.

Wang, W. (March 14, 2011). The woes of injury at work. Law center draws attention to long delays over compensation claims, *China Daily*.

Wang, X., Chan, C., and Yang, L. (2021). Economic restructuring and migrant workers' coping strategies in China's Pearl River Delta, *Third World Quarterly* 42(4), 812–830.

Wu, L. (吴琳缤). (2007). 农民工职业健康意识消解话语机制 Nongmingong zhiye jiankang yishi xiaojie huayu jizhi (The mechanism of discourse that dispels the peasant workers' consciousness of work-related ill health) MA thesis, Department of Social Work, Sun Yatsen University, Guangzhou.

Ye, Y., Zhang, S., Rao, J., Wang, H., Li, Y., Wang, S., and Dong, X. (2016), Analysis of national major work safety accidents in China, 2003–2012. *Iranian Journal of Public Health* 45(1): 6–13.

Yu, W., Yu, I., Li, Z., Wang, X., Sun, T., Lin, H., Wan, S., Qiu, H., and Xie, S. (2012). Work-related injuries and musculoskeletal disorders among factory workers in a major city of China, *Accident Analysis and Prevention* 48, 457–463.

Zhang, H.X.-Q. (2007). Conceptualizing the links: Migration, health and sustainable livelihoods in China, in Zhang, H.X.-Q., Wu, B., and Sanders, G. (eds.) *Marginalisation in China: Perspectives on Transition and Globalisation*, Aldershot: Ashgate, pp. 195–214.

Zhang, X. (张雪梅). (2021). 农民工工伤保险政策执行过程中的博弈分析 Nongmingong gongshang baoxian zhengce zhixing guocheng zhong de boyi fenxi (Game-theoretical analysis of the implementation of work-related injury insurance for migrant workers), 人才资源开发 (*Human Resource Development*) 6, 53–55.

Zhu, Y., Chen, P., and Zhao, W. (2014). Injured workers in China: Injustice, conflict and social unrest, *International Labor Review* 153(4), 635–647.

Chapter 3

Emerging Spaces of Care and Party-State Securitisation Policies: The Rise and Fall of Migrant-Worker NGOs in the Pearl River Delta

> "When providing services, more and more organisations began to emphasize the idea of community and of solidarity among the workers themselves."
>
> "The authorities who visited us … wanted us to move out, they disturbed our work and put us under pressure."

Introduction

Migrant-worker NGOs began to emerge in the Pearl River Delta (PRD) in the late 1990s. At that time, investment from overseas Chinese, low-cost land provided by local governments and migrant workers moving from rural to urban areas were key drivers in the development of the PRD into a booming centre of export manufacturing. As discussed in Chapter 2, the lack of occupational safety, work-related injury insurance and responsible trade unions left the migrant workers largely unprotected in their new working and living environments. However, this was also the time when a wide range of grassroots NGOs began to appear all over China, particularly in the PRD.[1] Participation by many civil society organisations in the 1995 UN World Conference on Women in Beijing was an important catalyst in this process. We can divide the development of migrant-worker NGOs in the PRD into five general phases[2]:

- **1996–2002:** Migrant-worker NGOs emerged as a specific type of NGO in China.
- **2003–2007:** Migrant-worker NGOs proliferated in connection with the more pro-migration policies of the Hu Jintao and Wen Jiabao administration. They saw themselves as representing the rights and interests of migrant workers and attracted the attention of local media and international observers.
- **2008–2012:** Government support was given only to those NGOs considered to have no other objectives than providing social services and social work. So-called *weiquan* (rights-protecting)[3] migrant-worker NGOs, however, were treated differently and closely monitored, resulting in a rapid decline in both their visibility and activities in urban public spaces.
- **2012–2015:** Public security cracked down on NGOs defending the individual and collective labour rights of migrant workers, especially targeting those advocacy NGOs that promoted strike activities by migrant workers in the PRD.
- **Since 2016:** A new architecture of NGO legislation has taken shape, which is characterised by increasing securitisation. This policy coincided with preparations for Hong Kong's National Security Law, which came into effect in 2020 and directly affected the close relationship between Hong Kong labour organisations and migrant-worker NGOs in the PRD.

---

[1]Early examples of migrant-worker NGOs in the PRD referred to in most of the literature include the Chinese Working Women Network (女工关怀), the Shenzhen Institute of Contemporary Observation (深圳当代社会观察研究所) and the Panyu Migrant Worker Documentary Centre (番禺打工族文书处理服务部). While the first two organisations worked on behalf of migrants (as Howell put it, 2009:178, 186), the latter was organised by migrant workers themselves.

[2]Different authors use different periodisations for the development of migrant-worker NGOs (Deng, 2009:286; Chan, 2010:160/61; Ling and Ngok, 2011:77; Luo and Gu, 2008:1–11; Howell, 2021).

[3]Consisting of 维(护) and 权(利).

This chapter has two main aims. The first is to explore how migrant-worker NGOs created spaces of care and support for their fellow migrant workers in large cities of the PRD such as Guangzhou, Shenzhen, Dongguan and Foshan. The second is to examine the politics of state space that the Chinese party-state employed to restrict the activities of migrant-worker NGOs, while at the same time attempting to selectively incorporate such activities into its own agenda of creating a Chinese-style service-oriented non-profit sector. The analysis of the dynamics of care activities related to migrant workers in urban areas is based on Henri Lefebvre's threefold conceptualisation of space-making (lived, conceived and perceived space) (1991), Martina Löw's critical refinements of the relation of agency and structure within the production of social space (2008), Marielle Gleiss's conceptualisation of care work in the context of migrant-worker NGOs in China (2019) and Neil Brenner's conceptualisation of the politics of state space (2003). The first part of the chapter is based on eleven interviews (2011–2012) with eight migrant-worker organisations[4] in Shenzhen (7), Panyu (2) and Guangzhou (2). The organisations concentrated on providing legal information, advice, training and aid in the context of labour laws and regulations, arranging hospital visits to injured migrant workers, conducting occupational safety training, factory surveys and urban integration training (hotline), as well as facilitating cultural and entertainment activities.[5]

The chapter begins with a brief discussion of previous research on migrant-worker NGOs in China. It then undertakes a conceptualisation of care in relation to the agency of migrant-worker NGOs in urban areas. The third section elaborates on how the work by migrant-worker NGOs can be read as creating and claiming urban spaces for and with "migrants in the city." The everyday concerns of these NGOs take the concrete form of visiting hospitals to counsel injured migrant workers, representing

---

[4] See the list of interviews at the end of the chapter. These interviews were not recorded, only notes were taken.

[5] As usual, the names of the NGOs, managers and staff interviewed are anonymised. A certain ethical dilemma admittedly arises in that almost all the leaders of the organisations we spoke to not only had no reservations about giving their names but on the contrary were convinced of the legality and social importance of their activities and explicitly advocated being named. Nevertheless, I am following academic etiquette here, not least because since these interviews were conducted there have been several arrests of leaders and staff of migrant-worker NGOs.

workers at court in disputes over unpaid wages, benefits or compensation, and preparing factory workers for collective bargaining with employers and factory management. The fourth section conceptualises state space as the politics of space, and the fifth section then applies this approach to analyse how the party-state securitised state space during both the Hu/Wen (2002–2012) and Xi/Li (2012–2022) administrations by regulating migrant-worker NGOs according to its own ideas. It is argued that the securitisation of state space includes (1) soft and coercive interventions into the economic, political and legal frameworks of migrant-worker NGOs; (2) imaginaries of state transition through the creation of a self-sustaining Chinese non-profit sector as part of a long-term vision of "new social policies"; and (3) treating International NGOs (INGOs) that provide funding to domestic migrant-worker NGOs as potential non-traditional security threats. The chapter concludes with a reflection on the relationship between spaces of care and spaces of securitisation in China's urban development.

Earlier Research on Migrant-Worker NGOs

Research on migrant-worker NGOs in China has thus far placed a premium on analysing tensions between grassroots NGOs and the authoritarian Chinese state (Zhang and Smith, 2009; Chan, 2012; Elfstrom, 2021). From a governmental perspective, Deng Guosheng analyses the "hidden rules" governing China's unregistered NGOs.[6] Deng identifies the "Three 'No' Policy" towards unregistered NGOs ("no recognition, no banning, no intervention") instead of applying existing laws and regulations as the core government policy. This means that as long as NGOs do not harm state security or social stability, the government will not interfere with their internal affairs or ban them (Deng, 2010:190). Howell (2015) introduces the concept of "welfarist incorporation" to describe efforts to develop a professional non-profit civic sector of welfare provision and argues that the government does not want to cooperate with all labour

[6]According to Deng, there were at least one million unregistered domestic NGOs in China and over 1,000 foreign NGOs, a number that increased ever more rapidly after 2000 (Deng, 2010:190). According to official statistics in China, there were 664,800 registered social organisations in 2016 and 900,914 in 2021. https://chinadevelopmentbrief.org/reports/china-social-organisation-network-published-new-data-of-social-organisations-in-china/.

NGOs (e.g. those relying on foreign funding) while not all labour NGOs want to cooperate with the government (for fear of losing their identity as workers' organisations). Beyond a focus on the relationship between the Chinese state and civil society organisations, and based on long-term participant observation, Anthony Spires (2024) provides a definition of hegemonic authoritarianism (inspired by Antonio Gramsci) and argues that a counter-hegemonic discourse is emerging in the everyday democracy of voluntary associations, driven mainly by the engagement of young people.

Labour NGOs' focus on defending the individual rights of migrant workers has been critiqued by Lee and Shen (2011) via the provocative question of whether these NGOs should be described as an "anti-solidarity machine," splitting the evolving Chinese labour movement and preventing workers from organising themselves. They argue that between cooptation by the state and commercialisation via the market, labour NGOs have little room to manoeuvre and foster civil society in China (Lee and Shen, 2011:187). According to Franceschini and Lin (2019), controversies in the field of labour studies revolve around optimistic versus pessimistic evaluations of labour NGOs' relations with official trade unions, workers and the party-state. Some of the scholars contributing to the debate are activists themselves or doing action research and have positioned themselves in favour of "collective bargaining" by workers with employers, management and local authorities as the main focus of labour NGOs' activities (e.g. Froissart *et al.*, 2019), while others take a more cautious stand on NGO interventions. Zhou and Yan (2019) argue that some Hong Kong donors' intent to channel migrant-worker NGOs towards a movement approach or some lawyers' eagerness to present influential cases of successful labour actions on social media could result in a loss of trust in labour NGOs and put worker representatives at risk of being detained.

Building on her earlier study (2012), Hsu (2017) categorises the interactions between different layers of the local state and migrant NGOs as strategic, asymmetric and symbolic. She sees the state and NGOs as mutually constitutive and argues that both state and NGOs may have joint ownership of the space in which NGOs conduct their activities (Hsu, 2017:160, 165). In a book-length study, Darcy Pan investigates the dynamics of state control towards labour activities in South China. Pan argues that deliberately keeping labour NGOs in a state of uncertainty promotes self-censorship on the part of these organisations. Proposing a new model of bottom-up change in labour politics within China's authoritarian system, Elfstrom's book (2021) starts with different patterns of labour protests. For the PRD (in contrast to the Yangtze Delta), Elfstrom identifies reactive, experimental and crackdown as the main control models used by local governments. Other more recent studies on labour NGOs tend to focus less on labour issues and more on the formation of citizenship. Jakimow (2021:239) identifies "resistance through accommodation" as a labour NGO strategy that can transform citizenship within state-prescribed channels. Chu (2021) takes a similar course in analysing the transformation of a self-organised labour NGO in Hangzhou into an integration project for "new urban citizens."

Most of the examples from this incomplete overview of the rich research in this field use the concept of "labour NGOs"[7] when in fact discussing primarily NGOs that were founded by migrant workers and provide services or advocacy[8] for these workers in urban areas. While there is excellent research on pressing issues such as labour rights, labour conflicts, industrial relations, and labour organising and movements, there is somewhat of a tendency in labour studies to neglect the specific context of migrant workers in cities as individuals, citizens and people from the countryside in search of a better life and in need of a broad variety of services. But the self-organisational efforts and collective actions by migrant workers – focusing not only on wages but also on legitimate social benefits, housing funds and pensions – all indicate that these actions are also a struggle for their right to the city (Lefebvre, 1968/2016). This is why the term "migrant-worker NGOs" is preferred to "labour NGOs" and why their agency is conceptualised in this chapter as care work.

Conceptualising Migrant-Worker NGOs' Activities as Care Work

Migrant-worker NGOs in the PRD provide care primarily in connection with occupational health issues, labour conflicts and compensation payments. In crisis situations of this type, migrant workers need information,

---

[7]The term "labour NGO" is used especially in English-language literature: Howell, 2015; Chen and Yang, 2017; Froissart *et al.*, 2019; Franceschini and Lin, 2019; Zhou and Yan, 2019; Pan, 2020; Elfstrom, 2021. Exceptions include He and Huang, 2015; Hu and Martin, 2020. Chinese literature more often uses concepts such as 农民工组织 (Luo and Gu, 2008; Deng, 2009), indicating organisations of migrant workers.

[8]On transnational advocacy networks in China, see Noakes, 2018.

particularly knowledge of labour laws and related regulations, as well as administrative knowledge and emotional support. Some of the founders of migrant-worker NGOs have experienced work-related accidents themselves. The knowledge they provide also helps empower other workers. The workers generally do not need to pay for the NGOs' services, but many of those who receive assistance later support the organisations as volunteers. This implies a reciprocal understanding of the relationship between care givers and care receivers.

In the research literature on the intersection of care and migration, Turcatti (2021) identifies two main directions: one focuses on the paid and unpaid care work done by migrants and the other on the extent to which migrants have access to care. This dichotomised construction, she argues, means that understanding migrants solely as care givers obscures the question of "who cares for migrants?" while understanding them only as care recipients has been used to label them as burdens on the welfare state. She makes the following critical observation: "Seldom have these directions explored the practices through which migrants care for each other" (Turcatti, 2021:651).[9] In research on care in connection with Chinese rural-to-urban migrants, the situation is similar. On the one hand, there is a body of literature on care work as a specific form of service provided by (often female) migrant workers to urban middle-class households (Connelly *et al.*, 2018). On the other hand, there is another set of research on the problem of social security and social insurance provision (or lack thereof) for migrant workers (Liu and ten Brink, 2022). In the Chinese context, too, the question of who cares for migrants is often unanswered.

A general conceptualisation of care that goes beyond established feminist discourse on female care work is suggested by Amelita King-Dejardin who defines it broadly as "consisting of activities and relations involved in meeting the physical, psychological and emotional needs of adults and children, old and young, frail and able-bodied" (King-Dejardin, 2019:41). She thereby highlights an understanding that focuses not only on a set of (paid or unpaid) tasks or activities but also defines it as a network of relationships between individuals and relevant institutions, such as individuals in need and their families, care workers and their organisations, government agencies supporting and regulating the provision of care, and private and non-profit providers of care services. These social relations and activities have to be seen as embedded in normative,

[9]An exception is Barglowski and Bonfert (2023).

socio-political, economic and legal frameworks for providing care (King-Dejardin, 2019:45).

Recent debates on care and the crisis of care in China do not focus particularly on migrant workers and their situations in the cities but more on family and kinship care in the countryside in relation to care provided by the state (Lammer, 2023; Feuchtwang, 2023; Steinmüller, 2023). An exception is Gleiss *et al.* (2019), who identify "care" as one of four modalities of civil society engagement in China (in addition to positioning, advocacy and identity formation). Care here refers to how civil society actors care for social groups and issues.[10]

In the wake of the COVID-19 pandemic, Gabauer *et al.* discuss an urban care crisis that has revealed multiple dimensions of vulnerability in urban societies (without, however, referring to Chinese cities). Their intent is to introduce existing debates on care "as an analytical prism on the urban crisis" (2022:4) in urban studies and thus to bring care research into dialogue with urban studies. To this end, they suggest exploring the spatiality of care regimes under different urban conditions. The authors argue that the retreat of the welfare state and the lack of institutional care on an urban scale are manifesting themselves in a crisis of care that reproduces and aggravates the urban crisis. Quoting Chatzidakis *et al.*, they call this "neoliberal uncaring by design" (2020:4). A possible key for engaging with urban studies, the authors suggest, is to uncover the "inherent spatiality of caring" (Gabauer, 2022:12) found in places and social networks, extending across different scales and in multiple social divisions of contemporary cities. At the intersections of city and space, Gabauer argues, "a perspective of care may enable just, productive and ethical engagement with urban transformations" (2022:12).

In contrast to Gabauer *et al.* (2019), Li Shiqiao addresses the concept of care from a comparative perspective between Western and Chinese cities. Li doubts that care in an urban context is understood in the same way in Western and Chinese cities. With its roots in the ancient Greek polis, the Christian idea of *caritas* and the more recent ideal of social welfare in the Western city, Li argues, are characterised by an understanding of "universal care" that includes citizens, strangers and public spaces.

[10] *Advocacy* refers to how civil society actors represent social groups and issues, *positioning* refers to how civil society actors use specific strategies to position themselves in a restricted political space and *identity formation* is about how civil society actors engage in processes by which both their own identities and those of the social groups they work with are socially constructed (Gleiss *et al.*, 2019:8–17).

The Chinese city, he says, is "constructed through degrees of care" (Li, 2014:98) with the presence of walls as its clearest manifestation.

At the centre of this conceptualisation of ranked care in urban China, Li sees "the body in safety and danger" with its desire to barricade itself against a potentially hostile exterior. The body is seen as surrounded by three circles of spaces of intensive care. The first circle is the family and the protected home, the second is the expanded home or the apartment blocks in contemporary Chinese cities known as *xiaoqu*[11] responding to the model of the extended family, and the third represents the state (literally the state family[12]) as a provider of intensive care in the form of prestige projects or mega-events such the Three Gorges Dam, the Olympic Games or the high-speed railway network (Li, 2014:102–107). Spaces of intensive care are surrounded by yet another circle of care, which Li calls spaces of regular care. The archetype of the space of regular care is the walled village, a space of kinship and a unit of economic interest. While family relations offer access to intensive care, it is through relational circles (*guanxi*)[13] that one may access economic resources (which are hard to find outside social networks). *Guanxi* relations must be cultivated and cared for to maintain their reciprocal effectiveness.[14] During the Mao era (and beyond), the ubiquitous space of regular care was the work unit (*danwei*),[15] which was both a unit of production and a system of care (as well as a method of human management) (Li, 2014:107–111).

In contradistinction to the inside spaces of intense and regular care, Li locates *jianghu* spaces, meaning outside spaces without care.[16] With the development of modern film-making in the 20th century, the *wuxia* genre

---

[11] 小区, a micro district.

[12] 国家.

[13] 关系.

[14] Care by relational circles in contemporary China takes place in dining rooms, particularly in enclosed (or private) rooms (包间) within a restaurant, separated from common spaces (Li, 2014:108).

[15] 单位.

[16] *Jianghu* (江湖, literally "rivers and lakes") stands for an unpleasant place outside the social order. The meaning of *jianghu* was elaborated in the highly popular Ming Dynasty (14th century) novel *Water Margin* (*Shuihu zhuan* 水浒传) set in the Southern Song Dynasty (12th century) about 108 rebellious characters and their followers, gathering in the Liangshan marsh, acting against the Imperial court but always with the noble goal of reestablishing a just order. While Li Shiqiao translates *jianghu* as "spaces of carelessness" (Li, 2014:111/112), I prefer "spaces of uncare" (see also Gabauer, 2022) to avoid misunderstanding "carelessness" here as "lightheartedness."

as an indigenous narrative gave rise to *jianghu* as the spatial framework for many martial arts films (Li, 2014:112). The concept of *jianghu* became translated into an urban context in the Hong Kong gangster and police films of the 1980s, Li continues, and was established as a characterisation of the underworld of the (Hong Kong) megacity. With several hundred million migrants having reached urban areas in China since the 1980s, *jianghu* has reconstituted itself in the Chinese city (Li, 2014:114). The demarcation line between spaces of care and uncare in large Chinese cities is the *hukou* system, which sorts the urban population into one of these two spaces. Urban villages (*chengzhongcun*)[17] belonging to village collectives whose agricultural land had been acquired when the cities expanded became the habitat of many migrants and have been described as typical *jianghu* spaces (Li, 2014:114; Ma and Wang, 2011).[18]

In conclusion, defining care as practices consisting of activities and (reciprocal) relations between care givers and receivers can serve as a lens to identify spaces of care provided by migrant-worker NGOs in urban areas. Similar to Gabauer (2022), care practices are understood here in the three dimensions of providing, interacting mutually in relations and reflecting on care. To be more precise about the activities of migrant-worker NGOs, we follow Gleiss (2019) who defines care in this context as being about social groups and items, including advocacy as an extension of caring for others (Gleiss, 2019:11). From the perspective of migrant workers, the neoliberal traits of their urban environments may be perceived as "uncaring" (Gabauer, 2022; Li, 2014).

Migrant-Worker NGOs: Creating Urban Spaces of Care

This section will introduce migrant workers' care activities, how and with whom they interact while providing such services and how they make sense of what they are doing. The scope and scale of migrant-worker NGOs' care practices depend on different types of activities and different types of relationships with other stakeholders. The day-to-day routines of migrant-worker NGOs are part of broader processes of restructuring highly institutionalised yet highly fragmented urban spaces. Before exploring the various care

[17] 城中村.

[18] For more on *jianghu,* see also Chapters 4 and 5.

activities of migrant-worker NGOs in greater detail, we will briefly introduce the rapidly changing economic, political and legal contexts of their activities and the crucial role of the registration system for migrant-worker NGOs in relation to both their internal organisation and the larger society.

Institutional embeddedness of migrant-worker NGOs' agency

Since 2007, the government of Guangdong province has pursued a strategy aimed at eliminating the low-end manufacturing industry (such as clothing, toys, footwear and furniture) and advancing global value chains via industrial upgrading and innovation. These industries were to be replaced by large-scale high-end technology industries. Guangdong's approach was in line with the central government's policy of boosting domestic demand by increasing workers' purchasing power (*China Labour Bulletin*, 2011:55, 56). In keeping with Guangdong's economic strategy, Wang Yang, party secretary of the province (2007–2013), adopted a pragmatic and conciliatory political approach. It viewed migrant workers' demands for higher wages as timely, in concert with the strategy of industrial upgrading, broadening domestic consumption and promoting the expansion of the Chinese middle class. When a strike was held in 2010 at the Nanhai Honda automotive components factory in Foshan, the Guangdong Provincial Federation of Trade Unions made Nanhai Honda a pilot site for collective bargaining with workers, who elected their own representatives, presented their own demands and achieved some positive results (*China Labour Bulletin*, 2011:41, 66).[19] Using local officials experienced in labour conflicts, the Guangdong provincial government handled the 2010 automotive strikes as "work conflicts" and supported collective negotiations between workers and management (Zhang, 2019:130).

In late 2012, the incoming Xi/Li administration started to transform the field of domestic and international NGOs[20] including the subfield of

[19]The strike's successful outcome helped set off more than twenty further strikes at other automotive suppliers in the PRD within the following two months (*China Labour Bulletin*, 2011:26).

[20]In relevant legal regulations and official documents, the term NGO only appears in connection with foreign organisations. Domestic grassroots organisations are called social organisations, which take the form of membership-based social organisations (社会团体 *shehui tuanti*), foundations (基金会 *jijinhui*) and privately operated non-enterprise units (,民办非企业单位 *minban feiqiye danwei*). See General Offices of CPC (中共中央办公厅国务院办公厅印发) (2016), 关于改革社会组织管理制度促进社会组织健康有序发展

charity in a way that put an end to the previous kind of civil society NGO development in China (see Levy and Pissler, 2020). Structural reforms initiated in conjunction with the top-level design (Ahlers and Schubert, 2022) included transforming the previous civil society sector into a newly created and politically shaped NPO sector[21] and generating a series of new laws and regulations (see Table 1).

Table 1. Legal architecture of an emerging Chinese NPO sector (1998–2017).

Year (adopted)	Document	Main points
(1998) 2016 revised	Administrative Regulations on Registration of Social Organisations[a]	Dual registration system with requirements: • to register with local Civil Affairs department (with periodic inspections); • to seek professional sponsorship by a state agency or organisation in a related policy area (with possible influence on decision-making).
March (2010)	–	Transfer of funds from international donors to registered Chinese NGOs requires notarial certification.
November (2011) Guangdong Province new regulations (came into effect July 2012)	Plan Concerning Further Fostering and Regulating Social Organisations of Guangdong Province	Social organisations may directly apply for registration with Civil Affairs departments without the "dual registration system" of first having to secure sponsorship by a state agency or organisation.

的意见 (Opinion on the reform of the social organisation management system and promotion of the healthy and orderly development of social organisations). Available at: https://www.gov.cn/zhengce/2016-08/21/content_5101125.htm (accessed February 8, 2025).

[21] The term NPO (non-profit organisation) is used to distinguish such entities from NGOs (non-governmental organisations) in the context of services provided to the Chinese state. Both NGOs and NPOs are part of the third sector, which is defined as a distinct domain separated from the state and private sectors.

Table 1. (*Continued*)

Year (adopted)	Document	Main points
April (2016) promulgated by the National People's Congress and its Standing Committee on 16 March 2016	Charity Law[b]	Registration under the Ministry of Civil Affairs with the aim to: • restore trust in charity; • increase the level of private donations.
August (2016) CPCCC and State Council	Views on reforming social organisation management systems and promoting social organisations' healthy and orderly development[c]	• Simplified registration procedures; • Bureau of Management of NGOs under the Ministry of Civil Affairs.
April (2016) Standing Committee of the National People's Congress (came into effect January 2017)	Law on the Administration of Activities of Foreign NGOs within the Territory of China[d]	• Registration under the Ministry of Public Security; • Dual registration system (requiring a Chinese supervisory unit)[e]; • Prohibition on engaging in or funding political activities.

Notes: [a]社会团体登记管理条例.
[b]中华人民共和国慈善法.
[c]关于改革社会组织管理制度促进社会组织健康有序发展的意见.
[d]中华人民共和国境外非政府组织境内活动管理法.
[e]业务主管单位.

Easier registration requirements with the Ministry of Civil Affairs for domestic social organisations that were not seen as politically sensitive formed the core of an entirely new legal architecture for the emerging Chinese NPO sector. The reform basically established a hybrid registration management system in which industry associations, chambers of commerce, science and technology, public welfare and charity, and urban and rural community service organisations could register directly, whereas other social organisations required dual management (Ma, 2014).

Nearly all of the migrant-worker NGOs interviewed around 2012 had a registration with Industry and Commerce departments, and one was registered as a community library with the Education department. None was able to register with the Civil Affairs department, which meant most of their funding had to come from overseas foundations or other funding sources. Further changes to formal registration practices and protocols over the past decade have also had an impact on the position and self-positioning of migrant-focused NGOs.

Limited opportunities to successfully obtain official registration and the associated limited access to resources resulted in another serious problem, namely, finding qualified employees willing to work at low pay on primarily short-term projects in positions of lower social status. These constraints not only put migrant-worker NGOs lacking a formal registration with the Civil Affairs department in weak and vulnerable societal positions in general but also had the following specific effects: (1) difficulties in expanding and therefore becoming more efficient as organisations; (2) lack of access to government resources leading to low salaries, low job security, lack of scientific management and professionalism; and (3) absence of public trust in migrant-worker NGOs due to reasonable doubts that they can provide a career and income. This in turn fostered a vicious cycle consisting of a lack of government support and funding, a lack of organisational capacity and professionalism, and a lack of public trust in migrant-worker NGOs.

Invisibility and acting in informal spaces became the *sine qua non* for the development of grassroots NGOs in China in general and migrant-worker NGOs in particular. The fewer rights these organisations had because of their questionable legal status, the more they became dependent on the benevolence – the "closed eye" – of officials. The aforementioned constraints had an impact on their societal status and reputation. They also affected the quality of their internal management which made it challenging to meet their own standards.[22]

The migrant-worker NGO office: Organisational care work

Migrant-worker NGOs in the PRD normally run one or more project offices, usually located in Shenzhen, but also in Guangzhou, Foshan and Dongguan. Activities at or connected with the office cover a wide

[22] Generally speaking, this was the context in which our interviews were conducted.

spectrum that can include legal consultancy provided to migrant workers, trainings or lectures (on labour law, work safety or collective bargaining), running phone hotlines for migrant workers who need individual support or advice, workers' cultural activities, community services (such as libraries or after-school activities for migrant workers' children), networking among migrant workers, research such as industrial surveys or creating databases of migrant-worker NGOs, preparing informational materials for a broader audience, targeting the media and social media, management and administrative tasks for the organisation (such as project preparation, financial management and work plans), and meetings and recreational gatherings for staff and volunteers.

While many administrative tasks can be done electronically, the office is nevertheless an important meeting place and a symbolic anchor of the organisation itself. Its rooms are equipped for trainings and seminars, and it contains the documents and data collections which are meaningful sources of knowledge for its activities. The office is the workplace of the organisations' directors/leaders, full- and part-time staff, and student and worker volunteers. Above all, the office is a place to receive migrant workers seeking advice or participating in the organisation's activities and welcome members of other migrant-worker NGOs, researchers and other visitors. One leader of a migrant-worker NGO in Shenzhen described the office atmosphere (of another migrant-worker NGO) as follows:

> "As everyone has had the same misfortune [of a work-related accident], when all are gathering together, it is very friendly. It is not really acting like an agent for a client, just as a fellow, but such companionship is very meaningful for the co-workers. When providing services, more and more organisations began to emphasise the idea of community and of solidarity among the workers themselves. The workers' mutual aid network ... stands for it" (Interview B6/12/SZ/11).[23]

The office as a symbolic place generates an atmosphere of self-affirmation, self-empowerment and self-respect for members and visitors alike.

The founders of NGOs often assume leadership positions at these organisations. Over the years, more and more satellite migrant-worker NGOs have emerged from some "base-camp" organisations. The NGO leaders are accountable primarily to sponsors, local governments at

---

[23] See list of interviews at the end of the chapter.

various levels, academia and the media. Compared to others in their organisations, the leaders have broader social networks and interact in more complex domestic and transnational/international environments. This dominance raises questions about whether migrant-worker NGOs are institutionalised organisations or simply the personal networks of their leaders (Gransow and Zhu, 2016:190; Wu, 2008; Qian, 2010).

Normally, migrant-worker NGOs have 4–7 staff members (full- and part-time), sometimes dispersed across multiple project offices. As with other NGOs in the PRD, the migrant-worker NGOs are quite small in scale and have high staff fluctuation with employees often staying less than one year. In organisations with five full-time staff members, more employees stay for a year or longer. Volunteers (from 20 to 200 at some organisations) are a considerable resource for these NGOs. There are two kinds of volunteers: students who help prepare informational materials and newsletters, staff the office and help with charity activities and outings, and workers who visit injured migrant workers in hospitals. For worker volunteers, it is relatively easy to gain the trust of such patients (Gransow and Zhu, 2016:190).

Overall, the scope of migrant-worker NGOs and their activities depends on the type of registration, their internal management, their funding and last but not least the political environment which has often been more constricting than encouraging. When asked about their organisation's main problem, respondents regularly mentioned funding. But the interviews also revealed that unsatisfactory fundraising could to a large extent be attributed to insufficient internal management expertise, particularly financial management. In addition, problems with internal management often seem to be directly or indirectly related to the disguised nature of NGO registration.

Interactions related to hospital visits

Visits to injured migrants in hospitals are done mainly by worker volunteers who ask the patients about their situations and accidents. A leader of a migrant NGO in Guangzhou explained the following to us: "Worker volunteers visit hospitals on a regular basis, such as every ten days, or two to three days a week. ... Volunteers form a visiting group. They go to a hospital twice a month on average. According to their calculations, a worker is hospitalised for 20 days, so visiting once every 15 days can cover every worker as much as possible. This makes the organisation's work more streamlined because some areas are relatively remote and it isn't convenient for the staff to go by themselves, so we entrust volunteers in the area to visit and give them hundreds of sets of materials at a time.... And it is much better for these workers to do the work than the organisation itself; after all, they are all people who have had the same experience. This kind of work-related injury volunteer team has been established for two years, and it also has turnover. Some people leave, and the organisation will arrange new people to join it" (B11/12/GZ/16).[24]

When distributing informational material and telling patients with work-related injuries about free services by their organisation, the reaction is often amazement, scepticism and fear of falling prey to fraud. "Because the organisation does not charge money, many workers are worried that it is deceiving people, so they go to a lawyer.... Some people have sought out lawyers but the results were not good, especially because there are some 'black lawyers' who can take both sides, all the more so for relatively serious accidents. They not only charge the workers but also take money from the company. While litigating, they are not entirely on the side of the workers, of course.... The workers find out later that the lawyer is always in contact with the boss. When they suspect something is wrong, they find their way to the organisation again but often it is too late by then. The first trial may have been over.... However, as the worker volunteers have often had similar fates, it's not so difficult for them to gain the trust of more recent victims and establish a sense of solidarity."

In 2004, an accident insurance system was launched that also covered migrant workers. Since then, injured workers have been treated primarily in specially contracted hospitals, so migrant-worker NGOs and their volunteers have known where to find the injured workers. "Generally, a special team is assigned to each hospital, but there will always be problems. The hospital's security personnel will recognise people and will not let them in again, so two or three people will arrange to go in turns. Now the work of the organisation is very difficult, and all aspects are under some pressure, so it is difficult to do some things smoothly."

While a hospital as a profit-oriented entity has an interest in excluding the worker volunteers, its care personnel sometimes assist the volunteers in gaining access to the patients' rooms and introducing their services (Gransow and Zhu, 2016:195).[25] "But now there are some new problems,

[24] The following quotes in this subsection are also from Interview B11/12/GZ/16.

[25] See also Chapter 2 on injured migrant workers.

that is, the doctors in the hospital lack professional ethics. They tell patients not to trust the organisation, but in fact, they know that it provides free services. The purpose of doing so is to build a good relationship with the workers' company and protect its interests, so the company will send injured people to the hospital in the future. All hospitals are like this…."

But hospital staff sometimes secretly help the worker volunteers. Some nurses support the volunteers by spreading information about their organisation among patients. "Nursing volunteers can only do some work secretly because this practice conflicts with the hospitals' interests and they usually just tell the workers quietly. There are fewer than 20 hospitals to visit now, and only four or five have volunteer nurses."

Bringing cases of individual labour disputes to court

Some of the migrant-worker NGOs interviewed also represented individual workers in court. Their cases usually focused on compensation payments for work injuries or other labour disputes (up to 2013). The staff members of these organisations who engage in rights protection are not necessarily licensed to practice law. Before 2013, the Chinese Civil Procedure Rules allowed any Chinese citizen aged eighteen or above to provide civic representation in court. At that time, migrant workers could be represented in court by migrant-worker NGOs, i.e. by licensed practitioners, legal scholars or more or less self-educated lay people (Gransow and Zhu, 2016:194; Fu and Cullen, 2008:112–114). But the growing phenomenon of "citizens' legal agents" came under attack by Guangdong public security authorities. In January 2013, the Civil Procedure Law was amended to stipulate that the litigant or legal representative may entrust only lawyers, the litigant's relatives or employees, or citizens recommended by the litigant's community, employer or relevant social groups. As such, migrant workers are theoretically permitted as co-workers or social groups endorsed by the community or the employer to provide civic representation, but in practice, the amendment has been used to narrow civic representatives to professional lawyers, co-workers and relatives of the litigant. Faced with these legal constraints, migrant-worker NGOs gradually abandoned the "civic representation" channel to care for individual fellow migrants (Gransow and Zhu, 2016:194).

The existing formal system of administrative bodies, arbitration and courts cannot substitute the role of migrant-worker NGOs in representing individual migrant workers in court. This is because it has thus far proven ineffective as a tool for migrant workers in disputes with their employers. According to Hu and Martin (2020), the main obstacles for migrant workers in using the formal labour dispute resolution system effectively are twofold. First of all, it is often difficult to prove a labour relation with the employer. Secondly, official mediators of Labour Bureau arbitration committees at municipal and district levels are motivated primarily by the government's interest in economic growth and social stability. Such mediators are often regarded as more interested in "putting out a fire than assisting the migrant workers" (Hu and Martin, 2020:22). What makes migrant-worker NGOs such as "Little Bird Hotline"[26] more effective in handling workers' disputes than the formal labour dispute resolution system, they argue, is that the NGOs are funded only by donations; so, they can represent workers' interests without interference from the government or employers. This is what enables "Little Bird" to pressure employers to care successfully for migrant workers. But the authors also point to the dilemma that what works on a small scale would not necessarily succeed if expanded to the national level. In the latter case, they would need financial support from the government, and then "Little Bird" would face dependencies similar to those of the All-China Federation of Trade Unions (ACFTU) (Hu and Martin, 2020:22).

Preparing collective bargaining

Before 2012, while migrant-worker NGOs were dealing mainly with individual conflicts about occupational health and other work-related issues, some organisations wanted to scale up and support collective bargaining for migrant workers. Advocacy of this type makes a difference insofar as it not only tries to solve individual conflicts within China's existing legal framework but also seeks to influence the policies and agendas of state actors. "In a way," Gleiss argues, "advocacy is an extension of … caring for others … in that the knowledge and experiences gained while caring for a particular social group or issue are used as a springboard to defend their rights and interests and call for changes in public policies that will benefit this group or issue" (Gleiss *et al.*, 2019:11). Like forms of care for individual migrant workers, advocacy means exercising agency from

---

[26] 小小鸟互助打工热线.

below. But unlike care for individuals, which is generally considered a relatively unpolitical activity by government officials, advocacy is perceived as politically sensitive (*mingan*)[27] or even as crossing a red line. Some migrant-worker NGOs in the PRD are involved in both forms of caring, others only in one or the other.

In addition to the legal constraints on NGOs' civic representation of migrant workers in court as mentioned in the previous subsection, two more reasons have led some NGOs to give up on bringing individual cases to the courts. First, some organisations rejected a focus on legal training, legal aid and cultural or recreational activities as a "legalistic strategy focused on individual cases" and therefore as insufficient. Second, they argued that a slowing economy and an ageing workforce have led to new collective threats such as factory relocations and non-payment to social security funds, and therefore workforce needs have been shifting from individual to collective care activities (Franceschini and Lin, 2019:78).

To engage more strongly in collective bargaining, in May 2012, a platform was established under the Guangdong Provincial Workers' Union called the "Federation of social service organisations for Guangdong workers." Under the joint supervision of the Provincial Union and the Civil Affairs Bureau, the Federation should have served as an umbrella organisation, embracing not only associations and individual members but also migrant-worker NGOs that had applied for membership (Gransow and Zhu, 2016:188).[28] Hong Kong and foreign NGOs played a supportive role in offering capacity building and training courses for migrant-worker activists, lawyers and scholars. But while access to resources from abroad such as funding, organisational expertise and transnational networks helped migrant-worker NGOs in the PRD to survive and maintain a certain degree of independence from employers and local governments, it also raised the risk of dependency on the international sponsor who might expect to push the migrant-worker NGOs towards a labour movement orientation (Gransow and Zhu, 2016:189). The new platform could have paved the way for cooperation between trade unions and migrant-worker NGOs and was welcomed by grassroots organisations. But the fact that

---

[27]敏感. On the politics of *mingan*, see Pan (2020, Chapter 4).

[28]In addition to 34 associations including industrial organisations, university legal clinics, foundations and local trade union agencies, plus 55 individual members such as lawyers and union members, the umbrella organisation covers 20 organisations including migrant-worker NGOs that have applied for membership (cf. Franceschini, 2012).

the platform's founding coincided with an unprecedented clampdown on migrant-worker NGOs by authorities in the PRD raised doubts as to whether this model would survive and could be successfully implemented in the future (cf. Franceschini, 2012).

The embryonic process of collective bargaining met with harsh resistance from the Hong Kong business federations (*China Labour Bulletin*, 2011:57, 58). The ability of NGOs to mobilise migrant workers' collective action was a major reason why governments and business circles perceived the organisations as politically sensitive and wanted to keep them under control. With political and social stability remaining the primary concern of the Chinese government, in 2012, Guangdong authorities increasingly turned to repressive measures and used riot police and safety guards to break up workers' protests by force. In subsequent years, the situation became even more acute.

In 2014, there were extensive and prolonged strikes in the shoe industry, first at the Yue Yuen shoe factory in Dongguan, involving more than two-thirds of the 60,000 workers (Blecher, 2014:665), and later at the Lide factory, part of which was to be relocated from Panyu to Nansha in Guangzhou. While the Yue Yuen strike was about pension payments, around 1,000 workers at the Lide factory feared for their jobs (Han, 2016). In both cases, established migrant-worker NGOs had successfully prepared and promoted collective bargaining through worker representatives and were able to achieve considerable success for the workforce. However, NGO leaders and worker representatives were subsequently arrested and some of them were convicted.

Interim conclusion

It has been argued that in an "uncaring" urban environment, migrant-worker NGOs provide care activities such as legal information and support in the event of labour conflicts. While their services are mostly free of charge (which initially made them untrustworthy in the eyes of some migrants), the relationship between the organisations and the workers who benefitted from them often later became one of reciprocity between the NGO and worker volunteers. The trust established via mutual interaction in care relations is an asset for these NGOs, in contrast to the relationships between migrant workers and trade unions or labour administration representatives who are on the payroll of the Chinese government. As long as migrant-worker NGOs were not funded by official Chinese institutions, they were able to wholeheartedly support and represent workers' interests in court. Later on, restrictions on receiving funds from foreign donors through the requirement of notarial certification since 2010 and restrictions on representing migrant workers in court since 2013 narrowed the scope of their activities and significantly increased competition among them. Additionally, some NGO activists viewed this form of care work for individual migrants as insufficient and aimed for more substantial approaches, such as engaging in collective bargaining (instead of collective consultations) with factory management.

The year 2012 marked a turning point in many ways. The creation of a joint platform of official trade unions and numerous migrant-worker NGOs created favourable conditions for linking the trust-based relationships between NGOs and a broader stratum of migrant workers with departments of the official trade unions, thus not only creating more sustainable conditions for collective bargaining at the workplace level but also initiating a long overdue reform of the trade unions into an interest representation body. This would have meant considerable expansion of urban care spaces in the interests of migrant workers. In addition, Hong Kong NGOs were acting as intermediaries between Western foundations and Chinese migrant-worker NGOs in the PRD. But such an empowerment of migrant workers was opposed by local Chinese and international business circles in the PRD. And the incoming Xi administration embarked on a new policy course in late 2012. Beyond potential economic losses, it saw the platform as a weak point that could be exploited by INGOs as funders for the migrant-worker NGOs. The following section shows how the Xi administration has responded to the spontaneous emergence and expansion of NGO care spaces for migrant workers by imposing a spatiality of party-state power.

Conceptualising State Space

In their activities and interactions with a wide range of actors, migrant-worker NGOs have often operated on the terrain of the Chinese party-state. But how can the party-state itself be conceptualised as a space-generating actor? To this end, we draw on the work of Brenner *et al.* (2003), who have explored the spatiality of state power. They begin by distancing themselves from a naturalising understanding of state space in the sense of Max Weber (and twentieth-century social science), whereby the territoriality of the state is taken for granted. Against the backdrop of

Table 2. Conceptualising state space.

State space (Brenner *et al.*, 2003)	Production of space (Lefebvre, 1991)		
State space in the integral sense	Representational space	Social space	Lived space
State space in the representational sense	Representations of space	Mental space	Conceived space
State space in the narrow sense	Spatial practise	Physical space	Perceived space

Source: Brenner *et al.* (2003:6), Lefebvre (1991:33, 38–40), Elden (2007:110) and the author's compilation.

debates on globalisation, including critiques of methodological nationalism, the crisis of the national welfare state and the (re)discovery of subnational and supranational scales, the authors focus on the political economy of scale by (1) calling into question the taken-for-grantedness of nation-state space as the necessary arena of political life; (2) suggesting a relativisation of scale and the increasing importance of subnational and supranational levels of state space; and (3) analysing "struggles to establish new scales as sites of state regulatory activity under conditions of rapid geo-economic change" (Brenner *et al.*, 2003:5).[29]

As shown in Table 2, Brenner *et al.* (2003:6–11) consider the following three dimensions and dynamics of state space (which seem to be based on Lefebvre's conceptual triad): (1) *State space in the integral sense* refers to state spatial strategies claiming to accomplish a unified and hence homogeneous society. Explorations are directed to scale-specific ways in which state institutions regulate and reorganise social and economic relations and related modes of state intervention into social and economic processes. (2) *State space in the representational sense* refers to competing spatial imaginaries that represent state and political spaces.

[29]Brenner *et al.* conceptualises state space as "dynamically evolving spatial entities that continually mold and reshape … the very social relations they aspire to regulate, control and/or structure. This continual production and transformation of state space occurs not only through material-institutional practices of state spatial regulation but also through a range of representational and discursive strategies through which the terrain of sociopolitical struggle is mapped and remapped by actors who are directly involved in such struggles" (2003:11).

Explorations of these spatial imaginaries provide an important basis for the politics of representation. (3) *State space in the narrow sense* refers to the spatialities of the state itself, regarded as legal and political institutions and regulatory capacities grounded in the territorialisation of political power. Explorations in this dimension of state space comprise the changing organisation of state territoriality in the modern interstate system and the internal administrative differentiation.

To apply this approach to analysing the dimensions and dynamics of state space in relation to the spatiality of the Chinese party-state, an obvious limitation is that Brenner *et al.* (2003) explicitly focus on the history and contemporary formations of capitalism. This needs to be considered accordingly. Another limitation is that the reflections go back more than twenty years and are embedded in the context of the globalisation discourses of the time. Against the background of more recent tendencies of asymmetrical renationalisation, they must be read in both respects. In the next section, all three dimensions of state space are seen as belonging together but will be addressed one by one to better understand the seemingly paradoxical and contradictory reactions of various Chinese state institutions towards the emergence and development of migrant-worker NGOs.

Party-State Politics: Securitising Chinese State Space

We will start the analysis of the (re)production of Chinese party-state space by examining the state's intervention in the social and economic realms of the migrant-worker NGOs. How did the Chinese state (in the capacity of different levels and functional institutions) intervene and regulate the evolving field of migrant-worker NGOs over time? This first dimension of party-state space corresponds to Brenner's "state space in the integral sense," directed to the domestic situation, and to Lefebvre's "social space/lived space."

Soft and forcible interventions: Regulating migrant-worker NGOs

Rather than using existing laws and regulations as its core policy from the early 2000s onwards, the Chinese government adopted a soft policy of keeping "one eye shut and one eye open,"[30] first to regulate unregistered

[30] 睁一眼闭一眼.

foreign NGOs and later also to target domestic NGOs by similar hidden rules (Deng, 2010:192). This policy dominated until around 2012 when some puzzling and disconcerting political signals were sent to the NGO community. As of 1 July 2012, Guangdong province loosened its registration requirements for NGOs such that a single registration procedure with the local Civil Affairs Bureau should suffice. Initially, such loosening of the local registration regulations was interpreted as a positive sign and nurtured the expectation within the NGO community – albeit not without scepticism – that more organisations (possibly including migrant-worker NGOs) could become legal with all the associated opportunities regarding fundraising, solving human resource problems and so on. Since creating a joint platform for trade unions and migrant-worker NGOs at the time marked a turn towards legal forms of collective bargaining, the migrant-worker NGOs involved in this process felt a certain sense of optimism. Less optimistic was the fact, mentioned earlier, that only those NGOs on a special list of eligible organisations could register as social organisations directly with the relevant levels of the Ministry of Civil Affairs. Groups engaged in advocacy, rights work or political issues were not on the list. The targeted exclusion of advocacy groups, including migrant-worker NGOs, became increasingly evident with more frequent raids by public security organs on individual organisations' offices, especially in Shenzhen. Given what looked like liberalisation (simplified registration, cooperative approaches with the ACFTU and a comparatively open attitude by the provincial government towards civil society activities), these attacks seemed erratic and disturbing.

Pan (2019:159, 160) provided three possible explanations based on speculations by migrant-worker NGOs and NGO circles in Hong Kong: (1) power plays within the provincial government which under Party Secretary Wang Yang stood for the relatively liberal "Guangdong model" but which harboured a certain envy of Wang; (2) a carrot-and-stick policy of trying to steer migrant-worker NGOs towards providing services (funded by Chinese sources); and (3) tensions between ACFTU and migrant-worker NGOs.[31] A quite different explanation for the conflicting

[31] At that time, no analysis was really convincing. In retrospect, however, all three aspects were linked to deeper developments which will only be touched on here in a few words: Party Secretary Wang who was "promoted" to the central government in 2013; the ambitious transformation of China's NGO landscape into a politically tame and welfare-oriented third sector; and the ACFTU's continued lack of capacity to reform.

signals sent to migrant-worker NGOs is given by Diana Fu who argues that the government mandate to maintain social stability was executed differently by different local state agencies according to their bureaucratic functions, additional informal mandates and the level of information on migrant-worker NGOs' labour activism (Fu, 2017:453). To describe these divergent and conflicting forms of state governance, she develops the concept of "fragmented control" and illustrates the divergence of control strategies across local agencies using the examples of the Public Security Bureau ("soft repression"), Labour Union ("cooptation") and Labour Bureau ("neglection").[32] Fu's explanation fits what we were told by harassed migrant-labour NGO staff members in 2013. They said, "The authorities who visited us included labour administration departments, the commerce ministry, fire control and others. They didn't do anything violent; they just exercised their right to inspect. But more and more people came, the inspections didn't stop; furthermore, they sat around forever in our office, they wanted us to move out, they disturbed our work and put us under pressure" (Interview 13/SZ/29 in Gransow and Zhu, 2016:192). As it turned out, the crackdown on migrant-worker NGOs in 2012 was not just a moment in time like the violent interventions some organisations had experienced previously. The pressure from public security officials to move out immediately despite legal leases went on for years. Some migrant-worker NGOs had to find new office space every few months (Franceschini and Nesossi, 2019:120).

After successful strike actions and collective bargaining in the shoe industry in 2014 (see above), some of the migrant-worker NGO activists were criminally charged and even sentenced in late 2015 for "the crime of gathering a crowd to disturb social order" (*juzhong raoluan shehui zhixu zui*).[33] This harsh treatment of labour activists shows some similarities to the campaign against prominent *weiquan* lawyers in an earlier crackdown campaign in July 2015 (Franceschini and Nesossi, 2019:121–122; see also Zhu, 2022). It looked like labour activists' success in collective bargaining (proper compensation to the employees of a shoe factory that was

[32] Besides these three agencies, Fu identified five additional state organs interacting with migrant-worker NGOs under the political mandate of upholding social stability: Ministry of Civil Affairs, Industry and Commerce, State Security (国保, part of the domestic security department of the Ministry of Public Security B.G.), subdistrict offices and neighbourhood committees – Fu (2017:453, footnote 1).

[33] 聚众扰乱社会秩序罪.

planning to relocate its factory) was to be turned into defeat by punishing those who ignored the government's mandate to maintain social stability.

After Xi Jinping came to power in late 2012, the methods of repression and control changed significantly. Franceschini and Nessosi note that unlike previous forms of repression against migrant-worker NGOs, which were local affairs, the 2015 crackdown on labour activists was presented as part of a nationwide campaign against cooperation between foreign donors and Chinese grassroots NGOs. Unlike previous attacks on migrant-worker NGOs, which used extra-legal means such as intimidation, violence and informal pressure on landlords to evict migrant-worker NGOs, in the 2015 crackdown, the Chinese government used the new NGO laws and regulations (see Table 1) and the Criminal Law to enforce the policy of maintaining social stability through the police in order to reinforce the demarcation between China's "official" and "unofficial" civil society. (Franceschini and Nesossi, 2019:122). The changing tools of state intervention (from soft to rough to repression by legal means) that strongly impacted the care activities of migrant-worker NGOs can be explained from three angles: (1) as an expression of the incoming Xi administration's need to make a difference; (2) as an attempt to protect the economic interests of companies and investors by cracking down on strikes; and (3) as an attempt therefore to prevent closer cooperation between migrant-worker NGOs and official trade unions.

Imaginaries of state transformation: Creating a self-sustaining NPO sector

This subsection examines the party-state's imaginaries of the politics of state space in the field of care/welfare and the transformation of state-society relations over the long term. What is the party-state's broader vision of creating a China-specific NPO sector alongside the state and the market and what kind of state transformation would this process imply? The second dimension of the party-state space corresponds to Brenner's state space in the representational sense and Lefebvre's "conceived/ mental space" (representations of space or the space of planners).

The legal framework for adapting the NGO sector to the politics of party-state space can be interpreted as an initial step in achieving the macro-strategy of "new social policies." Under this heading, Wang and Lan (2017) summarise three key strategies of a programme of social policy reforms, namely, of the NGO system, of the social services system and of the social governance system. The authors view them as a sequence on the one hand and as interdependent on the other.

The first key strategy, the NGO reform, was already established by the laws and regulations described earlier. This clearly limits the areas in which migrant-worker NGOs can still legally register and receive state funding. Conversely, labour advocacy activities, which had become increasingly important since the wave of strikes in 2010, were excluded and in some cases even criminalised.

The heart of the second key strategy, i.e. the reform of the social services system, is the idea of the government purchasing services.[34] According to Wang (2017:119), this idea was inspired by the new public management campaign[35] by which public services should be outsourced to all kinds of NPOs. Public services here include education, medical care, culture, elder care, assistance for the disabled and comprehensive community-level services. This should establish a new mechanism for providing and developing public services. The resulting mode should be one in which the government does not directly participate in the production and provision of these services. Instead, a new type of supply-and-demand relation is to be formed, involving the government (on the outsourcing side), taxpayers (on the demand side) and non-profit organisations (on the supply side). The transformation of government functions could therefore accelerate social structural reform (Wang, 2017:120).

The aim of the third key strategy is to establish a modern social governance system "which represents the masses, allows unobstructed expression of opinions, responds quickly and solves disputes at the source" (Wang and Lan, 2017:10). To achieve this goal, the trade unions, the Communist Youth League and the Women's Federation should be reformed to play their roles in representing the people and contributing to the resolution of social conflicts. In Wang and Lan's account, the mass organisations had failed in their governance function and needed to be modified. In a similar vein, they see the established top-down regime for maintaining stability as no longer compatible with the current pattern of social development (Wang and Liu, 2017:10). But they also have to admit

---

[34] 国家购买服务.

[35] New Public Management was created in the public sector and is based primarily on the use of business methods and instruments such as target agreements, project management, decentralisation, customer/citizen orientation and output/outcome control.

that they do not expect these three reforms to be achieved as an integrated macro-strategy any time soon.

Protecting state power: Perceiving INGOs as a non-traditional security threat

The third dimension of the (re)production of state space has to do with protecting the territory and national borders of the Chinese party-state and the organisation of the state itself. Framing INGOs as a possible non-traditional security threat means that the sovereignty of the Chinese state needs to be protected against the assumed undermining effects of INGOs on the state and society. How did the Chinese party-state frame INGOs as a potential non-traditional security threat and draw a line between domestic and international NGOs? This dimension of party-state space corresponds to Lefebvre's concept of "perceived/physical space" (spatial practice) and Brenner's "state space in the narrow sense," directed towards the foreign world outside the state's territory.

The creation of a legal framework to contain and transform China's burgeoning civil society into a politically adapted third sector was accompanied by the framing of the advocacy activities of domestic and international NGOs as potential security risks. International funding for advocacy NGOs made them suspects in the eyes of the party-state as potential threats to national security. In the spring of 2013, leaked internal party documents branded civil society[36] as an instrument of Western anti-China forces (Holbig and Lang, 2018:2; *Chinafile*, 2013).

Enactment of the INGO Law in January 2017 reinforced the trend towards securitisation of the state space *vis-à-vis* the NGO sector. Instead of the Ministry of Civil Affairs, the Ministry of Public Security and its subordinate agencies are now responsible for registering INGOs. Although the dual registration system has been eliminated for many Chinese NGOs, it still applies to INGOs. Accordingly, the number of Chinese "professional management units" (*yewu guanli danwei*)[37] willing to act as supervisors for INGOs' day-to-day operations has dwindled. This makes it particularly difficult for smaller INGOs to register legally. Further restrictions include a prohibition on political activities and the threat of arrest of INGO staff if they support advocacy activities (article 5, INGO law).

[36] 公民社会.

[37] 业务管理单位.

The reason for this trend can be assumed to be the influence of the National Security Committee (*guojia anquan weiyuanhui*),[38] newly established in 2013 and one of several powerful party organs chaired personally by Xi Jinping (see Holbig and Lang, 2018:3). According to Patricia Thornton, the Committee does not distinguish between traditional and non-traditional threats to China's political security, territorial sovereignty or social stability in an overall system of national security (Thornton, 2015:65).[39]

With the end of the Cold War and the rise of globalisation discourses, the concept of non-traditional security (*fei chuantong anquan*)[40] emerged in the 1990s (Yu, 2011:295, 296). It was a time when academia and political circles were in search of a broader non-military security concept.

In 1994, the concept of human security appeared in the UN Human Development Report and was also introduced in China. But the concept of human security has not been endorsed in Chinese government documents. The concepts of non-traditional and human security overlap in that both focus on an understanding of security that goes beyond its military defence core to include, for example, pandemics, terrorism or climate change as security threats. However, the two concepts differ in that the concept of non-traditional security emphasises collective human rights, while the human security agenda focuses on the security of individuals. (Breslin, 2018:26–28). The Chinese government has been selective in its acceptance of the non-traditional security concept and has been keen to avoid any associated threats to national sovereignty or integrity (see Goldstein, 2012:7).

As of the early 2000s, "security" aspects became the object of ever greater discussion in China, including social, energy and financial security, and the term non-traditional security became something of a trend (Goldstein, 2012:7). The concept has since been extended to ever more fields of public affairs, often in the wake of non-military crisis situations

---

[38] 国家安全委员会.

[39] Thornton (2015:64) draws on a statement by Xi Jinping about the creation of the committee, namely, that the nation is under simultaneous pressure to protect its sovereignty, security and development interests externally and its political security and social stability internally. This phrase, it should be added, corresponds to the Chinese idiom "内忧外患" (*neiyou waihuan*), which stands for "domestic trouble and foreign aggression," and reflects a broad understanding of security that includes both foreign policy and domestic security.

[40] 非传统安全.

(e.g. the SARS epidemic in 2003, "colour revolutions" in Eastern Europe in 2004 and the Wenchuan earthquake in 2008 – Thornton, 2015:65).[41] After 2018, i.e. the 13th National People's Congress and the associated efforts to institutionalise tighter top-down control of societal actors, propaganda materials began to frame INGOs as a potential security risk (Holbig and Lang, 2022:582, 583). The restrictive regulations on INGOs reflect the distinction already made with regard to domestic NGOs between desirable charities and undesirable advocacy groups and were now reinforced by the institutional assignment of INGOs to the departments of the Ministry of Public Security. This is a warning signal to INGOs and their staff as well as to domestic NGOs working with INGOs.

Overall, from the perspective of state politics of space, the activities of migrant-worker NGOs and their interactions with different actors are perceived as potential non-traditional security threats, which can be divided into internal and external threats. Domestically, the challenge of migrant workers' protests and strikes, which can have a strong impact on the economy, is framed as a threat to social stability. Externally, the challenge of foreign donor funding and its influence on migrant worker NGOs is framed as an undermining of China's national security. From the perspective of the party-state, migrant-worker NGOs represent two major "security gaps." The first is their potentially significant influence on large groups of migrant workers and thus on the possible expansion of protest and strike movements (social movement trade unionism). The second is the financial support they receive from foreign donors who might be working for regime change in China.

Overall, since 2012, there has been a trend towards the 'securitisation' of state space, which has since dominated the Chinese party-state's perception of migrant-worker NGOs not only domestically, but also in terms of their external relations. In particular, national security concerns have been raised about their relations with foreign donors and intermediary organisations in Hong Kong. In this context, the Chinese state was conceptualised here as a powerful actor reshaping the emerging spaces of care created by migrant worker NGOs. Neil Brenner's reflections on the spatiality of state power, adapted to the Chinese party-state, have been

[41]From 2001 to 2019, the non-traditional security threats mentioned most often in the *People's Daily* were terrorism (declining after 2017), environmental security and cybersecurity (increasing) (Liu, 2021:512). Additional areas of non-traditional security threats include climate change, food security, pandemics, transnational crime and maritime security.

Table 3. Securitising Chinese state space.

State space (Brenner *et al.*, 2003)	**The party-state's spatial policy towards emerging migrant-worker NGOs**
State space in the integral sense (social/lived space)	**Aim:** Claiming to accomplish a unified society **Strategy:** State intervention to deprive migrant worker NGOs of the legal and material basis to operate
State space in the representational sense (mental/conceived space)	**Aim:** State imaginaries of an NPO sector that includes only "welfarist" or community migrant-worker organisations **Strategy:** Transformation of state-society relations through social policy reforms
State space in the narrow sense (physical/perceived space)	**Aim:** Territorialisation of political power **Strategy:** State perception of foreign funding for migrant-worker NGOs as an non-traditional security threat to the Chinese nation

Source: Brenner *et al.* (2003:6), Lefebvre (1991:33), Elden (2007:110) and the author's findings.

used as an analytical tool to highlight the party-state's policy aims and strategies towards the emerging migrant-worker NGOs. As summarised in Table 3, these aims and strategies have been mapped onto the three dimensions of state space identified by Brenner (2003).

The strategy of using various kinds of state intervention to deprive migrant-worker NGOs of their legal and material bases of operation has been used to achieve the aim of a unified society (corresponding to the state space in an integral sense). The strategy of transforming state-society relations through socio-political reforms (NGO reforms, reform of social service systems, and social governance) has been aimed at creating a self-sustaining NPO sector that includes only charitable and community-based migrant-worker NGOs (corresponding to the state space in the representational sense). And the strategy of framing foreign funding for migrant-worker NGOs as a non-traditional security threat to the Chinese nation-state has served the aim of territorialising the political power of the party-state (corresponding to the state space in the narrow/physical sense).

Conclusion

The spontaneous and vibrant development of migrant-worker NGOs and their function as care givers for rural migrants working and residing in PRD cities helped to compensate for the lack of social security provided by governments and companies in the areas of health, labour issues and legal education, at least to a certain extent. The reciprocal relationship that developed between the NGOs and the "care recipients turned worker volunteers" was a relationship of trust and an important component of the incorporation of migrants into the city through their own agency. The most serious setbacks experienced by migrant-worker NGOs began late into the Hu/Wen administration and worsened under the Xi/Li administration when the role of national security was upgraded to a "comprehensive national security framework" in terms of scope and areas, institutions and political ideology. This securitisation of the party-state space had serious implications for migrant-worker NGOs in the PRD. Pressure from various public security departments accelerated a bifurcation into welfare-only NGOs on the one hand and advocacy NGOs on the other hand.

Domestic and international advocacy NGOs sought to go beyond caring for individual workers and advocate for collective labour rights. Their advocacy activities were then perceived as a security risk by local governments. Encouraged by Hong Kong-based labour organisations, some migrant-worker NGOs tried to expand the scope of their activities by pushing for collective action in some factories. While they were quite successful in their endeavour, some of their leaders and members were arrested or even convicted. Some migrant-worker NGOs responded to overtures from local governments to serve as publicly funded social workers and organise welfare-oriented community work. But the transition from activism to urban citizenship and integration projects funded by governmental agencies was not necessarily a smooth one for such organisations. As discussed previously, such domestication of migrant-worker NGOs by transforming them into community organisations (while perhaps with the best intentions of better integrating migrant workers into the urban society) could ultimately have a destructive effect on their innovative, creative and inclusive agency, similar in degree to the radical crackdown on advocacy activists in other migrant-worker NGOs.

The overlap between the spaces of care constructed by the agency of migrant-worker NGOs and the government's policy of securitising state space reflects, first and foremost, the asymmetrical power relations between the party-state and an emerging civil society, of which migrant-worker NGOs were a part. From the perspective of a China characterised by compressed modernity and a complex risk society, this overlap or collision of different perceptions and constitutions of space could also be identified as an example of "risk entanglement" (von Scheve and Lange, 2023), which even more clearly expresses the contradictory dynamics of spatial and risk configurations. As has been argued, for the party-state, migrant-worker NGOs represent a non-traditional security threat (a "risk object") that is expressed in two "security gaps," i.e. trust relationships with migrant workers, with the potential to mobilise them for strikes or other collective action, and funding from foreign donors, with the potential to make them dependent on foreign funding and expose them to potentially unwanted ideological influences. From the perspective of the migrant workers, who had experienced the activities of the NGOs as a contribution to reducing the risks of their own precarious situation, which was characterised by a lack of occupational safety and social security, as well as inadequate labour and civil rights, the party-state's "de-risking" strategy now poses a significant threat to the very existence of migrant worker NGOs, turning them into an "object at risk" in the eyes of migrant workers.

Appendix

List of interviews with migrant-worker NGOs in Shenzhen und Guangzhou (2011–2012)

Interview number	Interview code	Established in year	Fields of activities	Full-time staff	Funding
B1	11/SZ/6	2006	1. Labour culture 2. Legal information and training 3. Industrial injury visits 4. Legal aid	3	International
B2	11/SZ/7	2006.4	1. Legal advice 2. Labour dispute mediation 3. Legal information and training 4. Training on urban integration 5. Culture and entertainment	3	International

B3	11/SZ/8	2003.8	1. Labour culture 2. Occupational safety training 3. Law education 4. Legal aid	7	Hong Kong
B4	11/GZ/9	2005.1	1. Law information and training 2. Legal advice 3. Culture and entertainment	7	International
B5	11/GZ/10	1998.8	1. Industrial injury visits 2. Legal advice 3. Legal aid 4. Culture and entertainment	7	International
B6	12/SZ/11	2004.3	1. Legal information and training 2. Legal aid 3. Industrial injury visits 4. Factory survey 5. Culture and entertainment	3	International 70%; self-raised 30%
B7	12/SZ/12	2003.8	1. Labour culture 2. Occupational safety training 3. Law education 4. Legal aid	7	Hong Kong
B8	12/SZ/13	2004.9	1. Legal information and training 2. Legal consultancy service 3. Industrial injury aid	3	Small fund; self-raised
B9	12/GZ/14	1998.8	1. Industrial injury visits 2. Legal advice 3. Legal aid 4. Culture and entertainment	7	International

B10	12/GZ/15	2012.3	Culture and entertainment for female workers	3	Small fund
B11	12/GZ/16	2005.1	1. Law information and training 2. Legal advice 3. Culture and entertainment	7	International

References

Ahlers, A. and Schubert, G. (2022). Nothing new under "top-level design"? A review of the conceptual literature on local policymaking in China, *Issues and Studies* 58(1), 1–34.

Barglowski, K. and Bonfert, L. (2023). Migrant organisations, belonging and social protection. The role of migrant organisations in migrants' social risk-averting strategies, *International Migration* 61(4), 72–87.

Blecher, M. (2022). The Yue Yuen strike 2014, in Franceschini, I. and Sorace, C. (eds.), *Proletarian China. A Century of Chinese Labour*, London: Verso, pp. 664–673.

Brenner, N., Jessop, B., Jones, M., and MacLeod, G. (2003). *State/Space. A Reader*, Oxford: Blackwell Publishing.

Breslin, S. (2018). Non-traditional security for who/what? Between the International, the National and the Human, in Sieckmann, I. and Triebel, O. (eds.), *A New Responsible Power China? China's Public Diplomacy for Global Public Goods* (ifa Edition Culture and Foreign Policy). Stuttgart: IfA (Institut für Auslandsbeziehungen), https://nbn-resolving.org/urn:nbn:de:0168-ssoar-59038-7.

Chan, C. K.-C. (2010). *The Challenge of Labour in China: Strikes and the Changing Labour Regime in Global Factories*, Routledge: London.

Chan, C. K.-C. (2012). Community-based organisations for migrant workers' rights: The emergence of labour NGOs in China, *Community Development Journal* 48(1), 6–22.

Chatzidakis, A., Hakim, J., Littler, J., Rottenberg, C., and Segal, L. (2020). *The Care Manifesto. The Politics of Interdependence. The Care Collective*, London: Verso.

Chen, F. and Yang, X. (2017). Movement-oriented labour NGOs in South China: Exit with voice and displaced unionism, *China Information* 31(2), 155–175.

ChinaFile. (2013). Document 9: A ChinaFile translation. How much is a hardline party directive shaping China's current political climate? November 8, https://www.chinafile.com/document-9-chinafile-translation (accessed August 2, 2022).

China Labour Bulletin. (2011). *Unity is Strength. The Workers' Movement in China (2009–2011)*, Hong Kong: China Labour Bulletin.

Chu, J. (2021). *Von "Grassroots zu Volunteers". Aushandlungen von urban citizenship im Transformationsprozess der Land-Stadt-Migration Chinas*, Doctoral Thesis, Georg-August Universität Göttingen.

Connelly, R., Dong, X.-Y., Jacobsen, J., and Zhao, Y. (2018). The care economy in post-reform China: Feminist research on unpaid and paid work and well-being, *Feminist Economics* 24(2), 1–30, https://doi.org/10.1080/13545701.2018.1441534.

Deng, B. 邓保国 (2009). 珠三角农民工民间组织发展研究, Zhusanjiao nongmingong minjian zuzhi fazhan yanjiu (Research on the development of migrant NGOs in the Pearl River Delta), *Guangdong nongye kexue* (*Guangdong Agricultural Science*) 7, 283–287.

Deng, G. (2010). The hidden rules governing China's unregistered NGOs: Management and consequences, *The China Review* 10(1), 183–206.

Elden, S. (2007). There is a politics of space because space is political. Henri Lefebvre and the production of space, *Radical Philosophy Review* 10(2), 101–116.

Elfstrom, M. (2021). *Workers and Change in China. Resistance, Repression, Responsiveness*, Cambridge, UK: Cambridge University Press.

Feuchtwang, S. (2023). Care as critique of care: Public services, social security and ritual responsiveness, *China Quarterly* 254, 354–365.

Franceschini, I. (2012). Another Guangdong model: Labour NGOs and new state corporatism (posted August 4, 2012), *The China Story*, Australian Centre of China in the World, (accessed June 15, 2013).

Franceschini, I. and Lin, K. (2019). Labour NGOs in China. From legal mobilization to collective struggle (and back)? *China Perspectives* 1, 75–84.

Franceschini, I. and Nesossi, E. (2018). State repression of Chinese labour NGOs – A chilling effect? *The China Journal* 80, 111–129.

Froissart, C., Yan, L., and Quan, M. (2019). Trade-offs between state organisations and workers' organisations, Chinese unions in search of authoritarian collective bargaining, *China Perspectives* 2, 29–38.

Fu, D. (2017). Fragmented control: Governing contentious labour organisations, *China Governance* 30(3), 445–462.

Fu, H. and Cullen, R. (2008). Weiquan (rights protection) lawyering in an authoritarian state: Building a culture of public-interest lawyering, *The China Journal* 59, 111–127.

Gabauer, A., Knierbein, S., Cohen, N., Lebuhn, H., Trogal, K., Viderman, T., and Haas, T. (eds.) (2022). Care, uncare and the city, in *Care and the City. Encounters with Urban Studies*, London: Routledge, pp. 3–14.

Gleiss, M. S., Saeter, E., and Fürst, K. (2019). Re-theorizing civil society in China: Agency and the discursive politics of civil society engagement, *China Information* 33(1), 3–22.

Goldstein, L. (2012). *Not Congruent but Quite Complementary: U.S. and Chinese Approaches to Nontraditional Security*, CMSI Red Books, Study No. 9.

Gransow, B. and Zhu, J. (2016). Labour rights and beyond – How Chinese migrant worker NGOs negotiate urban spaces in the Pearl River Delta, *Population, Space and Place.* Special Issue: *Migrants' Agency and the Making of Transient Urban Spaces* 22(2), 185–198.

He, A. J. and Huang, G. (2015). Fighting for migrant labour rights in the world's factory: Legitimacy, resource constraints and strategies of grassroots migrant labour NGOs in South China, *Journal of Contemporary China* 24(93), 471–492.

Holbig, H. and Lang, B. (2018). Europäische NROs in China: Schwierige Abwägungen und Chancen der Zusammenarbeit, *GIGA Fokus. Asien* 6, 1–14.

Holbig, H. and Lang, B. (2022). China's overseas NGO law and the future of international civil society, *Journal of Contemporary Asia* 52(4), 574–601.

Howell, J. (2009). Civil society and migrants in China, in Murphy, R. (ed.), *Labour Migration and Social Development in Contemporary China*, Routledge: London, pp. 171–194.

Howell, J. (2015). Shall we dance? Welfarist incorporation and the politics of state-labour NGO relations, *China Quarterly* 223(September), 702–723.

Howell, J. (2021). From green shoots to crushed petals: Labour NGOs in China, *Made in China Journal* 6(1), 102–107.

Hsu, J. (2012). Layers of the urban state: migrant organisations and the Chinese state. *Urban Studies* 49(16), 3513–3530.

Hsu, J. (2017). *State of Exchange. Migrant NGOs and the Chinese Government*, Vancouver: UBC Press.

Hu, J. and Martin, D. (2020). Labour dispute resolution and migrant workers' legal rights protection in China, *Chinese Journal of International Review* 2(1), 1–24.

Jakimow, M. (2021). *China's Citizenship Challenge. Labour NGOs and the Struggle for Migrant Worker Rights*, Manchester: Manchester University Press.

King-Dejardin, A. (2019). *The Social Construction of Migrant Care Work. At the Intersection of Care, Migration and Gender*, Geneva: International Labour Office (ILO).

Lammer, C. (2023). Care scales: Dibao allowances, state and family in China, *China Quarterly* 254, 310–324.

Lee, C. K. and Shen, Y. (2011). The anti-solidarity machine? Labor nongovernmental organisations in China, in Kuruvilla, S., Lee, C. K., and Gallagher, M. (eds.), *From Iron Rice Bowl to Informalization. Markets, Workers, and the State in a Changing China,* Ithaca: ILR Press, pp. 173–187.

Lefebvre, H. (1968/2016). *Das Recht auf Stadt*, Hamburg: Nautilus.

Lefebvre, H. (1991). *The Production of Space*, Oxford: Blackwell Publishing.

Levy, K. and Pissler, K. (2020). *Charity with Chinese Characteristics. Chinese Charitable Foundations between the Party-State and Society*, Cheltenham: Edward Elgar Publishing.

Li, S. (2014). *Understanding the Chinese City*, Los Angeles: Sage.

Ling, L. and Ngok, K.-L. (2011). Report on the status quo of public health of migrants in China, Guangzhou: Sun Yatsen University Press.

Liu, H. (2021). The role and logic of nontradtional security in China's engagement in global governance mechanisms under Xi Jinping's regime, *Journal of Chinese Political Science* 26, 505–523.

Liu, T. and ten Brink, T. (2022). Social protection for migrant workers in China, in Nullmeier, Frank, González de Reufels and Herbert Obinger. (eds.), *International Impacts on Social Policy. Short Histories in Global Perspective*, Palgrave Macmillan, pp. 489–499.

Löw, M. (2008). The constitution of space: The structuration of spaces through the simultaneity of effect and perception, *European Journal of Social Theory* 11(1), 25–49.

Luo, G. and Gu, J. 罗观翠，顾江霞 (2008). 华南农民工 NGO 的组织环境分析 Huanan nongmingong NGO de zuzhi huanjing fenxi (Analysis of the organisational environment of migrant NGOs in South China), 青年研究 *Qingnian yanjiu* (*Youth Research*) 10, 1–11.

Ma, H. 马航 and Wang, Y. 王耀武. (2011). 深圳城中村的空间演变与整合, *The Space Evolvement and Integration of Villages-in-the-City in Shenzhen*, Beijing: 知识产权 Zhishi Chanquan Press.

Ma, H. (2014). Guangdong's new registration policy for social organisations: Progress and challenges, *China Development Brief*, https://chinadevelopment-brief.org/reports/guangdongs-new-registration-policy-social-organisations-progress-challenges/ (accessed November 10, 2023).

Noakes, S. (2018). *The Advocacy Trap: Transnational Activism and State Power in China*, Manchester: Manchester University Press.

Pan, D. (2019). Thinking like a state: Doing labour activism in South China, in Teresa, W. (ed.), *Handbook of Protest and Resistance in China*, Cheltenham: Edward Elgar Publishing, pp. 151–165.

Pan, D. (2020). *Doing Labour Activism in South China. The Complicity of Uncertainty*, London: Routledge.

Qian, Y. (Karina). (2010). *Poor Internal Governance in Chinese Environmental NGOs: Chinese Social Activity as Uncivil*, BA Thesis, Stanford University.

Spires, A. (2024). *Everyday Democracy. Civil Society, Youth, and the Struggle Against Authoritarian Culture in China*. New York: Columbia University Press.

Steinmüller, H. (2023). Introduction. Crises of care in China today, *China Quarterly* 254, 301–309.

Thornton, P. (2015). China's non-traditional security, in Dittmer, L. and Yu, M. (eds.), *Routledge Handbook of Chinese Security*, London: Routledge, pp. 64–77.

Turcatti, D. (2021). Migrant-led organisations as caring communities: Towards a re-appreciation of the reciprocal dimension of care, *International Journal of Care and Caring* 5(4), 651–667.

von Scheve, C. and Lange, M. (2023). Risk entanglement and the social relationality of risk, in *Humanities and Social Sciences Communications* 10 (170): 1–10.

Wang, M. (2017). On government purchasing services, in Wang, M. (ed.), *A Discussion on Chinese Road of NGOs. Reform and Co-Governance by Society*, Singapore: Springer Nature, pp. 119–123.

Wang, M. and Lan, Y. (2017). An analysis of "new social policies" and the realization path, in Wang, M. (ed.), *A Discussion on Chinese Road of NGOs. Reform and Co-Governance by Society*, Singapore: Springer Nature, pp. 3–12.

Wu, Q. (2008). *Whither New Social Organisations in Urban China? The Structural Politics of Social Organisations in Urban China, Post 1989*, Dissertation, University Duisburg-Essen.

Yu, X. (2011). The emergence of non-traditional security issues in China and corresponding strategies, in Wang Yizhou. (ed.), *Transformation of Foreign Affairs and International Relations in China 1978–2008*, Leiden: Brill, pp. 283–332.

Zhang, H. and Smith, M. (2009). Navigating a space for labour activism: Labour NGOs in the Pearl River Delta of South China, in Schwartz, J. and Shieh, S. (eds.), *State and Society Responses to Social Welfare Needs in China*, Routledge: London, pp. 70–76.

Zhang, L. (2019). Worker protests and state response in present-day China: Trends, characteristics, and new developments, 2011–2016, in Wright, T. (ed.), *Handbook of Protest and Resistance in China*, Cheltenham: Edward Elgar Publishing, pp. 119–136.

Zhou, M. and Yan, G. (2019). Advocating workers' collective rights: The prospects and constraints facing 'collective bargaining' NGOs in the Pearl River Delta, 2011–2015, *Development and Change* 51(4), 1044–1066.

Zhu, Y. (2022). *Initiating Agenda-Building under Authoritarian Settings. The Public Debate on the Abolition of "Re-education through Labour" (Laojiao) System in China (2010–2013*), Doctoral Dissertation, FU Berlin.

Chapter 4

Entangled in *jianghu* Spaces: Becoming Urban *xiaojie* in the City of Shenzhen

"I do this to make a living – people are not voluntarily in the *jianghu*."
"Here we are doing this voluntarily, mainly regular work."

Introduction

The city of Shenzhen is associated not only with creativity and innovation, high-speed urbanism and rapid economic growth but also with fake products and a high crime rate. Shenzhen is the site of China's first Special Economic Zone (SEZ),[1] established in 1980 as an experiment in connection with Deng Xiaoping's "market socialism." It was to Shenzhen that Deng returned in 1992 for his famous "Journey to the South" (*nanxun*)[2] to signal the end of the post-Tiananmen period of austerity. Jonathan Bach describes Shenzhen as having "bloomed through the production of objects of desire (via export)" and as producing itself "as an object of desire for the migrants of all classes who have flocked to its factories, urban villages, white collar jobs, luxury villas and underground economy" (Bach, 2011:415).

[1]For thirty years, the SEZ covered only Shenzhen's central districts of Futian and Luohu, as well as Nanshan to the west and Yantian to the east, all of which border Hong Kong. After 2010, the SEZ covered all nine districts of Shenzhen, including the larger districts of Bao'an and Longgang in the north.

[2]南巡.

Migrants arrived in Shenzhen in three waves. The first wave constituted people who came from regions within Guangdong province. The second wave consisted primarily of young and unmarried girls and women. Known as *dagongmei,*[3] their harsh factory working and living conditions have been researched widely (Pun, 2005; Lee, 1998; Gaetano and Jacka, 2004; Han, 2021). Then gradually, in a third wave, many male migrants came to work in construction and various manufacturing industries.[4] While the *dagongmei* lived in factory dormitories (called the "dormitory regime" by Smith and Pun, 2006), most of the later migrants, whether trained or untrained, male or female, employed or unemployed, found shelter in Shenzhen's urban villages (Wang, 2016:75–76).[5] A considerable percentage of young female migrants moved – voluntarily or involuntarily – into the entertainment and sex industry in various cities of the PRD, particularly Guangzhou, Dongguan and Shenzhen. Some came directly from rural areas to the sex industry, whereas others entered it after living and working as *dagongmei* – in larger numbers after many were laid off during the global financial crisis of 2008/2009.

In the literature on prostitution in contemporary China, Ding and Ho identified four main perspectives associated with different ideological positions: (1) moralistic accounts of prostitution as a residual phenomenon of capitalism counter to the principles of socialism and/or of the women involved as undermining family values; (2) early feminist approaches regarding them as victims of a still patriarchal culture and prostitution as a form of oppression; (3) liberal feminist standpoints advocating decriminalisation of prostitution and legal rights for sex workers; and (4) medical-centred perspectives taking the women as research subjects in need of

[3] 打工妹 (working sisters).

[4] In 2011, Shenzhen had a rural-to-urban migrant-worker (农民工) population of 6.13 million (with formal employers) or 58.6% of Shenzhen's 10.46 million permanent population (常住人口), plus 2.17 million informally employed migrants (excluded from formal employment, unemployed or non-working age) (Shenzhen, 2014). 25.6% (or 2.68 million) of Shenzhen's permanent population in 2011 had a Shenzhen *hukou* (户籍人口) (Shenzhen, 2012). 58.1% of the migrants were male and 41.9% were female. The 17–20 age group had more women (17.8% of all female migrants) than men (11.6% of all male migrants). This difference also holds for the 17–23 group with 36.8% female and 27.8% male migrants (Shenzhen, 2014). No numbers are available on the percentage of female migrants among the 2.17 million informal migrants including those under 16.

[5] Urban villages were called 城中村 *chengzhongcun* (villages in the city). In this chapter, *chengzhongcun* and urban villages are used interchangeably.

education (Ding and Ho, 2012:44). In addition, with the spread of HIV/AIDS, debate arose on the extent of a "bridging effect" and whether women providing sex services should be seen as victimisers or victims (Lau *et al.*, 2002; Choi, 2011).

But none of these standpoints reflect the self-understanding of the young migrant women themselves who work in the entertainment and sex industry. According to Ding and Ho, they did not want to be considered immoral or as sexual victims, nor did they wish to be called "sex workers." Instead, "they preferred the term *xiaojie*, a respectful way to address wealthy young unmarried women since ancient times in China … that remained appropriate for addressing urban women after China's economic reform although the term is now used mainly to refer to prostitute women" (Ding and Ho, 2012:44). This observation has been confirmed by our own interviews with thirty young female migrants (most of them between 18 and 22 years of age) providing sex services in Shenzhen city.[6] In preparing our fieldwork on a group of female migrants at high risk for health issues, we started out with the term "female sex worker," but the interview documentation (records and notes) and comments by the interviewers made it quite clear that the interviewees preferred to address themselves and their colleagues primarily as *xiaojie, jiemei* (older and younger sisters) or *nü haizi* (the girls).[7] Not one of them called herself or the others a "female sex worker" (*nüxing xing gongzuozhe*)[8] during the interviews. But what, then, are the implications of a self-understanding as *xiaojies*?

The entertainment and sex industry in the PRD has boomed in conjunction with rapid urbanisation, particularly in Shenzhen and Dongguan. In virtually no other Chinese city is the gap between legal norms and everyday practices as obvious as here between the prohibition on prostitution and the easy availability of commercial sex at all levels of society.

---

[6]The interviews were conducted in September–October 2009 as part of a research project on migration dynamics, global change and urban health in the PRD. See the list of interviews at the end of the chapter. More details on the project and its broader research programme framework can be found in the introductory Chapter 1. The project outputs included a doctoral thesis by Yuan Yuan-Ihle analysing these interviews with a focus on health issues and health policies (Yuan-Ihle, 2017).

[7]小姐, 姐妹 or女孩子. Sun (2021:112, 113) introduces the term *jiejie* (姐姐 older sister) as a polite way of addressing female migrants working in the entertainment and sex industries.

[8]女性性工作者.

The aim of this chapter is to expand knowledge about the adaptation process used by a very young and highly vulnerable group of rural female migrants to the mega-urban environment of Shenzhen city. It takes their own agency and self-understanding as a starting point for analysing the interrelations of migration and mega-urban development. What kind of urban spaces are produced and reproduced by female migrants providing commercial sex services in the PRD? The term *xiaojie* is used as a lens to explore what "becoming urban" means for this group of migrants in the city for whom there has thus far been no blueprint for integration. The question of the production of urban spaces by this specific group of female migrants will be linked to Li Shiqiao's (2014) understanding of the Chinese city as characterised by his conceptual framework of "ranked care," i.e. spaces concentrically ordered around the "body in safety and danger," including spaces of intensive (family) care, regular (economic) care and *jianghu* spaces (or spaces of uncare).

This chapter has two main sections. The first section uses our interview material to analyse the process of becoming urban *xiaojie* in terms of producing limited spaces of care within an environment of uncare. The second section discusses the urban, legal and political environment of rural migrant girls and women becoming urban *xiaojie*. The conclusion drawn is that the transformation from rural female migrant to urban *xiaojie* embodies an ambiguous process of adapting to urban *jianghu* spaces while contributing to the urban growth machine of Shenzhen.

Part One: Agency and Self-Perception of Rural Migrant Girls Becoming Urban *xiaojies*

The first part of this chapter is closely based on the interview material and aims to explore the everyday behaviour, everyday life, agency and self-image of the predominantly very young rural–urban migrant women in Shenzhen's entertainment and sex industry. The focus is on (1) three main pathways of becoming urban *xiaojies*; (2) their working and living conditions within the hierarchy of *xiaojie* categories regarding inner and outer venues of commercial sex; (3) shrinking family networks; (4) establishing something like "surrogate family" networks in the city; and (5) *xiaojies'* views of the future.

Pathways into prostitution

Our interviews revealed three different basic pathways into prostitution: (1) the intentional decision to work in the sex industry (which can be based on very different motives); (2) being tricked into it by "boyfriends" who seek to live off the work of young women and even girls; and (3) involuntary and coerced forms of submission/obedience in the sex industry based on human trafficking, rape, drugs, violence or the threat thereof.

(1) Interviewees who intentionally entered the commercial sex industry more or less all anticipated high incomes combined with relatively easy work, but also had quite different motives. First, some girls and women from very poor rural families felt they had very few options in the labour market. XJ 11 (age 20), who had finished junior middle school in Henan province and had been working for four years at a "hair salon" in urban village A in Shenzhen, was sending 3,000 yuan a month in remittances to her family (from a monthly income of around 8,000 yuan). She said, "First I worked in a toy factory. I don't do this any longer, because one day I had stomach pain and asked if I could leave. That was not allowed. Then, when I finished my work, I was fired. [I am doing this here] to make a living. People are not voluntarily in the *jianghu*.[9] Although my family does not need me to take care of it, its circumstances are really not good." XJ 1 was in a similar situation. Also aged 20, she had left Sichuan province four years earlier without finishing elementary school and was now working in a brothel in urban village B, Shenzhen. "I was the only one in our home who could earn money. As a waitress (*fuwuyuan*),[10] I could make only around 200 yuan a month … I entered this industry on my own. The elder members of my family had very strenuous work, with my father and mother tilling the fields. Pa's body is quite weak, he is only 40 years old. At first, Ma could work outside, but my Pa didn't want her to go out for work. At home … I didn't have my own room. The money that my family owed, I sent to them; now their debts are paid off and new rooms have been built in the house."

---

[9] 江湖.

[10] 服务员.

Second, the experience of factory work played a major role in the decision by young rural-to-urban migrants to work in an industry with fewer hours, less supervision and the opportunity to earn considerably more money. To what extent these expectations were fulfilled depended strongly on the specific conditions of their activities. Particularly with increasing age, it becomes more difficult to live up to the standards expected. XJ 3, who is nearly 35 years old, came from Guizhou province and is now working in a nightclub in urban village B. She complained, "A *laoxiang* (a woman from my own region)[11] told me I could earn money much faster this way [than in the factory], so I came here.… Business went well in the past and I could make 5,000 to 6,000 yuan a month. Now, it's not so good and I earn only 2,000 or 3,000 yuan a month."

For XJ 12 (age 22) from Henan, who had finished junior middle school and was now working in a hair salon and KTV bar in urban village B, working in a factory had also influenced her decision to enter the sex industry. Unlike the earlier interviewees, however, she did not mention the high income as the most appealing aspect of the industry but rather the expected freedom. This was a third type of motivation specified for voluntarily turning to the sex industry. One should note that her monthly income of over 10,000 yuan (after paying for housing and food) was relatively high. She said, "My earlier work [as a waitress and in a factory] was very exhausting. In addition, I am somebody who appreciates her freedom. At first, I came here with a girlfriend to have some fun…[12] Besides, I do this work only occasionally; usually, I go to learn something about beauty and so on."

(2) A mixture of curiosity, adventurousness, carelessness and "looking for Mr. Right" can pave the way for young women to enter the entertainment and sex industry. Some are still teenagers who have not worked in a factory (or elsewhere) before. Often, these girls had met "boyfriends" (*nan pengyou*)[13] at a very young age who later turned out to be pimps or "chicken heads" (*jitou*)[14] who manipulated them into the sex industry so they themselves could make an easy living from their girlfriends' lucrative work. For the girls, this leads to major disappointment as well as greater or lesser degrees of suspicion towards

[11] 老乡.
[12] 一起出来玩吧.
[13] 男朋友.
[14] 鸡头.

men in general later. Some stay in the industry even after breaking up with their "boyfriends." This was the case with 21-year-old XJ 28, for example, who came to Shenzhen from Hunan with her parents at the age of 12, finished junior middle school and entered the sex industry at 16 after her first boyfriend fooled her into thinking he was her great love. She continued working and was at a KTV club in urban village A, but she didn't want to be with a boyfriend anymore. XJ 16 (age 22), from Hunan, came to a hair salon in urban village A through the introduction of a friend of her *laogong* (老公 husband) who was back in Hunan. She reiterated that she was earning much more now than at the factory before. XJ 17, an illiterate 22-year-old from Jilin, worked in a brothel in urban village A to sustain her Korean husband. She argued that in *Dongbei* (northeastern China) it would be very difficult for poor girls like her to find a husband without providing some money. She saw this view confirmed by the fact that many of her sisters (姐妹 *jie mei*, fellow *xiaojies*) also had *laogongs* whom they were supporting financially.

(3) Finally, various types of force are used to compel girls and young women into the sex industry. Our interviewees who were violently forced into prostitution later stayed more or less voluntarily in the sex industry. They were very young when they were forced into prostitution and most landed in the lower tiers (5 and 6) of sex work venues. XJ 19 (age 20) from Hubei, who had finished primary school and was now working in a brothel in urban village B, said she had been working as a housemaid back in Hubei for a couple who offered her a better job in Shenzhen. Not suspecting a thing, she agreed. After arriving in Shenzhen, she continued working as a housemaid for the couple but started wondering about their type of business. Then, she said, the householder gave her a glass of water with drugs, raped her while she was semi-conscious and forced her into prostitution. She later escaped, but then returned to the sex industry to find the man who had given her the drugs to report him to the police. It is unclear why she did not simply file charges against him. XJ 4, a 17-year-old from Guangdong who had not finished senior middle school and was now working in a brothel in urban village B, said that during summer vacations she would go out with friends to have fun. Then, a friend of a friend gave her ecstasy (*yaotouwan*),[15] raped her and forced her into

[15] 摇头丸.

> prostitution. "I didn't dare to think of escaping. They know where my family lives and they are very aggressive. They beat up people and knock them around; if I didn't do something willingly, they beat me up." XJ 8, an 18-year-old who hadn't finished junior middle school and was now working in a brothel in urban village A, told her story as follows: "First I worked in a factory.... That I'm working here is because I myself became a victim.... Together with another girl ... we met a man from Sichuan. He said he wanted to go out with us to have some fun. When we got into his car, he brought us to Buji. We were sold and [you can be] sure [that we were] watched. If we didn't behave well, we could expect to be beaten ... After arriving in Buji, I had to receive clients, then couldn't rest, receiving guests continuously every day, very tiring and painful, my body was messed up... The daily quota there was 8 clients; anyway, day and night you had to work ... Later I could escape. Then, I lost my identity card and had no choice but to come here. I intend to stop very soon." XJ 7 (age 27) from Hunan, who had finished junior middle school and was now working in a hair salon in urban village A, described her entry into the sex industry in similar terms: "I was forced by a man. If I didn't do it, he would beat me. He said he knew my home address. If I tried to escape, he would go there and talk to my parents. I was small and scared. Originally at that time, I wanted to join the army ... now there is no way (*meiyou banfa, yijing xiahai*)."[16]

To combat different forms of human trafficking including forced prostitution, the Chinese State Council adopted a National Action Plan on Combating Trafficking in Persons (2013–2020) with a long-term integrated series of preventive and counteractive measures, rescue operations and rehabilitation efforts, including allocation of responsibilities to relevant authorities, offices and organisations. It prescribes crackdowns in areas that have a history of human trafficking. The action plan also calls for more serious measures against prostitution and heightened inspections by public security organs of entertainment locations in suburbs and urban villages (Guowuyuan, 2013). The plan has been criticised for combining the fight against human trafficking with crackdowns against prostitution in ways that increase general anti-prostitution measures and thereby undermine

---

[16]没有办法，已经下海.

more targeted approaches against forced prostitution and third parties who exploit first parties engaged in commercial sex (see also Ling, 2018:66).

Working in the Sex Industry: A Job Like Any Other?

Urban spaces related to female sex providers' work and private lives are closely connected with different tiers or categories of their work. This hierarchy is based on age, education, appearance and body shape, manners, experience in singing and dancing, type of employment, income, organisation of labour and the type of clients they cater to. The Chinese sex industry can accordingly be divided into eight tiers.[17]

The venue-based hierarchical order of the sex industry

Mistresses or second wives (*ernai*)[18] who are sustained by a single client or benefactor for a period of time and provided with a hotel room or apartment by him constitute the highest category in the sex industry. The second category is the high-class prostitute working, e.g. in expensive hotels and clubs. While the age and education of the mistresses may vary, they not only have a considerably high and stable income but also have relatively easy and safe working conditions. High-class prostitutes are normally quite young and educated. Both groups of women work for themselves. Regarding the first tier, i.e. the second wives, there is disagreement on whether they can be viewed as sex workers as this is an individual relationship between two adult persons (without frequent changes in partners), which more closely fits the definition of transactional sex.

The third tier consists of young women who provide massages in leisure centres and (foot) massage salons. They usually have professional training in, e.g. *tuina*,[19] a type of traditional Chinese medicinal massage. Their income may vary widely, depending on whether they also offer sex services. While simple massages are provided in ordinary rooms, sex services are offered in separate VIP rooms.

[17] On the hierarchy of female sex work, see also Burger (2012:81–84).

[18] 二奶.

[19] 推拿.

Young women employed at karaoke bars and nightclubs in the entertainment industry constitute the fourth tier. Income in this category can be quite varied, depending on whether only *zuotai* services are provided or also *chutai* services. *Zuotai* services (sitting at the table/on stage) mean accompanying guests by chatting, singing and drinking (*zuotai xiaojie*,[20] hostess without sex services). *Chutai* services (leaving the table/the stage) mean those provided in a different room on a different floor (*chutai xiaojie*,[21] hostess with sex services). Venues in this tier may have different but fixed prices for sex services. The *xiaojies* are managed by a "*mami*" (madam)[22] and have some freedom in choosing the guests to whom they will provide services.

In the fifth tier, i.e. underground brothels which are less visible from the outside, the *xiaojies* are normally not allowed to reject clients introduced to them by the *mami*. In general, the *xiaojies* have to serve more clients per day than in fourth-category venues and more clients from mainland China who are said to be ruder than those from Hong Kong and Macao. Their income is less than in the fourth tier.

The sixth tier consists of the countless beauty salons and barber shops (*falang xiaojie*/ *falangmei*)[23] that serve as façades for sexual services. *Xiaojies* in these venues are managed by *mamis* and/or bosses (*laoban*, *dage*).[24] Their (young) age and educational background are similar to those of *xiaojies* in tiers 4 and 5.

The last two groups in the sex industry include streetwalkers (*zhanjienü*)[25] in tier 7 and women who offer sexual services in work sheds on construction sites (*gongpengnü*)[26] in tier 8. Streetwalkers solicit clients in public spaces, outside hotels or entertainment centres and in parks, railway stations, pedestrian malls, overpass bridges and truck stops. While streetwalkers work with pimps or on their own account,[27] the women providing sex services in work sheds to rural migrant workers are managed

---

[20] 坐台小姐.

[21] 出台小姐.

[22] 妈咪 The *mamis* are also called *mamasan* or *laoma*.

[23] 发廊小姐/发廊妹.

[24] 老板, 大哥.

[25] 站街女.

[26] 工棚女.

[27] On streetwalkers in Dongguan, see Tsang, 2018.

by pimps. The educational level of these women is relatively low, they are markedly older, sometimes married and have children. The work-shed women have the lowest incomes.[28]

The hierarchy of categories in commercial hostessing and sex work at different venues also entails different work environments, working hours, incomes and to a certain extent different health risks as well. From the interview material, we can observe a certain upward and downward mobility among these categories. This is due in part to ageing (downward mobility with increasing age) and to the fact that *xiaojies* from category 6 hair salons and beauty parlours (more rarely from category 5 brothels) were also working in category 4 nightclubs and KTV bars. In addition, a *xiaojie* working in a nightclub or KTV bar might become the mistress of a client. As such, demarcation lines between different sex work categories as well as between sex work and transactional sex appear more blurred from the perspective of the *xiaojies'* practices in everyday life (see also Yu, 2018:149).

The incomes at category 6 beauty parlours and hair salons were generally the lowest among our interviewees (4,000 to 8,000 yuan a month). At category 5 brothels, monthly incomes were from 5,000 to 10,000 and at category 4 nightclubs and KTV bars from 2,000 to 20,000 yuan (or sometimes higher). Depending on whether the services included sex, the income range in category 4 was considerably broader than in the lower categories. More generally, one might say that the higher the category of a *xiaojie*, the higher her freedom to select clients for sex services on her own and the lower the number of her clients (compared to category 5 and 6 brothels). The duration and rigidity of working hours could vary (for all these categories) and ranged between 5 and 12 hours a day/night. The most desirable places of work from the perspective of *xiaojies* were nightclubs and KTVs, which were seen as less boring than places in categories 5 and 6. But jobs at nightclubs and KTV bars are reserved for the youngest, prettiest and most cultivated girls.

[28] Most interviewees in our fieldwork were in tiers 4 to 6. One was a second wife and one was a *mami*.

Earnings, spending and lifestyle

Because the income of *xiaojies* in all categories was considerably higher than average factory wages,[29] moving to the sex industry was not without appeal for some female factory workers in the PRD. In comparing their own work and life in Shenzhen with the situation of *dagongmei*s, the *xiaojies* interviewed highlighted not only their higher incomes but also their more relaxed and flexible working conditions and considerably fewer working hours. In addition, the *xiaojies* were living in apartment rooms instead of factory dormitories and could afford an urban lifestyle with fashionable and sexy clothes, high heels, makeup from international brands, fitness studio visits and the luxury of urban consumption. In this regard, they accommodated their desire to become part of the high-speed urbanity of Shenzhen city (see also Ding and Ho, 2012:56, 170; Lin and Gu, 2014; Ding, 2017; Tsang, 2018).

Different price categories were reported for different tiers, venues and services. For example, at Brother X's beauty parlour, clients could choose from the following three kinds of services: Firstly, "without comfort" (*bu fangbian*),[30] i.e. 200 yuan per commitment/guest to be accompanied by a hostess/*xiaojie* while chatting, singing and drinking – of the 200 yuan, 50 went to the boss and 50 to the *mami*; secondly, "with comfort" (*fang-bian*) to include sex services in a different room (*yaoqu fangjian*)[31] for 300 yuan; and thirdly, "the whole night" (*baoye*)[32] including sex services in a different room for the entire night at a cost of 600 yuan. At KTVs, restaurants and clubs, there was a similar tiered system but prices were usually higher, e.g. 200 – 500 – 800 or even 300 – 600 – 900 yuan (XJ 21, XJ 22). Differentiation among services was quite similar, e.g. at KTV bars: Firstly, "sitting at the table" (*zuotai*) accompanied by a *xiaojie* while

[29]Production line workers in the PRD in 2011 could earn no more than around 2,800 yuan a month, even with overtime and bonuses (*China Labour Bulletin* (*CLB*), 2011). This was much more than a few years previously when there had been no wage increases at all for a long time. One should note that the interviews took place not long after the global financial crisis (2008/2009) hit the export production industries in the PRD and many young women working in factories had lost their jobs.

[30]不方便.

[31]要去房间.

[32]包夜.

chatting, singing and drinking, without sex services: "*Zuotai*" is paid when a guest rents a room (开房*kaifang*). Normally, one hostess would accompany one guest in a room. But to make more money, some *xiaojies* were operating 2–3 rooms at the same time (see also Zheng, 2006). Secondly, "leaving the table or going to a room (*shangfang*)[33] for sex services. Thirdly, "the whole night" including sex services in a different room: If the price for the whole night is, e.g. 600 yuan, the *xiaojie* may keep 400 and the rest is given to the boss and/or the *mami* (XJ 29). Fourthly, the most money could be made by *xiaojies* selling their virginity. The so-called "virgin opening fee" (*chunü kao bao fei* or just *chuye* for a virgin night)[34] was 3,000 yuan. "Whether real or faked, it is 3,000 yuan.… Normally, if the client sees blood, he will think it is real" (XJ 29).

Responses to the question of how the *xiaojies* spent their incomes provide some clues to their self-understanding, ideas of life and life plans. Seventeen of the 30 interviewees gave more detailed answers here, and nine said that they were (more or less) regularly sending remittances to their families back home. Like with the remittances sent from young female factory workers, the families of the *xiaojies* used this money mainly for renovating and expanding their houses, for school fees for siblings and similar purposes. Despite their relatively high incomes, most of the *xiaojies* did not dare send more than 1,000 yuan per month because they feared their families might become suspicious (almost none of the families of the *xiaojies* knew – or wanted to know – about the real origins of the incomes of their daughters and sisters).[35]

Room rental costs in urban villages (apartment rentals were the exception) had to be paid by the *xiaojies* themselves or were deducted if they lived in the apartment of a *mami* (normally, two *xiaojies* in one room). Some of the *xiaojies* invested larger sums in fashionable clothing and expensive branded cosmetics. This might have contributed to their self-understanding as modern, urbanised and at home in the glamorous city of Shenzhen (see also Tsang, 2018; Tsang *et al.*, 2018). Depending on their personal priorities, the range and content of their daily living costs could differ widely. In addition, those *xiaojies* who for one reason or

---

[33] 上房.

[34] 处女开苞费/处夜.

[35] The *xiaojies*' relationships with their families back home will be discussed below.

another wanted a man at their side spent a considerable part of their income on the living costs of their "boyfriends." In the eyes of the more established *xiaojies*, teenage girls tend to earn more and spend more, e.g. by playing cards or mahjong, in their early twenties, the young women save some money and think about their future more often.

Health and safety risks

The downside of the high earning potential in the sex industry lies in the many physical and psychological/emotional risks the girls and women face. While interviewees working in venues such as KTV bars and nightclubs complained largely about the unhealthiness of smoking and drinking and always working night shifts, the primary physical risks of the job include sexually transmitted diseases (STDs) and HIV/AIDS, unwanted pregnancies and gynaecological diseases such as cervicitis, pelvic inflammation and ovarian cysts. Condoms were commonly used by the *xiaojies* interviewed[36] but more detailed knowledge about health risks or the quality and choice of clinics was limited and differed widely. Regular preventive health checks were more the exception than the rule and reflected individual behaviour under specific circumstances.[37]

Another type of health risk is posed by drunken and/or violent clients who do not hesitate to beat or injure *xiaojies*. Usually, the *mamis* encouraged the *xiaojies* not to engage in conflict too readily with guests or clients and did not interfere in minor quarrels. If clients acted excessively, the *mami* or boss would come out to find a solution. But the *mamis* seemed reluctant to call the police. The safety and anonymity of their guests and customers was important to them, not least for the sake of their own business. Only if the company could not solve the problem would they call the police. XJ 14, a 22-year-old from Hubei working de facto as a *mami* at a KTV bar in urban village A, said, "In one case, a *xiaojie* who had been annoyed by a client and whose company did not solve [the problem], gave her own "chicken head" a call and ordered him to have many people waiting outside the bar to beat the client up. For the

[36]Here, it should be noted that the AIDS prevention activities of a local NGO in Shenzhen's entertainment industry could have had some results.

[37]Health checks and treatment for STDs or other diseases as well as abortions (which were done quite frequently) could cause considerable expense. Yuan-Ihle (2017) includes a detailed discussion of health risks, institutions and related policies.

company, the most important thing is the safety of the clients. At least the clients should be brought safely out of the door, then the police could be called to deal with it." If a *xiaojie* is injured, the boss of the company decides whether the client should pay compensation (XJ 16). The danger of being beaten by a client was seen as considerably higher for *xiaojies* working in hair salons or streetwalkers who are more visible than *xiaojies* working in inside spaces (XJ 15). The worst forms of violence were experienced by girls and women who were raped and forced into prostitution (XJ 19, 5, 7, 8).

Finally, there is the risk of easy access to various kinds of drugs. Drug experiences were reported mainly by teenage *xiaojies* (age 17 to 20), who viewed them primarily "as part of entertainment" (XJ 12) and tried ecstasy, crystal meth/ice (*bingdu*)[38] and ketamine (K fen). "The girls took ketamine and gave it to me to try. After I inhaled it, my whole body felt light and happy. The whole second day I couldn't eat or drink anything, I felt very excited and nothing bothered me. But something was strange: If other people hit or beat you, you will feel nothing.[39] When the effect wears off you become sleepy. That is hard to bear and you immediately want to inhale again" (XJ 21). XJ 1 described her use of different drugs to meet different emotional challenges: "If you take [ketamine], you are not thinking about what you will have to do tomorrow, and if you want to forget what happened, you take ecstasy. And when I am sad, then I sit down at the bar." The girls generally got the drugs from their boyfriends whom they supported and who used the money from the *xiaojies* to buy drugs (XJ 16). On the one hand, the *xiaojies* were living in environments with easy access to drugs, and on the other hand, they were under psychological pressure from working in the sex industry, which in turn made them more susceptible to using all sorts of substances.

Besides the physical risks, the interviewees emphasised the emotional pressures of working in an industry that is illegal, morally condemned and socially discriminated against. The situation of *xiaojies* therefore led to estrangement from family and friends at home as well as to many lies and feelings of isolation and loneliness. The interviewee who seemed to feel the most isolated was XJ 18, a 20-year-old from Fujian province, who hadn't finished senior middle school, left home after a quarrel with her

---

[38] 冰毒.

[39] K 粉 Ketamine, which was originally a medication for initiating and maintaining anaesthesia, is used as a recreational drug.

mother and was working in a brothel in urban village A. Not only did her family not know about her work but she also withdrew from her earlier social networks. At the same time, she broke up with her "boyfriend" by whom she felt betrayed. In addition, and unlike most other *xiaojies*, she was not willing to make friends with the other girls or "sisters" (as the *xiaojies* often call each other) because she thought of herself as somewhat superior to them. "Here I don't want to make friends. Because, here … everyone is doing this, therefore I don't want to make friends here." So her only contacts were some online friends.

The process of becoming a *xiaojie* is accompanied by the experience and fear of discrimination. XJ 12 (age 22), working in a hair salon in urban village A, expressed her feelings as follows: "I guess that other people and I are not on the same level, not in the same world. If the people around me looked at me as being on the same level, then I wouldn't feel such great stress." XJ 11, also working in a hair salon, said the following: "The work in our industry is the most despised in the whole world. There are people who are able to appreciate something about killers but they despise *xiaojies* … I am feeling very exhausted emotionally… Every day I perceive that I am here, I meet with strangers … I don't know how to put it; I do not have the words for it … Sometimes, if a client berates me, I think I'm still so young; then these old men come to do it. I've done this since I was fourteen, now I am twenty." XJ 4, a 24-year-old from Fujian working in the foot massage room of a nightclub (without providing sex services), complained about her boyfriend whom she had known for nine years since meeting as colleagues at a factory in Fujian. She felt sadness and discrimination from him: "My boyfriend does not want to talk in front of his friends about me working in the foot massage parlour. He fears other people could think it is not a regular place.[40] I think that's not right. What I do is a formal occupation … I previously trained in *tuina*; it is all completely official."

Shrinking social networks: The family at home

"In the family, nobody knows what I am doing" (XJ 15). These and similar statements were frequently made by the girls and young women interviewed. Practically all of them hid their work of providing sex services

[40] 不是一个正规的场所.

from their families and friends who usually lived far away from them. Their fear of discovery and possible fury on the part of their families was enormous. "They would kill me," said XJ 19 who fled forced prostitution but later returned to the sex industry on her own. "If it came to light, it would be a disaster" (XJ 10). Others feared their families would worry about them if they knew (XJ 9), while yet others feared the whole family in their village back home could lose face. XJ 15 said, "The family is living in the countryside. There are many people who could say something very ugly. Because it is quite feudal in the family, they wouldn't be able to bear it." For XJ 12 who regularly goes back to visit her family in Henan province, her work in Shenzhen is a taboo subject not discussed in her family. "If I did so," she said, "they would no longer have anything to do with me; they would despise me. Their judgements definitely have an impact on my emotional state." "I also have close girlfriends," said XJ 15, "but even if they are my close friends, I still cannot tell them that I work in this business."

Another interviewee highlighted her fear of meeting clients in the streets: "Normally, I cannot go out shopping; if you work in this business, you do not necessarily want to be seen by other people. I am afraid I could bump into clients whom I know" (XJ 3). Individual strategies for dealing with such fears were quite different. For example, XJ 29 feared that people from her hometown who had seen her in Shenzhen could blurt out at home what she was doing there. As a result, she said she returned home less and less. XJ 30 did not share such fears. On the contrary, she argued, "Those who can see me here must themselves be entangled with commercial sex in one way or another. Thus, in their own interest, they won't talk about it." To prevent their families back home from learning about their work in the sex industry, *xiaojies* were eager to hide their true identities in the event of a police raid. XJ 29, who worked in a nightclub in urban village A, had already been apprehended by the police during a crackdown campaign against prostitution. To protect her real identity, she did not reveal her true address. She also suggested never carrying a real identity card so her family could not be informed following a police check.[41]

If a *xiaojie's* work does come to light (XJ 1 learnt about her pregnancy only when she visited home and her mother recognised the signs and explained the matter to her daughter, which set the ball rolling), the

---

[41] Given the increasing use of facial recognition technologies, this strategy might already be outdated.

parents then face a dilemma, particularly if they are poor and dependent on their daughter's remittances. On the one hand, they want to uphold morals, norms and values (which might also be their own, and in the case of XJ 1, led the parents to pressure their daughter to marry as soon as possible), yet on the other hand, they might desperately need the remittances. The situation is no less ambivalent for the girl, which led XJ 1 to defend herself by shaming her parents for their poverty: "When my parents started to realise [in which industry I am working], they were full of objections but then I told them: 'Look at you, you cannot make any money. Where should the money come from if I didn't work in this industry. I am doing this for the family!'"

Overall, *xiaojies'* relations with their families at home were becoming more distant – despite the remittances many of them sent back – and the social networks with their earlier friends were shrinking too.

Establishing a "Surrogate Family" in the City

While female migrant networks tend to uphold "strong" family ties as opposed to "weak" ties with friends, colleagues, etc., in comparison to male migrant networks,[42] the *xiaojies'* social networks seem to be even smaller and more self-contained than those of other female migrants. The girls and women interviewed have social relations primarily with other *xiaojies*. They go for work together and some share rooms or apartments together (with or without a *mami*). They spend their leisure time playing cards or mahjong, or going swimming or hiking outside the city. The interviewer of XJ 10 described the small brothel in urban village B where XJ 10 was working and living as follows: "From the outside, this is a very ordinary family. The only thing which is different is that 6–7 *xiaojies* are living in this 'family'." The seemingly small social networks of the *xiaojies* consist mainly of "surrogate families." This means a quasi-family, sometimes called "fictive" kinship (Osburg, 2016:160), a social bubble, in which the *xiaojies* live and are exploited. In many cases, the most important person in the network is the *mami*. She is a procuress of the girls, a

[42]According to Granovetter (1973), the so-called weak ties are in fact strong ties because they represent broader social networks with greater reach into other spheres of society and thus may provide more information, mobility and other opportunities; with reference to China, see Gransow (2006:80, 81).

caregiver and the first contact if there is trouble with clients (XJ 9). If clients are violent, the *xiaojies* can also turn to the "boss" or "elder brother" (XJ 28). Some of the *xiaojies* receive (or at least expect) emotional support from "boyfriends" whom they provide for. Except for those among the "sisters," all of these everyday relationships are characterised by forms of exploitation: the *mamis*, the boss, the boyfriends and the "chicken heads" all profit from the income of the *xiaojies*.

Mamis and bosses

In the eyes of a *mami*, "her" *xiaojies* are valuable resources. She therefore cares for them (at least as far as seems necessary for the business) and scolds them if she feels they need to be disciplined. The *mami* introduces the *xiaojies* to the clients, ensures that they comply with the working hours and manages their finances. She makes efforts to protect the *xiaojies* against violent clients and undercover policemen, provides some health knowledge and guidance on health clinics, and is sometimes also their landlady.[43]

From the *mami*, the young women learn how to behave like *xiaojies*. "Acting as a *mami* primarily means teaching them how to behave, only then can they act as *xiaojies* to you" (XJ 12). The *mami* provides information on contraceptives and protection against sexually transmitted infections (STIs), especially on always using condoms. She urges caution and suggests clinics if the *xiaojies* need an abortion (XJ 5, 10, 29). "If the girls discover they have STDs, they should rest, see a doctor and not keep working. But there are some girls without any self-protection awareness. Even if they are pregnant, they still want to work; the *mamis* don't like this [either]" (XJ 14). Some of the *mamis* accompany the girls and women to more or less regular health checks (XJ 27). But this definitely does not mean that the *mami* feels responsible in all cases of *xiaojie* illnesses.

What *mamis* normally do not care about is whether *xiaojies* consume drugs. The only exception is if women who live in the apartment with them are consuming drugs in their home, "because they [the girls] could be seen by policemen in civilian clothes and then be picked up [by police]; it is also not good for their health" (XJ 14). In addition, the *mami* herself would risk being caught by the police; so, she tries to educate the *xiaojies*

---

[43] On the protective role of *mamis*, see also Yi *et al*. (2012:850–851).

to avoid situations that could attract police attention. But outside her own apartment, she doesn't care: "Most clients do not like *xiaojies* who take drugs but what the girls do after business hours is not my affair" (XJ 14).

The *mami* decides which clients the *xiaojies* should serve. This decision-making power may lead to rivalry among *xiaojies* who are eager to be introduced to clients to make money. As Zheng Tiantian has reported about hostesses in a Dalian bar, they had to bribe the "madam" so she recommends or promotes them. Otherwise, they will be left with little chance of being chosen for services (Zheng, 2006:137–138). According to our interviews in Shenzhen, there is a difference between brothels and nightclubs/KTV bars. If a *xiaojie* in a brothel rejects a client on her own, the *mami* would get angry with her "because … the *xiaojies* are all brought by the *lao ma*"[44] (XJ 17). But in nightclubs and KTV bars, the *mami's* decision-making power might be on *zuotai* (i.e. accompanying a client with chatting, singing and drinking), while the *xiaojies* have some freedom to agree to sex services wanted by their clients.

The *mami* controls whether the *xiaojies* comply with the working hours. It was reported that some *xiaojies* would try to meet regular clients during their leisure time outside the usual workplace to avoid paying the commission to the *mami* and possibly also the boss. If such behaviour comes to light, the *xiaojie* at least has to pay the missing commission to the *mami*. A *mami's* regime might be perceived very differently by individual *xiaojies*. For example, two *xiaojies* at a brothel in urban village B voiced quite different evaluations of their *mami*: XJ 5, who was 17 years old and had just had an abortion, said, "The *mami* is very good to me, she does not force me [to work] … the abortion was now one month ago, I will rest for a few weeks." XJ 1, who was 20, saw the *mami* more critically: "If I feel unwell, I will not go to work. But it may happen that the *mami* requires me to work."

*Mami*s might cooperate with a boss or manager of another sex venue. The interviewer of XJ 21 describes the collaboration between a *mami* at a nightclub and the boss of a beauty salon in urban village A as a type of joint venture by which the two pool their resources and share the profit (i.e. the commission fee that is deducted from the *xiaojie's* income). According to XJ 21, who was living at the beauty salon, the commission for the boss already included her rent fee. Some *mamis* manage all of their *xiaojies'* income. XJ 27 (age 18), who lived with three other girls in a

---

[44] 老妈, same as *mami*.

mami's apartment, said, "The *mami* stores all the money. If you need it, you can demand it. If a girl is out of cash but needs money, for example, to see a doctor or if she loses a card game with the *mami*, then she will lend you some (without interest!)" (XJ 27).

Boyfriends, chicken heads, small white faces

Emotionally the most important – but often also most disastrous – relationships the girls and women have are with their boyfriends – who only later turn out to be "chicken heads." Quite a few girls have been tricked into the sex industry by boyfriends (who often were also their first sex partners). XJ 21, a 19-year-old from Chongqing, was 14 when she moved to Shenzhen with her parents. Two years later, she met a boy at an ice-skating rink, fell in love with him and they started to live together. When her boyfriend pretended to be injured and unable to work, she looked for a job and started to work in the "beauty salon" of Brother X. She didn't want to return to the electric assembly factory because the work there had been very tiring and the wages would not be enough to also support her boyfriend. Later, she realised that he had lied to her and she broke up with him. Because she then didn't know where to go (her mother had meanwhile returned to Chongqing and she felt ashamed to move back in with her father still working in Shenzhen), she returned to the beauty salon of Brother X.

Especially in the eyes of very young women or girls, their boyfriends are of such crucial importance for their emotional equilibrium that they don't hesitate to support them. XJ 25 (age 18), also from Chongqing, who had finished junior middle school and started working in a KTV club in urban village A not long before the interview, said she is doing this work for the sake of her boyfriend and that she would not provide any sex services there. She describes her boyfriend as follows: "After he was cheated out of a large sum of money by his very best friend did things go downhill for him and I wanted to help."

When they enter their twenties, fewer *xiaojies* seem willing to spend their money supporting a boyfriend. XJ 28 (age 21) said she had also supported a boyfriend when younger and she didn't mind spending her money on him. But after realising that this first boyfriend had cheated her, she no longer wanted to have a man by her side (*nanren lai pei*).[45] XJ 29 showed a similar attitude: "Some girls already know that their

---

[45] 男人来陪.

boyfriends are fooling them and just want them to pay for their living." Her guess was that around 20% of the girls and women did not have a boyfriend.

XJ 8 (age 18), who entered the sex industry via forced prostitution and later returned on her own to a brothel in urban village A, wanted a boyfriend mainly to feel safer: "In our métier, we look for a boyfriend, and we will pay for his livelihood. Right after escaping, I looked for a boyfriend. Because I was very afraid, I wanted to have somebody who listens to me and whom I can rely on."

The "chicken head" is defined by two "tasks." The first task consists of recruiting prospective *xiaojies* from their (or his) hometown (consensually, with false promises or by force) and escorting them to places of prostitution. According to Pan Suiming, during this recruitment process, the "chicken head" controls the freedom of the girls and young women, although the scope and measures might differ widely. The second task of the "chicken head" is to guarantee the *xiaojies* three things (*san bao*)[46] in exchange for their freedom: namely, food, shelter and client introductions (*baochi baozhu baolake*).[47] The "chicken head" generates his income directly from *xiaojies* in the form of fees or from relatives who might be involved in such negotiations. Few of the *xiaojies* report their "chicken heads" to the police, either because the two are a couple or because they fear subsequent revenge.

If "chicken heads" collaborate with bosses of sex venues, they might receive a commission for recruiting "sisters" (*meizi* as they are called at this stage)[48] on the condition that the women are managed by the boss and his venue. Pan notes that this has been described as "fertilising another man's field" (*feishui zhuanjiao wairen tian*).[49] It implies that the "chicken head" himself will also become dependent on the boss. His income is directly related to the number of clients he introduces and the hourly rate the clients pay to the boss. If the boss wants to see new faces, the "chicken head" has to exchange *xiaojies* with those of other "chicken heads" or come under pressure to recruit new women (Pan, 1999:144–150; see also Pan, 2000:211–218).

---

[46] 三包.

[47] 包吃包住包拉客.

[48] 妹子.

[49] 肥水专浇外人田.

Then, there are *xiaojies* who can afford a toy boy (*xiao bailian*, literally "little white face"),[50] a handsome guy who might be younger than they are and depend on them. In a way, such a relationship is the reversal of or compensation for the often humiliating and/or discriminating encounters with people the *xiaojies* know only too well. Among the interviewees, *xiaojies* with a positive attitude towards *xiao bailian* were the exception. XJ 1 stated the following: "I have no boyfriend … I also do not support a *xiao bailian*. I have the feeling I don't need that. If other people pay for them, it's because they do not have any elderly people in their family they have to care for, and no economic pressure. They want to have a man by their side, a tall one or a smart one, so other people won't harass them. I think people who keep a *xiao bailian* don't have troubles in their head but families with money. I definitely couldn't afford to pay for a boy's living; the family conditions are not good. When boys want to borrow 300 or 500 yuan, they would certainly get nothing from me. Of course, 300 or 500 yuan is nothing here, but at home it means something completely different."

In conclusion, the concept of "boyfriend" has quite different connotations and the transition from boyfriend to chicken head is fluid. Even if boyfriends act more or less as pimps (e.g. by tricking girls into prostitution and living on their income), it may be too simplistic to equate every "boyfriend" with a "pimp." It is not entirely clear from the interviews to what extent boyfriends are involved in acquiring clients for the *xiaojies*, and if so, whether and how this overlaps with the role of the *mami*.

Among xiaojies: *Girls and sisters*

When talking about other *xiaojies*, the interviewees also referred to them as "little girls" and more often "sisters." There was nearly no mention of rivalries among the *xiaojies* except some reservations by higher-age *xiaojies* towards younger ones. Supporting and comforting each other if necessary has often been mentioned. The *xiaojies* share their knowledge (or assumptions) on health issues and risks in the sex industry (XJ 14) and pass on information about illnesses, abortions and clinics to visit or avoid (XJ 15). XJ 21 moved up the ladder of sex service tiers to "second-wife" status soon after starting to work as a *xiaojie* in a beauty salon in urban

---

[50] 小白脸.

village A. Because her patron from Hong Kong was visiting her only once or twice a week, she had a lot of leisure time. Despite living in a convenient hotel, she often returned to her "sisters" in the beauty salon to play mahjong with them. Only XJ 3, who is in her mid-30s, expressed a little distance regarding her much younger colleagues: "I think the people out there are quite young; they came here by deception. I don't know whether they can make money here at all. They don't understand how things work (*tamen bu dong shi*).[51] Here, we are doing this voluntarily, mainly regular work. We are chatting with our guests; if we feel it works, we do it (*juede keyi jiu zuo*).[52] If things go well, they tip more."

Guests, clients, johns

In the interviews, the visitors of nightclubs and KTV bars were usually called "guests" (*keren*)[53] and those of brothels, hair salons, etc., were called "clients" (*kehu*)[54] or "johns" (*piaoke*).[55] Most of the guests at tier-4 venues were from Hong Kong (80% according to XJ 21; 50–60% according to XJ 14) and the others were from mainland China. Foreigners are rare and were seen only in KTV bars (XJ 27). The *xiaojies* interviewed clearly preferred guests/clients from Hong Kong. Compared to mainlanders, they were described as more cultivated, more reliable in paying the bill and more generous when it came to tips (XJ 29). Their sophistication (*you suzhi*)[56] was also measured by their high willingness to use condoms (XJ 21). XJ 14 explains this with reference to the fear of clients from Hong Kong and Macao of getting STIs or HIV/AIDS and potentially destroying their families upon returning. XJ 12 (age 22) said approvingly that "these people [clients from Hong Kong] are pretty decent [men] who have manners and behave respectfully … If you want to get into the car of somebody from Hong Kong, he will first go [around the car] and open the

[51] 她们不懂事. "'Dong shi' [literally, knowing things] becomes a must-have quality – it means knowing how to deal with complicated relationships and recognizing one's responsibility. Think before you leap. Accumulate experience. Be able to utilize your body and sex to earn a place in the cities. Above all, being young and rural should not be an excuse" (Ding, 2017:852).

[52] 觉得可以就做.

[53] 客人.

[54] 客户.

[55] 嫖客.

[56] 有素质.

door and let you enter first; this is so attentive, I feel it is very touching. The higher the people's level, the more respectful they are – [this does] not necessarily [mean that] those people who have a lot of money are [also] very respectful; instead, those middle-class people I see here know best how to respect people. Those big bosses, on the contrary, do not know how to respect people."

The interviewees did not have much to say about the occupations and social backgrounds of their guests/clients. Their average age was estimated at "around 40" (XJ 29) or "between 30 and 50" (XJ 22). "The older the clients are," said XJ 29 (age 24), "the more they like very young girls." XJ 14, a *mami* from urban village A, described the level of the Hong Kong guests/clients as relatively high overall: "The clients from Hong Kong come from all kinds of occupations and social status groups. They may include garbage collectors as well as office clerks. In general, most of the guests/clients come from the lower middle class. People from the middle and upper middle classes do not come to urban village A." "Many of my clients," said XJ 12 from urban village B, "are working in the administration/management of companies and they usually have monthly incomes of around 10–20,000 (HK$ or yuan); there are really some with over 100,000."

Clients from the mainland were doing less well in the eyes of the *xiaojies*. Their payment habits left a lot to be desired, especially if they came from Hunan and Sichuan provinces. They were also considered to be bold or rude. Precisely these clients had to be exhorted more often by the *mami* to use condoms. If a *xiaojie* agrees on her own to services without condoms or if a client secretly strips off a condom, then the client has to pay a surcharge or a risk premium so to speak that is used, e.g. to buy morning-after pills (XJ 14).

With regular dates, the relationship between a *xiaojie* and a client may change, becoming more trustful, and the clients may become boyfriends (XJ 3), just friends (XJ 12) or benefactors for second wives (XJ 21). XJ 3, in her mid-30s, said, "I have two boyfriends. They are very good to me. I have known them for 5 or 6 months.... Together with them I feel very relaxed. One comes once a week, the other every two weeks. When they come, they sleep here but I cannot go to their place. I trust them because every day they call me to chat … It cannot be that they're lying to me (*pian wo*)."[57] One of the two boyfriends knows that there is another one; the other does not. Neither thinks of marrying her. Unlike many other *xiaojies*, XJ 3 does not

[57] 骗我.

support either one of these boyfriends: "No," she said, "they support me. If the business is not going so well, I ask them to come over and give me some money." XJ 12 counted some of her regular clients among her circle of friends. "Besides the sisters," she said, "I have social contacts with some clients, particularly those who see me as their (girl)friend; with them, I can also interact as friends. If they saw me only as a tool, then I couldn't socialise with them." XJ 21 (age 19) had been sustained by a former client from Hong Kong as a "second wife" for one year. "[He is] very good [to me], food, housing, he takes care of everything very well. He regularly accompanies me to have a health check and I get an injection. [The boss] and the sisters all say that I am lucky. I eat and live at his expense, and spend his money, [in addition] he provides me with pocket money of 5,000 yuan per month." But XJ 21 wouldn't see her benefactor as her boyfriend because of the age difference alone of more than twenty years.

Overall, the *xiaojies'* social networks are quite limited and dominated by their urban "surrogate family" ties around workplaces. Self-contained as these networks are, they do not provide many options to connect with urban social life in Shenzhen, even less so as more entertainment venues move out of the city centre. The isolation of the girls and young women is reinforced by their evening and night working hours and by the disillusionment many of them experience with their boyfriends. The *xiaojies* also feel entrapped by the secrets and lies that dominate their communication with family members back home and with friends and colleagues from before they entered the sex industry. Often, the *xiaojies* wanted to stay in the business for only a limited period of time. Considerations of exit strategies were closely related to ideas and plans for a life after working in the sex industry.

Imagining the Future: An Exit Strategy or Not?

Following the tradition of a patrilocal marriage system in rural China, the *xiaojies* – like other rural–urban female migrants – see the phase between leaving school and their generally expected marriage as a special time in their lives. At marriage age,[58] they are expected to return home, marry into the bridegroom's family, have children and care for them. Sometimes, they also have to care for elderly and/or ill family members. It is only after

[58]According to the 2020 Census, the average age of marriage for women in rural China was 23 in 2010 (25 for men) and had risen to 27.6 in 2020 (29 years for men). https://www.yicai.com/news/101472657.html. Over two-thirds of our respondents were under the age of 23.

this period that they go out to work again. The patrilocal transfer from the parental home to the home of the husband and his family is linked to the interruption of their work and migration biographies. In the case of male migrants, marriage has a much smaller impact. Another aspect that influences the *xiaojies*' imagination of the future is the sending of remittances back home. As we know from China-related gender-sensitive migration research, young rural female migrants make greater use of their incomes to financially support other family members by sending remittances than their male counterparts. In stark terms, male migrants care primarily for themselves while female migrants care more about other family members (see Chiang *et al.*, 2015). As seen from our interview material, many *xiaojies* also send remittances to their parental families. But despite their high incomes, these are quite unstable; so, they sometimes have to borrow money themselves to send remittances as regularly as possible.

The reality of a fractured female migration biography in China is also mirrored in the *xiaojies'* visions of their future. But unlike those of other rural female migrants, *xiaojies'* considerations of marriage become more complicated because they are inextricably linked with strategies for exiting the sex industry. *Xiaojies* in their early to mid-twenties face pressure on two sides: On the one hand, competition with younger *xiaojies* becomes tougher and making money more difficult with age; on the other hand, pressure from families and/or from the *xiaojies* themselves to marry becomes ever stronger with increasing age.

Asked about their plans for the future, nearly all of the *xiaojies* interviewed indicated a clear point in time or specific financial target after which they wanted to exit the sex industry, such as "the end of this year" or "50,000 yuan in savings" (XJ 28, 27). Others were not explicit about exiting the industry, particularly those who were paying for a boyfriend (XJ 10, 8). "Marriage" was a typical option given for the time thereafter (XJ 29, 28, 8), as was "looking for a good husband" (XJ 7, 22) or "looking for a husband who has money" (XJ 11). One 17-year-old girl just wanted to go back to her mother and father (XJ 5). Other interviewees included not only marriage in their future plans but also ideas for work or business (XJ 29, 22, 8, 2), while yet others focused on their future career aspirations. The latter had either dependent forms of employment in mind such as an electric car factory worker (XJ 18), a cosmetics consultant (XJ 9) or a skilled tradeswoman (XJ 21). Yet others wanted to start their own business if they could save the necessary starting capital (XJ 29, 19, 3, 2, 1). XJ 3 wanted to open her own kiosk and saw this as a way to earn her livelihood; she didn't want to marry at all, fearing for her personal freedom.

But whether the *xiaojies*' visions of the future were more marriage- and family-centred or more focused on employment and business plans, many saw themselves staying in Shenzhen and not going back to their home province (XJ 29, 21, 19, 18, 11, 7, 3). One exception was XJ 1, a 20-year-old who had not finished elementary school. She explicitly wanted to return to her home village in Sichuan to start a business. More important than the kind of business seemed to be the social status of having a business of her own in the village: "I want to open a shop, buy a car and go back home. You know, at our home village, if you open a shop there, whether it is small or large, then everyone in the village has to address you as [female] boss (*laobanniang*).[59] This is very different from opening [a shop] [somewhere] outside, even if it is a large shop, the others can still say you are only a [migrant] worker (*dagongzhe*)[60] – so, is it worth the effort?" This statement by XJ 1 makes it particularly clear that the money saved should enable the *xiaojie* to lead a life that hadn't been possible at home before and would be even less possible in the sex industry, i.e. to be respected by those around. In this sense, XJ 1's future plans clearly have a compensatory character. To a certain extent, however, this applies to nearly all future plans that simply seek a "normal biography" including marriage and family, working or running a business. And this normal biography should – at least in most cases – not take place in the countryside but rather in the city of Shenzhen, the city of strangers, anonymity and desire.

Part Two: The Urban, Legal and Political Environment of *xiaojies* in Shenzhen

The second part of this chapter focuses on the urban, legal and political environment of rural migrant girls and women who aspire to an urban lifestyle as *xiaojies* in Shenzhen's entertainment and sex industry. It includes a brief introduction to the transformation of Shenzhen's urban villages into shadow economy (*jianghu*) spaces and the emergence and development of a vibrant entertainment and commercial sex industry in the context of Shenzhen's economic reform policies; an overview of the legal framework and enforcement measures of the prohibition of

---

[59] 老板娘.

[60] 打工者.

prostitution in China's socialist market society (laws, regulations, police crackdown, custody and education system); a sketch of the public discourse on the pros and cons of legalising prostitution in China, and a conclusion summarising the main findings of the chapter.

Transforming Shenzhen's Urban Villages

In Shenzhen, the Chinese government separated land ownership from land use rights in 1987 and enacted land marketisation policies in 2009 and 2012 in urban villages (see Wang, 2016:99). A general model of development emerged in Shenzhen whereby the villages partnered with real estate developers for funds and projects. By owning hotels, restaurants and shopping malls, the villages not only assert their place in the expanding metropolis but also generate most of the funding for themselves and their welfare programmes (Wang, 2016:92–100). Formal integration of the urban villages was achieved in the inner districts in 1992 and in the outer districts (Bao'an and Longgang) in 2004 when the Shenzhen municipality owned all land within its borders (O'Donnell, 2017:118).[61] But it was incomplete or unfinished: Self-organisation of the urban villages in practice, which draws on a long administrative tradition as villages, turned out to be a double-edged sword for the Shenzhen municipal government. From the perspective of urban planning and redevelopment authorities, the villages were seen as an obstacle. But by solving the housing needs of millions of migrant workers, they relieved the Shenzhen government of having to provide affordable housing.

The influx of migrant workers from inland provinces and managers from Hong Kong created a demand for services from food hawkers, taxi drivers and sex workers (Bach, 2017:145). "Urban villages, in particular those near the boundary check points, transformed themselves to meet the market demands and commodified desires of Hong Kong day trippers" (Ma and Blackwell, 2017:127). At the Luohu border, several malls became well known for selling counterfeit designer goods and custom-tailored products, and "at the Huanggang checkpoint, spas, massage parlours, and the sex trade became particularly prominent" (Ma and Blackwell, 2017:127). Against this background and especially in terms of their social fabric, Shenzhen's urban villages have been characterised as

[61] In 2005, Shenzhen had 241 urban villages (Wang *et al.*, 2009:959).

spaces of ambiguity (Bach, 2017), informal development (Wang *et al.*, 2009), informality and creativity (Keith *et al.*, 2014), exceptionality (Ma and Blackwell, 2017) and anomie and *jianghu* rules (Ma and Wang, 2011).

Urban villages as **jianghu** *spaces*

In addition to the legal/formal businesses in the urban villages of Shenzhen, a considerable underground economy also emerged. Ma and Wang (2011) differentiate between underground economies related to activities that are per se legal and those that are per se illegal. The former include (1) tax evasion by villagers who rent out rooms and apartments; (2) tax evasion by businesses and services run by urban village joint stock companies; and (3) street hawkers/peddlers without business licenses. Because these peddlers would be subject to punishment in other urban places, many prefer to sell their goods in urban villages.

Underground economies related to per se illegal activities in Shenzhen's urban villages include smuggling, drugs, underground prostitution (*dixia maiyin*),[62] gangs and the production of counterfeit goods. In particular, illegal buildings in urban villages are an open secret. Most of these living spaces are rented out to migrants (Ma and Wang, 2011:75–76). In a spectacular move in May 2005, the city government blew up sixteen high-rise buildings in Yunong Village as a prelude to large-scale urban village redevelopment (Ma and Wang, 2011:101, 137; Bach, 2017:154).

Urban villages in Shenzhen are described as migrants' settlements with a high density of rental housing and an extremely mixed population consisting of white-collar and blue-collar workers, rich and poor people, artists, beggars and petty thieves. "This is where the city is full of chaos, vitality and desire" (Ma and Wang, 2011:28–29). The villages' mobile populations are seen as detached from their earlier lives, norms and values, entering a completely new social environment and subject to discrimination in housing, insurance and schooling. The diverse, heterogeneous and fluid composition of the population, the eagerness of villagers to rent out as much floor space as possible regardless of legality, the de facto self-governance of the villages and the commodified desires of Hong Kong (and other) consumers have made the urban villages a

[62] 地下卖淫.

convenient place for underground economic activities, including red-light districts with their beauty salons, barber shops, spas, massage parlours, nightclubs, KTV and leisure houses (Ma and Wang, 2011:30).

Similar to the official economy, Ma and Wang argue that the underground economy needs operating conditions and channels, specific orders and norms, and force constraining those who try to elude the unwritten laws of this shadow economy and society. But different from the formal economy, they cannot get the protection and guarantees of the state law and economic system. Instead, they need their own coordinators, protectors and "law enforcers," functions that will be fulfilled by "black society organisations" (*hei shehui zuzhi*).[63] These functions include defining the scope and distributing the shares of the underground market, formulating behavioural norms and penalties, establishing "law enforcement troops" capable of violent force, and organising *guanxi* and protection networks and, if need be, violent gangs to resist the government forces and maintain normal operations of various illegal economies. These organisational mechanisms of the underground world are also called "*jianghu* rules" (or etiquette) (*jianghu guiju*)[64] (Ma and Wang, 2011:30; see also Ma, 2006:73).

Spaces of entertainment and commercial sex in Shenzhen's urban villages

With the opening of the SEZ, Shenzhen became one of the first places in China where sex work more or less openly reappeared. Twenty years later, in the early 21st century, it is seen as a hot spot for sexual services (Dong and Cheng, 2017:172). With Dong and Cheng, we can divide the resurgence of commercial sex in Shenzhen into three stages (Dong and Cheng, 2017:174–175):

1979 to 1989: In addition to rural migrant workers, the mobile population that came to Shenzhen also included large numbers of urban professionals and Hong Kong residents. During this period, the predominate group of sex-service clients were regular male visitors from Hong Kong such as truck drivers and businessmen. Working as "mistresses" became fashionable. Sex-service locations were concentrated near Luohu crossing.

[63] 黑社会组织.
[64] 江湖规矩.

1990 to 2006: This was the most flourishing period of Shenzhen's sex industry. Rapid economic development increased the pool of potential providers and consumers. Well-known red-light districts were concentrated near Shuiwei checkpoint in Futian district, including Shangsha, Xiasha, Shazui and Shuiwei. These four urban villages were called *sansha yishui*,[65] indicating places of commercial sex. All were close to the Hong Kong border. Here, the phenomenon of so-called "mistress villages" flourished (Keith *et al.*, 2014:269). The number of female sex workers in Shenzhen was estimated at 110,648 in November 2006. For example, the urban village of Xiasha with a population of around 40,000 and a history going back to the Song Dynasty more recently acquired a reputation for confrontation between city authorities and original village families over drinking, drugs and sex workers. In the early 2000s, the village administration introduced and funded local policing patrols (Keith *et al.*, 2014:267). A Hong Kong resident who had moved to Xiasha because of the cheap housing said he was also attracted by its sex industry. "This street used to be full of prostitutes (*jinü*)[66] looking for business at night. I thought if I opened a convenience store here, I could earn some money, both from visitors and prostitutes. But nowadays you won't see prostitutes on this street anymore. In fact, the sex industry in Xiasha is no longer as active as it used to be, but you can still find prostitutes in the massage and entertainment parlors" (Ai, 2014:79).

After November 2006: Due to campaigns and crackdowns on prostitution in Shenzhen,[67] the geography and structure of the sex industry changed. After more than one hundred young women who had been arrested as prostitutes in November 2006 were paraded by police through the streets of Shenzhen, the well-known red-light districts in the city collapsed. This was well in the interest of the municipal government which wanted to develop Shenzhen into a "world-class city," access urban village land in the centre of the city and integrate the villages (but not the migrants populating them) into its urban governance system. With a master plan for redeveloping villages in the city (2005–2010),[68] the city government

[65] 三沙一水.

[66] 妓女.

[67] For more details, see the section on "Crackdowns on prostitution" in the following.

[68] 深圳市人民政府关于深圳市城中村（旧村）改造总体规划纲要 (2005–2010), https://www.sz.gov.cn/zfgb/2005/gb463/content/post_4948685.html.

expanded its planning power to intervene in what it perceived as spaces of disorder (such as prostitution, gambling and drug trafficking) (Chung, 2009:269). The gentrification process initiated by this plan strongly impacted the situation of female migrants providing sex services in these central locations. In the early 2020s, Shuiwei and Xiasha were described as "well-known foodie hangouts" (O'Donnell, 2021:64). Some of the *xiaojies* shifted to places further from the city centre, including Guanlan village in Bao'an district, Nantou village in Nanshan district (near the Shenzhen Bay checkpoint) and Shawan village in Longgang district, while others left Shenzhen, especially those who had been most visible on the streets. This development was especially obvious in Shazui village where before 2006 the streets were lined with sex workers publicly soliciting clients. Businesses supporting the sex industry, such as restaurants and beauty salons, were typical of the neighbourhood. But afterwards, conspicuously attired female sex workers disappeared and more businesses unrelated to the sex industry became established in Shazui. At the same time, the number of female migrants providing sex services in upscale entertainment venues increased (Dong and Cheng, 2017:175).

Regulating Prostitution in China's Socialist Market Society

At the beginning of China's transformation to a market economy, only two articles (140, 169) of the Criminal Law dealt with prostitution. These articles were directed primarily at third-party attempts to organise and profit from prostitution as a business and made no explicit reference to consensual commercial sex between adults. Since the PRC was established under Mao Zedong, the elimination and the prohibition of prostitution were construed as visible success in liberalising Chinese women from their plight in pre-socialist societies before 1949 (Jeffreys and Yu, 2015:106).[69]

The most recent Shenzhen master plan for urban village redevelopment covers 2019–2025: 深圳市城中村综合整治总体规划（2019–2025）, http://www.sz.gov.cn/cn/xxgk/zfxxgj/ghjh/csgh/zt/content/post_1344686.html.

[69] Shortly after the Communist government took power in 1949, the People's Congress ordered the closure of all brothels in China. Female sex workers were viewed as working-class victims and sent to newly established Female Rehabilitation and Treatment Centres

Legal framework since the 1980s

With the apparent resurgence of prostitution in China in the 1980s, not the Criminal Code but primarily a system of administrative sanctions was used, i.e. the vast majority of prostitution-related offences were handled by the police. The "Regulations of the PRC on Administrative Penalties for Public Security" (1986) prohibited not only the introduction of third parties into prostitution and the provision of accommodation for that purpose, but also the sale and purchase of sex services (Article 30). In other words, unlike the Criminal Law, the "Regulations" also focused on first-party offenders (i.e. *xiaojies* and their clients) (see Table 1). The criminal justice system now only dealt with cases of organised or forced prostitution (Jeffreys and Yu, 2015:107).

With the "Decision on Strictly Forbidding the Selling and Buying of Sex" in 1991, the National People's Congress (NPC) issued a prostitution-specific law which later became incorporated into the revised Criminal Law (1997). Following up on the "Decision" in 1993, the State Council released the "Measures on the Custody and Education of Prostitutes and Their Clients" (*maiyin piaochang renyuan shourong jiaoyu banfa*).[70] The "Measures" authorised public security organs to sentence sex workers and their clients to custodial penalties ranging from six months to two years if their offences did not qualify for "reeducation through labour" (*laodong jiaoyang*, or *laojiao* for short) (§7, 9).[71]

The custody and education system imposes legal and moral education on arrested sex workers and clients, including their participation in production work and testing and treatment for sexually transmitted infections (STIs) (§2; see also *Asia Catalyst*, 2013). Stephen Noakes interprets the "Measures" as a predecessor to the recent trend under Xi Jinping of a more diversified model of legal control of political dissent and social challenges (such as prostitution and drug abuse) after abolition of the *laojiao* system in 2013 (Noakes, 2018:201). Prostitution had been the main reason for incarcerating women in *laojiao* facilities, but after 1999, sex workers

---

for moral education and vocational training. By 1953, nearly all brothels in China had been closed and, in 1958, the Chinese government declared victory over prostitution, gambling and opium (Tucker *et al.*, 2010:122).

[70] 卖淫嫖娼人员收容教育办法.

[71] 劳动教养 – The reeducation through labour system is a form of administrative punishment in China which was launched in the 1950s and abolished in 2013.

Table 1. Regulating prostitution in China (1979–2019).

Date	Department	Document	Main points
1979	National People's Congress (NPC)	Criminal Law of the P.R. China (中华人民共和国刑法)	Articles 140 and 169 targeted third-party attempts to organise and profit from prostitution as a business.
1986	State Council	Regulations on Administrative Penalties for Public Order (中华人民共和国治安管理处罚条例)	Administrative sanctions to curb prostitution in China, with a focus not only on third-party offenders but also on commercial sex providers and their clients.
1991	Standing Committee of the NPC	Decision on Strict Prohibition of Prostitution and Visiting Prostitutes (全国人大常委会关于严禁卖淫嫖娼的决定)	Reaffirmed the previous administrative regulations and cleared the way for the "Measures" (1993).
1993	State Council	Measures on the Custody and Education of Prostitutes and their Clients (卖淫嫖娼人员收容教育办法)	Authorised public security organs to sentence sex workers and their clients to custodial penalties ranging from six months to two years.
1997	NPC	Revised Criminal Law 中华人民共和国刑法 (1997年修订)	Incorporated the "Decisions" (1991).
1999 (2006 revised)	State Council	Regulations Concerning the Management of Public Places of Entertainment (娱乐场所管理条例)	Article 25 prohibited organising, forcing, soliciting, harbouring or introducing prostitution; articles 39, 40 and 42 focussed on related penalties.
2005	Standing Committee of the NPC	Administration Punishments Law for Public Order (中华人民共和国治安管理处罚法)	Replaced the "Regulations" (1986).

Table 1. (*Continued*)

Date	Department	Document	Main points
2015	NPC	Amendment to the Criminal Law 中华人民共和国刑法修正案(九)	Reclassified the crime of "sex with underage prostitutes" as "rape."
2019	Standing Committee of the NPC	Decision on Repealing the Legal Provisions and Systems of the Custody & Education System (关于废止有关收容教育法律规定的决定)	Abolished the Measures (1993) and Article 4, §2 and §4 of the Decision (1991).

were diverted to custody and education centres set up in large and medium-sized Chinese cities which meant their number in *laojiao* declined. Only those women who organised prostitution were apparently still sent to the *laojiao* (Fu, 2005:824). An estimated 450,000 sex workers were held in detention in 2010 (Noakes, 2018:214).[72]

In 2005, the "Public Security Administrative Punishment Law" replaced the 1986 "Regulations." This was a relief for first-party engagement in adult and consensual commercial sex. The period of administrative detention for prostitution-related offences was lowered from a maximum of 2 years in serious cases to 10–15 days, and in less serious cases to up to 5 days, with the additional possibility of a fine (art. 66 and 67). Average fines for prostitution offences were lowered from 5,000 to 500 RMB, and on-the-spot fines (which needed a receipt) were limited to 200 RMB (art. 100) (Jeffreys and Yu, 2015:111). Nevertheless, the "Measures" with their detention period of six months to two years continued to exist.

In 2015, after years of advocacy, an amendment to the Criminal Law (which focused mainly on removing the death penalty for various crimes) reclassified the crime of "sex with underage prostitutes" as rape. This new

[72] Other estimates are even higher with over one million people held in around 200 custody and education camps in first- and second-tier cities (http://blog.dwnews.com/post-417057.html). For comparison, the number of female sex sellers in China is estimated at 2 to 10 million. The problematic nature of these estimates is discussed in Jeffreys and Yu, 2015:98.

classification also raised the previous maximum penalty of 15 years in prison to a life sentence or in some cases did introduce the death penalty.

The latest move to ease the criminalisation of sellers and buyers of sex involved a report by the Legislative Affairs Commission of the NPC Standing Committee suggesting revocation of the regulation that prostitutes and their customers should face detention of six months to two years when apprehended by public security authorities (Cao, 2018). Again, it needed years of advocacy until the NPC in December 28, 2019 decided to abolish the Custody & Education system (which had been in force for more than 25 years) and the related Article 4, §2 and §4 of the Decision on Strict Prohibition of Prostitution and Visiting Prostitutes (1991). Prostitution is still illegal in the PRC and prostitutes and their customers face up to 15 days' detention and fines up to 5,000 Yuan.[73]

Crackdowns on prostitution

For decades, the Chinese government attempted to implement its legal and administrative framework to abolish – or at least curb – prostitution through two kinds of police-led crackdowns: "strike hard" (*yanda*) and "sweeping away the yellow" (*saohuang*).[74] *Yanda* campaigns target prostitution as part of reducing a broad range of criminal activities, including drugs, gambling, organised crime, trafficking and prostitution. Nationwide "strike hard" campaigns were launched in 1996, 2000–2001, 2010–2011 and 2014. *Saohuang* campaigns target prostitution and pornography more specifically. These campaigns normally last a couple of weeks. The police raid entertainment venues, hair salons, massage parlours and other spaces with sex services and detain large numbers of women suspected of selling sex.

These campaigns have not been without reaction from the public. When massage parlours and discos were raided as part of a *saohuang* campaign in Shenzhen in early 2006, more than 3,000 people went onto the streets to protest and thousands of armed police were deployed to maintain order. Even more people were outraged when around one hundred women and their alleged clients were paraded down the streets accompanied by television cameras and loudspeakers announcing their names and accused misdeeds following a crackdown on prostitution in karaoke bars, saunas and hair salons in Futian district in November 2006.

[73] "China abolishes 'custody and education' system", *China Daily*, December 28, 2019.

[74] 严打 and 扫黄.

Internet chatters sympathised with the accused female sex workers and attacked the violation of their privacy and the Cultural Revolution-like tactics of the police during this "shame parade."[75] The next crackdown in 2011 occurred just before the Universiade, an international sporting event for college athletes in Shenzhen (Dong and Cheng, 2017:175).

Another anti-prostitution campaign (which appeared to be orchestrated from Beijing) started from Dongguan (close to Shenzhen) in early 2014 and then spread to other cities in China.[76] It was speculated that up to 10% of the GDP in Dongguan, which is short on land, water and electricity, was based on income from the sex industry (Lo, 2016:107, 110). Three months after this campaign, Dongguan's economic performance dropped markedly. One-third of the estimated 300,000 sex workers had left for other locations in southern China (such as Fujian, Macao and Hong Kong), and the associated industries such as cosmetics, fashion, taxis, restaurants and beauty parlours felt the impact. Beijing police headquarters sent secret teams to investigate a possible criminal–political nexus (Lo, 2016:108, 109). Following the campaign in 2014, China initiated tight controls over the internet in 2015. Messages considered obscene were monitored, problematic websites closed and pornographic content deleted (Lo, 2016:112). At the same time, following rigid crackdowns on prostitution, more advertising and communication with potential clients shifted online.

Public Discourse on the Pros and Cons of Legalising Prostitution

Starting in the late 1990s, criticism of crackdowns on prostitution as ineffective and corrupt triggered a public discourse on the pros and cons of legalising prostitution in China. A broad range of people has been involved in this discourse, including academics, bloggers, journalists, police, sex workers and some political celebrities. Should commercial sex be legalised to

[75] "China to end 'shame parades' of criminal suspects", *The Guardian*, July 27, 2010.

[76] After Xi Jinping mentioned social problems in Guangdong province, state television reported on prostitution in Dongguan and the *People's Daily* criticised Dongguan for tolerating such an immoral business as prostitution, the province government was pressured to respond by closing saunas and nightclubs, arresting hundreds of female sex workers and dismissing Dongguan's deputy mayor and police chief, Yan Xiaokang, for his failure to control prostitution (Lo, 2016:105).

promote tourism, raise tax revenue, prevent the spread of STIs and provide better protection to sex workers? (Jeffreys and Yu, 2015:12). Some local officials who dealt *de facto* with the sale of sex on a day-to-day basis advanced another argument, namely, that it would generate a significant source of revenue for local governments and other self-financing authorities (McMillan, 2006:113). Against a backdrop of socioeconomic insights from the voices of some migrant sex workers themselves, Sun uses examples from the media and popular culture to critique their normative moral, cultural and political frameworks of transgression as stigmatising (Sun, 2022:129).

Discussion heated up when health officials from the CDC (Centre of Disease Control) in Harbin ran a training session for sex workers in October 2006 on how to use condoms correctly. This generated a debate among journalists on whether such training would undermine China's policy of abolishing the prostitution industry. Some senior officials responded that the two tracks of combating prostitution while expanding health training for sex workers were complementary, not contradictory. Similarly, the PRC's five-year action plans for controlling, preventing and treating HIV/AIDS (2006–2010 and 2011–2015) were following WHO suggestions (on reaching out to sex workers for condom use) and encouraging such dualistic policies (Jeffreys and Yu, 2015:114–115). But few government officials who agreed with the need for suitable policies to prevent STIs and HIV/AIDS among specific target groups dared to call into question the central government's policy on prostitution. While some simply repeated the ideological arguments that legalisation would violate the rights and personal dignity of women in China, undermine family values and contravene the basic principles of socialism (Liu, 2010:9), others saw a way out of the dilemma by encouraging educational programmes by specialised NGOs on specific health risks and corresponding measures for sex workers (Yuan-Ihle, 2017:144, 186).

More nuanced positions were taken by academic experts in sexology and sociology such as Li Yinhe and Pan Suiming. Li argued that both prohibition and legalisation of prostitution would be equally problematic. Legalising it to control disease would probably result in more monitoring of sex service providers to ensure relevant health checks and licenses. But such monitoring, she argued, could result in greater corruption and render sex sellers open to economic and sexual exploitation. Instead, she recommended "laissez-faire" decriminalisation (*feizuihua*)[77] based on removing

[77] 非罪化.

legal restrictions on sexual activities for consenting adults, including those involved in commercial sex (which, she suggested, could be handled discreetly in terms of advertisement and meeting). This would not only decriminalise and legalise sexual activities for consenting adults but also considerably reduce the costs of policing. Assuming the unlikelihood of legalising prostitution in China but arguing in a similar direction as Li Yinhe, Pan Suiming favoured a policy of allowing sex sellers to run single-person businesses from private dwellings (such as in Hong Kong and the UK) (Jeffreys and Yu, 2015:116–117).

With the constraints on civil society in China and the new NGO legislation,[78] it is unclear to what extent Chinese health institutions in cooperation with NGOs will be able to effectively provide health education and services to sex workers in the future. In addition, voices criticising the crackdowns and public humiliation of sex workers have become louder. Just before the campaign in Dongguan in 2014, some members of the NPC raised the idea of proposing a bill to legalise prostitution in China. "However, this view remained politically sensitive and morally controversial in the PRC where prostitution is legally banned, although de facto prostitution persists" (Lo, 2016:109). It seems that another round of debate on legalising prostitution in China is inevitable.

Conclusion

Becoming urban *xiaojies* in Shenzhen's *jianghu* spaces has been discussed in this chapter as an ambiguous process of inclusion into the mega-urban environment with its high-speed development, glittering nightlife and hopes of making quick money and at the same time of exclusion from spaces of care and privilege connected to formal urban citizenship in terms of education, employment, affordable housing and social recognition. While the *hukou* system functions in a sense as a demarcation line or sorting machine between urban spaces of care for formal citizens and urban spaces of uncare for migrants in the city, for *xiaojies*, this line is

[78]The "Charity Law of the People's Republic of China" of 2016 and the "Law on Administration of Activities of Overseas Nongovernmental Organizations in the Mainland of China" of 2017; see Chapter 3, Table 1.

even more pronounced as a result of weakened family ties, the illegality of prostitution, moral discrimination and a patriarchal culture. "*Xiaojie*" as an analytical lens helps to illuminate the ways in which young rural migrant women perceive their performance in Shenzhen's entertainment and sex industries as an informal way of integrating into the city without a formal channel.

Urban *xiaojies* in Shenzhen's *jianghu* spaces are largely on their own. The "body in safety" (Li, 2014) is challenged by a variety of physical and psychological risks. As already discussed, the *xiaojies* are at high risk of unhealthy work environments, STIs and HIV/AIDS, unintended pregnancies, abortions and gynaecological diseases. Another risk to the "body in safety" comes from violent clients who beat or otherwise injure *xiaojies*. There are additional risks of drug addiction in a social environment with not only easy access to drugs but also isolation, discrimination and the potential for harm, control or deception by others, particularly by "boyfriends," who are often seen by young girls as their most important source of emotional care.

As also discussed, the *xiaojies* show very different knowledge of and attitudes towards the multiple physical and psychological risks of working in the entertainment and sex industry. While some *xiaojies* appear to be very careful with their bodies in terms of nutrition, smoking and drinking habits, regular health checks and condom use, others, particularly the very young ones, seem much more careless in viewing their bodies as invulnerable.

Xiaojies entangled in *jianghu* spaces usually cannot build on their family networks. Due to their efforts to hide the source of their income, their ties and communication with family members back home shrink over time. Instead, *xiaojies* rely on urban *guanxi* networks connected with the entertainment and sex industry, regardless of whether they entered it voluntarily or were tricked or forced into it. Beyond the emplacement of rural migrants in urban villages/*jianghu* spaces, this chapter identifies – limited – spaces of care produced by the agency of *xiaojies*, including transregional spaces of care generated by the remittances *xiaojies* send to their families and their urban social networks established in the entertainment and sex industries. These relatively small and self-contained social networks have been called "surrogate family networks" consisting of *mamis*, other *xiaojies*/sisters, bosses/big brothers, boyfriends/chicken heads and clients from mainland China, particularly Hong Kong. While these networks provide some kind of care, with the exception of relations among the *xiaojies*/sisters themselves, the networks are overwhelmingly fuelled by an interest to participate in the revenue the *xiaojies* generate from their erotic and sexual resources. This is primarily an instrumental or parasitic type of care, limited mainly to maintaining the *xiaojie* as a source of profit.

Except for occasional health administration programmes (which triggered debate on whether sex workers should be seen as victims or victimisers), there is little in the way of government-provided social safety nets for *xiaojies* in the PRD. Because prostitution is illegal, *xiaojies* fear encounters with the state in the form of police raids, public shaming campaigns and (until 2019) possible detention in custody and education facilities. Even then, distorted forms of "protection" within *jianghu* rules play a role: Managers in the entertainment and sex industry might provide bribes to avoid police raids or at least be informed about the dates of police action, or individual arrangements might be made between a policeman and a *xiaojie* to "protect" her personally in exchange for her acting as his "girlfriend." Thus, various relations of personal dependency become established. As long as the custody and education facilities existed, individuals who had chosen the life of a *xiaojie* over toiling as a *dagongmei* might end up in working and living conditions even worse than those in a factory, with harsh labour, high prices for buying everyday conveniences, and even less freedom and income. From this perspective, the marketised custody and education camps appear to be just another way of exploiting *xiaojies* and a far cry from the original idea (at the time of founding the People's Republic of China) of prohibiting prostitution and installing reeducation facilities to integrate former sex workers into a newly built socialist society of working citizens without exploitation.

This chapter has described the lived space of migrant *xiaojies* in Shenzhen as *jianghu* spaces from different angles. The first is the perspective of academic research that identifies *jianghu* rules as dominating underground economies related to drugs, prostitution and counterfeit goods in urban villages. Second, these negative connotations of urban villages have been taken by urban planners, developers, government agencies and media as strong arguments for redeveloping villages in valuable central urban locations and thus influencing the distribution of entertainment and sex industry venues among city centres and peripheries, driving lower tiers of sex services out of central public spaces. Third, while rural female migrants in Shenzhen's sex industry are motivated in part by the desire to become urban *xiaojies* and thereby wealthy, stylish, modern and at home in the city, and often not less by the pressure of sending remittances to their needy families back home, they easily become entangled in urban *jianghu* spaces and rules.

Following Li Shiqiao's understanding of "ranked care" in the Chinese city, in which *jianghu* represents an external space without care that surrounds internal spaces of "regular care" (providing access to economic resources through relational circles) and circles of "intensive care" (from family relations) (Li, 2014: 98–115), one can conclude that spaces of regular economic care and *jianghu* spaces intersect in certain entertainment venues. For instance, in China's patriarchal business culture joint visits to KTV bars and nightclubs with business partners, including *xiaojie* services, are often seen as a prerequisite for successful business deals (Zheng, 2006:125). Such contributions by *xiaojies* to the urban growth machine have never been valued – unlike the contributions by migrant construction workers which at least sometimes have been acknowledged in connection with the high-rise skyline of the megacity. And finally, another sphere of regular care that urban *xiaojies* become involved in, particularly if they have higher incomes at their disposal, is the consumption of products, including luxury goods, contributing to their transformation and performance.

In any case, being a *xiaojie* is perceived as a transitional stage in the biography of female migrants providing sex services in Shenzhen's entertainment and sex industry. *Xiaojies* see themselves in a "normal life" with marriage, family and children, and/or a business of their own, sometimes back home but mostly in the city, in the near future. Finally, in the self-understanding of some *xiaojies*, sending remittances home and not revealing the source of their income or the attendant hardships and risks might not only be interpreted as legitimation for working in the sex industry but may also give rise to the feeling of being a secret hero fighting for a poor family and social justice in urban *jianghu* spaces.

Appendix

List of interviews with female migrant workers in Shenzhen's entertainment and sex industry (September–October 2009)

Xiaojie interview no.	Working site urban village (A/B)	Age	Education	Place of origin	Time of interview
XJ 1	B, brothel	20	Elementary school (unfinished)	Sichuan	u.k.
XJ 2	A, leisure centre	u.k.*	Senior middle school (finished)	Sichuan	u.k.
XJ 3	A, nightclub	~ 35	u.k.	Guizhou	u.k.
XJ 4	A, nightclub	24	u.k.	Fujian	u.k.
XJ 5	B, brothel	17	Senior middle school (unfinished)	Guangdong	u.k.
XJ 6	B, leisure centre	20	Junior middle school (unfinished)	Hunan	u.k.
XJ 7	A, hair salon	27	Junior middle school (finished)	Hunan	10.09.09, 09:00 P.M.
XJ 8	A, brothel	18	Junior middle school (unfinished)	Henan	11.09.09, 05:35 P.M.
XJ 9	A, hair salon	18	Junior middle school (finished)	Hunan	10.09.09, 06:00 P.M.
XJ 10	B, brothel	18	Junior middle school (unfinished)	Guangdong	09.09.09, 08:00 P.M.
XJ 11	A, hair salon	20	Junior middle school (finished)	Henan	11.09.09, 10:00 P.M.
XJ 12	B, hair salon	22	Junior middle school (finished)	Henan	10.09.09, 05:40 P.M.
XJ 13	B, brothel	22	Junior middle school (unfinished)	Jiangxi	09.09.09, evening
XJ 14	A, KTV	22	Junior middle school (finished)	Hubei	11.09.09, afternoon
XJ 15	A, hair salon	21	Junior middle school (finished)	Yunnan	10.09.09, afternoon

XJ 16	A, hair salon	22	Junior middle school (finished)	Hunan	10.09.09, afternoon
XJ 17	A, brothel	22	Illiterate	Jilin	11.09.09, afternoon
XJ 18	B, brothel	20	Senior middle school (unfinished)	Fujian	09.09.09, evening
XJ 19	B, brothel	20	Elementary school (finished)	Hubei	09.09.09, evening
XJ 20	A, KTV	23	Junior middle school (unfinished)	Henan	u.k.
XJ 21	A, beauty salon	19	Junior middle school (unfinished)	Chongqing	10.09.09, 06:00 P.M.
XJ 22	A, hair salon	21	Junior middle school (unfinished)	Chongqing	u.k.
XJ 23	A, hair salon	22	Senior middle school (finished)	u.k.	u.k.
XJ 24	A, hair salon	22	Junior middle school (unfinished)	u.k.	u.k.
XJ 25	A, KTV	18	Junior middle school (finished)	Chongqing	11.09.09, 05:30 P.M.
XJ 26	A, KTV	u.k.	u.k.	Guangdong	11.09.09
XJ 27	B, brothel	18	Junior middle school (finished)	Sichuan	09.09.09, evening
XJ 28	A, KTV	21	Junior middle school (finished)	Hunan	10.09.09
XJ 29	A, nightclub	24	Elementary school (finished)	Jiangxi	10.09.09
XJ 30	A, beauty salon	20	Junior middle school (finished)	Hunan	10.09.09

Note: *u.k.= unknown.

References

Ai, S. (2014). *Villages in the City. A Guide to South China's Informal Settlements*, Hong Kong: Hong Kong University Press.

Asia Catalyst. (2013). "Custody and education": Arbitrary detention of female sex workers in China, https://www.asiacatalyst.org/wp-content/uploads/2014/09/AsiaCatalyst_CustodyEducation2013-12-EN.pdf (accessed July 30, 2019).

Bach, J. (2011). Shenzhen: City of suspended possibility, *International Journal of Urban and Regional Research* 35.2(March), 414–420.

Bach, J. (2017). "They come in peasants and leave citizens": Urban villages and the making of Shenzhen, in O'Donnell, M. A., Wong, W., and Bach, J. (eds.), *Learning from Shenzhen. China's Post-Mao Experiment from Special Zone to Model City*, Chicago: University of Chicago Press, pp. 138–170.

Burger, R. (2012). *Behind the Red Door. Sex in China*, Hong Kong: Earnshaw Books.

Cao, Y. (2018). Prostitute re-education expected to end, *China Daily*, December 26. http://www.chinadaily.com.cn/a/201812/26/WS5c22c16aa310d91214050d51.html.

Chiang, Y., Hannum, E., and Kao, G. (2015). It's not just about the money: Gender and youth migration from rural China, *Chinese Sociological Review* 47(2), 177–201.

China Labour Bulletin (CLB). (2011). White collar workers lose out as factory wages rise in the Pearl River Delta, https://clb.org.hk/en/content/white-collar-workers-lose-out-factory-wages-rise-pearl-river-delta (accessed February 12, 2025).

Choi, S. (2011). State control, female prostitution and HIV prevention in China, *China Quarterly* 205(March), 96–114.

Chung, H. (2009). The planning of 'villages-in-the-city' in Shenzhen, China: The significance of the new state-led approach, *International Planning Studies* 14(3), 253–273.

Ding, Y. (2017). Eating the rice bowl of youth: *xiaojies*' everyday self-practises as doing citizenship from the margins, *Citizenship Studies* 21(7), 842–859.

Ding, Y. and Ho, P. S. Y. (2012). Sex work in China's Pearl River Delta: Accumulating sexual capital as a life-advancement strategy, *Sexualities* 16(1/2), 43–60.

Dong, W. and Cheng, Y. (2017). Sex work, migration and mental health in Shenzhen, in O'Donnell, M. A., Wong, W., and Bach, J. (eds.), *Learning from Shenzhen. China's Post-Mao Experiment from Special Zone to Model City*, Chicago: University of Chicago Press, pp. 171–190.

Fu, H. (2005). Re-education through labour in historical perspective, *The China Quarterly* 184(December), 811–830.

Gaetano, A. and Jacka, T. (2004). *On the Move. Women in Rural-to-Urban Migration in Contemporary China*, New York: Columbia University Press.

Granovetter, M. (1973). The strength of weak ties, *American Journal of Sociology* 78(6), 1360–1380.

Gransow, B. (2006). Risk employment and social risk management – Job searching strategies of rural-to-urban migrants, in Baur, M., Gransow, B., Jin, Y., and Shi, G. (eds.), *Labour Mobility in Urban China: An Integrated Labour Market in the Making?* Münster: Lit Verlag, pp. 75–88.

Guowuyuan Bangongting 国务院办公厅 (General Office of the State Council). (2013). 中国反对拐卖人口行动计划 2013/2020年 Zhongguo fandui guaimai renkou xingdong jihua 2013–2020 (Chinese action plan for fighting human trafficking 2013–2020), http://www.gov.cn/zwgk/2013-03/08/content_2349019.htm.

Han, Y. (2021). Bargaining with patriarchy: Returned *dagongmei*'s (factory girls') gendered spaces in neo-liberalizing China's hinterland, *Gender, Place & Culture* 28(12), 1673–1694.

Jeffreys, E. and Yu, H. (2015). *Sex in China*, Cambridge: Polity Press.

Keith, M., Lash, S., Arnoldi, J., and Rooker, T. (2014). *China. Constructing Capitalism. Economic Life and Urban Change*, London: Routledge.

Lau, J. T. F., Tsui, H. Y., Siah, P. C., and Zhang, K. L. (2002). A study on female sex workers in southern China (Shenzhen): HIV-related knowledge, condom use and STD history, *AIDS Care* 14(2), 219–233.

Lee, C. K. (1998). *Gender and the South China Miracle. Two Worlds of Factory Women*, Berkeley: University of California Press.

Li, S. (2014). *Understanding the Chinese City*, Los Angeles: Sage.

Lin, M. 林孟端 and Gu, X. 古小明 (2014). 深圳市娱乐场所女性性工作者工作，生活及维权情况 Shenzhen shi yule changsuo nüxing xing gongzuozhe gongzuo, shenghuo ji weiquan qingkuang Working, life and safeguarding rights of female sex workers in entertainment venues in Shenzhen City, 就业与健康 *Occupation and Health* 30(16), 2264–2270.

Ling, B. (2018). Prostitution and female trafficking in China, *China Perspectives* 1–2, 65–74.

Liu, W. (2010). Prostitution should never be legalized, *China Daily*, May 31.

Lo, S. S.-H. (2016). *The Politics of Controlling Organized Crime in Greater China*, London: Routledge.

Ma, E. X. and Blackwell, A. (2017). The political architecture of the first and second lines, in O'Donnell, M. A., Wong, W., and Bach, J. (eds.), *Learning from Shenzhen. China's Post-Mao Experiment from Special Zone to Model City*, Chicago: University of Chicago Press, pp. 124–137.

Ma, H. (2006). *"Villages" in Shenzhen. Persistence and Transformation of an Old Social System in an Emerging Mega City*, Dissertation at the Bauhaus-Universität Weimar.

Ma, H. 马航 and Wang, Y. 王耀武. (2011). 深圳城中村的空间演变与整合, Shenzhen chengzhongcun de kongjian yanbian yu zhenghe (*The Space Evolvement and Integration of Villages-in-the-City in Shenzhen*), Beijing: Zhishi Chanquan Press.

McMillan, J. (2006). *Sex, Science and Morality in China*, London: Routledge.

Noakes, S. (2018). A disappearing act: The evolution of China's administrative detention system, *Journal of Chinese Political Science* 23, 199–216.

O'Donnell, M. A. (2017). Laying siege to the villages: The vernacular geography of Shenzhen, in O'Donnell, M. A., Wong, W., and Bach, J. (eds.), *Learning from Shenzhen. China's Post-Mao Experiment from Special Zone to Model City*, Chicago: University of Chicago Press, pp. 107–123.

O'Donnell, M. A. (2021). The end of an era? Two decades of Shenzhen urban villages, *Made in China* 2, 56–65, https://madeinchinajournal.com/2021/12/01/the-end-of-an-era-two-decades-of-shenzhen-urban-villages/ (accessed March 20, 2024).

Osburg, J. (2016). Corruption, masculinity, and *Jianghu* ideology in the PRC, in Kam Louie. (ed.), *Changing Chinese Masculinities. From Imperial Pillars of State to Global Real Men*, Hong Kong: Hong Kong University Press, pp. 157–172.

Pan, S. 潘绥铭 (1999). 存在与荒谬 – 中国地下性产业考察 Cunzai yu huangmiu – Zhongguo dixia xingchanye kaocha, *Subsistence and Absurdity – An Investigation into the Chinese Underground Sex Industry*, Beijing: Qunyan Publishing House.

Pan, S. 潘绥铭 (2000). 生存与体验. 对一个地下红灯区的追踪考察 Shengcun yu tiyan. Dui yige dixia hongdengqu de zhuizong kaocha (Subsistence and Experience. A Follow-up Investigation on an Underground Red-light District), Beijing: Chinese Social Science Press.

Pun, N. (2005). *Made in China. Women Factory Workers in a Global Workplace*, Hong Kong: Hong Kong University Press.

Shenzhen dui Zhongguo nongmingong zhuanxing de zhuyao gongxian yanjiu 深圳对中国农民工转型的主要贡献研究 (Research on Shenzhen's Main Contribution to China's Rural Migrants). (2014). Renmin luntanwang 人民论坛网, People's Forum Network, http://www.rmlt.com.cn/2014/0714/291157.shtml (accessed April 16, 2025)

Shenzhen tongji ju 深圳统计局 (Shenzhen Bureau of Statistics). (2012). Shenzhen shi 2011 nian guomin jingji he shehui fazhan tongji gongbao 深圳市2011年国民经济和社会发展统计公报, Statistical bulletin on the national economy and the social development of Shenzhen city in 2011, https://tjj.

sz.gov.cn/zwgk/zfxxgkml/tjsj/tjgb/content/post_3085073.html (accessed April 16, 2025)

Smith, C. and Pun, N. (2006). The dormitory labour regime in China as a site for control and resistance, *The International Journal of Human Resource Management* 17(8), 1456–1470, doi: 10.1080/09585190600804762.

Sun, W. (2022). Dark intimacy and the moral economy of sex: Rural migrants and the cultural politics of transgression, *China Information* 36(1), 112–133.

Tsang, E. Y.-H. (2018). Finding hope as a "tempting girl" in China: Sex work, indentured mobility and cosmopolitan individuals, *Deviant Behavior* 39(7), 896–909.

Tsang, E. Y.-H., Lowe, J., Scambler, G., and Wilkinson, J. (2018). Peasant sex workers in metropolitan China and the pivotal concept of money, *Asian Journal of Social Science* 46, 358–379.

Tucker, J., Ren, X., and Sapio, F. (2010). Incarcerated sex workers and HIV prevention in China: Social suffering and social justice countermeasures, *Social Science & Medicine* 70, 121–129.

Wang, D. W. D. (2016). *Urban Villages in the New China. Case of Shenzhen*, New York: Palgrave Macmillan.

Wang, Y. P., Wang, Y., and Wu, J. (2009). Urbanization and informal development in China: Urban villages in Shenzhen, *International Journal of Urban and Regional Research* 33(4), 957–973.

Yi, H., Zheng, T., Wan, Y., Mantell, J. E., Park, M., and Csete, J. (2012). Occupational safety and HIV risk among female sex workers in China: A mixed-methods analysis of sex work harms and mommies, *Global Public Health* 7(8), 840–855.

Yu, Y. J., McCarty, C., and Jones, J. H. (2018). Flexible labors: The work mobility of female sex workers (FSWs) in post-socialist China, *Human Organization* 77(2), 146–156.

Yuan-Ihle, Y. (2017). *Health-Seeking Behavior of Rural-to-urban Migrant Women in Pearl River Delta, China: Sexual Health, Individual Behavior, Formal and Informal Institution and Policy Change*, Doctoral Dissertation (rer.pol.) at the Freie Universität Berlin.

Zheng, T. (2006). From peasant women to bar hostesses. An ethnography of China's karaoke sex industry, in Ching Kwan Lee. (ed.), *Working in China*, London: Routledge, pp. 124–144.

Chapter 5

Creating Transnational Urban Spaces and Migration Containment Policies: African Traders in Guangzhou

Introduction

A young trader from Mali, active in his uncle's trading company, was buying textiles and clothing in the Middle East and Asia at the end of the 1990s. When his uncle's business began to deteriorate due to the Asian financial crisis, the young man decided to start his own business. With a loan of 4,000 US$ from his uncle, he travelled to Hong Kong where he had some loose contacts with Chinese wholesalers. Upon discovering that most products came from mainland China, he decided to buy directly from the manufacturers in the Pearl River Delta (PRD). He then relocated his trading base to Guangzhou (Gilles, 2015:29).

Like this young man, many African traders from Southeast Asian cities such as Bangkok, Jakarta and Kuala Lumpur started moving to China after the Asian financial crisis in 1997–1998. A large number of them went to Guangzhou, where they set up shops and began shipping goods manufactured in China to their home countries. This development – and the increasing economic and trade cooperation between Guangzhou and African countries – encouraged traders in Africa to go to China to find manufactured goods there themselves (Bodomo, 2012:XXIX). In addition, some African students in China decided to remain in the country and enter the trading business. Moreover, African businesspeople in Hong Kong were attracted by the low prices of production sites in mainland

China and began to explore Guangzhou as a new trading base (Bork-Hüffer and Yuan-Ihle, 2014:581). All in all, a favourable business environment brought African traders from various backgrounds to the city of Guangzhou.

Guangzhou can look back on a long history as a major commercial and trading centre in China. It was the first Chinese port to be visited regularly by European traders. After joining the World Trade Organization (WTO) in 2001, China in general and the PRD in particular became an increasingly popular new destination for migrants from developed and developing countries. An active metropolitan marketplace with events such as the Canton Fair, which has taken place twice a year since the 1950s, Guangzhou has attracted many international merchants and traders, including from African countries (Qu, 2016:203). In fact, it has become the preferred destination for African traders (along with Yiwu in Zhejiang province), who often conduct business in the informal economy with relatively small amounts of capital (Lan, 2015:289).

While China's engagement in Africa has been accompanied by official Chinese rhetoric of South–South cooperation, mutual advantage, friendship and a win-win situation, African migrants who came to the country in ever greater numbers around the turn of the century had a somewhat different experience. It turned out that Guangzhou did not welcome them with open arms but instead with various forms of everyday discrimination (e.g. taxi drivers refusing to pick up black people) as well as harsh governmental constraints due to very restrictive visa policies that disproportionately affected this group of international migrants. Nevertheless, over the years and despite the often-precarious conditions, an African diaspora has emerged and developed in Guangzhou and the PRD. The concept of diaspora is used here in its more recent context as a signifier of multiplicity, fluidity, wildness or hybridity. Focusing on the transformations and dislocations created by movement and de-emphasising moral implications, diaspora is conceptualised "as a generalizable category applicable to the understanding and comparison of a wide variety of mobilities and dispersals" (McKeown, 1999:308/309).

The development of the African diaspora in Guangzhou can be divided roughly into five periods:

(1) **The beginnings (1990s to 2003):** During this first phase, trading centres and markets were established in new buildings such as the Tianxiu Building and the Guolong Building (built in 1994 and 1998 respectively). These served international traders.

(2) **A period of prosperity (2004–2007):** More specialised services appeared and several new markets opened in the Xiaobei and Sanyuanli areas, which expanded the local tax base (Li *et al.*, 2012:65). After the Forum on China–African Cooperation (FOCAC) was established (in 2000), the Chinese government signalled to immigrants in 2004 that its door was opening by offering a legal possibility to acquire permanent residency – but in practice the requirements were very tough.

(3) **A period of increasing surveillance (2008–2011/2012):** In 2007, the tone of the local press in Guangzhou became increasingly negative. That same year, the municipality began to build a networked information system for foreigner management. As the 2008 Beijing Olympics and the 2010 Asia Games in Guangzhou approached, the situation for foreigners and particularly for Africans became increasingly tense. The Guangzhou government has launched a policy targeting international migrants living, staying or working in China without the required legal documentation. In 2009 (when two Nigerians were seriously injured when trying to escape visa inspection) and again in 2012 (when an African died in police custody), large numbers of Africans demonstrated in the streets.

(4) **A period of legalised containment (2011/2012–2018/2019):** After local Guangdong regulations on the administration of foreigners (in 2011) and a national exit and entry law (in 2013) came into effect, the combination of a strict visa policy and law enforcement measures such as police controls led ever more foreigners to overstay their visas and others to leave either the city or the country.

(5) **A period of pandemic control and its aftermath (2020–2023):** Under the conditions of the COVID-19 pandemic, the coping strategies of the many African visa overstayers in Guangzhou – to be as invisible and untraceable as possible – came into conflict with the local authorities, who wanted to avoid a virus outbreak in the city's foreign community and experimented with new technologies of mass surveillance and mobility control (Castillo and Amoah, 2020). As part of the testing and tracking measures, Africans in Guangzhou were mistreated (e.g. evicted from their homes and denied access to commercial areas).

Although economic conditions in the PRD appeared to be promising, the early African traders missed a socio-cultural environment that enabled exchange with the local people. The newcomers faced many practical questions, such as where to find Ghanaian (or Kenyan, Senegalese, Congolese, etc.) food, when and where to report their residence status in Guangzhou, how to renew their visas, how to rent an apartment and how to avoid being cheated by their Chinese suppliers (Mathews, 2015:124). Rarely speaking Chinese or Cantonese, the African traders were limited in their ability to turn to local Chinese people about these matters and establish their own diaspora logistics in the economically attractive but not especially sympathetic local environment of Guangzhou city.

How was it possible for African migrants to put down roots in this seemingly unpleasant social environment? What kinds of urban spaces have been produced by African migrants? And what effects have local and national immigration policies and legislation had on African traders in Guangzhou? This chapter explores how African traders have created transnational urban spaces in Guangzhou and other places in the PRD and thus contributed – albeit not explicitly intended by either them or the municipal government – to Guangzhou's efforts to become a world city. The traders discovered the potential and opportunities Guangzhou offered in terms of business in a global setting, and they tried to continue working and living in the city for certain periods of time, despite an increasingly unfavourable legal environment marked by many instances of everyday discrimination, racism and exclusion.

This chapter is structured as follows: After briefly introducing how African migrants and their spaces in Guangzhou have been defined thus far, it examines the production of transnational urban spaces by African traders in different dimensions: as transnational business spaces, spaces of (informally organised) care and spaces of communication between African migrants and internal Chinese migrants. The second part of the chapter then analyses local and national immigration policy, including the construction and targeting of the so-called "triple-illegal" population among foreigners in Guangzhou, the content of and differences between local regulations and national legislation, and the impact of law enforcement measures on African traders in Guangzhou.

Defining African Migrants in Guangzhou and the Pearl River Delta

Any attempt to explore the agency of African migrants in Guangzhou must first raise the question of how this specific group of international or transnational migrants has been defined thus far. In general, African migrants in China include diplomats, students, professionals and businesspeople, with diplomats and students more concentrated in Beijing and traders (the largest group) concentrated in Guangzhou and Yiwu in Zhejiang province. While the traders in Yiwu often originally came from the Maghreb (e.g. Mauretania, Morocco, Libya, Tunisia and Algeria), those in Guangzhou came mainly from West African countries such as Nigeria, Mali, Senegal, Ghana and Guinea (Bodomo, 2012:10ff, 28).

Lyons *et al.* (2008) have described the African traders in China as a global counterflow to the rise of Chinese diasporas in Africa, part of the significant changes in African economies and societies, thereby creating new interactions with Chinese urbanity. They highlight the embeddedness of the emerging diaspora of private African traders in Guangzhou in a broader global context and characterise them as a "transient community" and "a third tier of globalization" (Lyons *et al.*, 2008:200, 205).[1] In a similar way, Gordon Mathews addresses this large group of mostly small traders from Africa (and the Middle East) in Guangzhou as part of low-end globalisation, or globalisation from below (Mathews, 2017:2; 2015:118; see also Mathews *et al.*, 2012).

Equally worth considering is the question raised by Niu (2015a and 2015b) of whether African migrants in Guangzhou are "real" migrants, given that African traders generally do not come to Guangzhou with the ultimate aim of staying there but rather of trading goods between China and Africa and also given their precarious social status and uncertain situation due to strict visa policies (Niu, 2015a:139). He therefore suggests defining the group of African traders in Guangzhou as "transients" (*guoke*)[2] rather than as immigrants (Niu, 2015a:140, 143). Castillo (2016), by contrast, has complained that existing research on Africans in Guangzhou tends to represent them as "a mass of traders" and their presence in the PRD as "a wave of immigration" (288). He suggests focusing more instead on the diverse rationales behind the multiple forms of mobility that drive individuals into transnational movements and activities.

---

[1] Drawing on the earlier discourse on global cities, Lyon et al. emphasise the role of private global actors, such as private African traders in Guangzhou, as a 'third tier of globalisation' alongside a transnational elite class (Sassen) and the local middle class (Hamnett).

[2] 过客.

The newly established transnational spaces of African migrants in Guangzhou have been socially constructed in different (yet interrelated) ways, depending on the researcher's subjective perspective and research approach. From the perspective of urban space formation, Lyons *et al.* (2016:027/028) have framed these transnational spaces as "international immigrant districts" (*guoji yiminqu*)[3]. Li *et al.* (2009) have addressed them as "ethnic enclaves" and as part of a global African diaspora, but without more detailed comparisons with African diaspora spaces in other megacities outside China. With a greater focus on international relations, Adam Bodomo has highlighted the potential of African migrant communities in Guangzhou to play a role as "bridges" in the development of African–Chinese relations (Bodomo, 2012:19; 2010).

Other authors, such as Jin *et al.* (2021) or Niu *et al.* (2020), have criticised the identification of the African diaspora in Guangzhou as "immigrant neighbourhoods" or "ethnic enclaves." Their point is that conceptualisations of African migrant settlements that have emerged in the global North are not necessarily applicable in the context of South–South mobility. Whereas Jin *et al.* see the situation of Africans in Guangzhou as a kind of "trading post" that "functions as a hub in the global circuit of South-South trade" (Jin *et al.*, 2021:10), Niu *et al.* highlight the significant role of the Chinese state "as one of the major forces that result in the transiency of African neighbourhoods in Guangzhou" (Niu *et al.*, 2020:215). The seemingly contested conceptualisations of African diaspora spaces in Guangzhou/China may be due (at least in part) to a focus on different time periods, with Bodomo's "bridge theory" looking at the early stages of formation (before 2007/2008), Li Zhigang looking at what he calls an already "collapsing enclave" in the period after 2007 (Li *et al.*, 2012:65), and Jin *et al.* (2021) and Niu *et al.* (2020) pointing to more recent developments.

From the perspective of spatial practices, Karsten Giese and Kelly Liang (2018) argue in a case study of Xiaobei that seemingly "African spaces" in Guangzhou can actually be identified as three overlapping territorial spatial orders: a visible African order based on trading activities; below the surface, a thriving informal economy of Chinese rural–urban migrants providing services to the African community and local residents renting out shops and accommodation; and a third spatial order in which the local state demonstrates its sovereignty over this "African" territory.

---

[3] 国际移民区.

In addition to these different perspectives and approaches, it should also be noted that African migrants in Guangzhou do not constitute a homogeneous group but instead are described as a mosaic of different national and socio-cultural backgrounds. Early migrants to Hong Kong, Guangzhou and other places in China who became the most established members of the African community in Guangzhou are largely from Mali and Guinea. Deep socio-cultural differences have been found between Anglophone (around 75% Christian) and Francophone (around 58% Muslim) Africans in Guangzhou (Lyons *et al.*, 2008:197, 200). Because few Chinese understand French, Francophone Africans formed relatively tight communities around mosques, while Anglophone Africans have looser social networks (Han, 2013:85). Africans in Guangzhou generally have some type of religious affiliation: Around 60% are Christians including Protestants and Catholics, 35% are Muslims and 5% have some kind of folk belief (Zhou, 2016:131).

As far as the local Chinese people are concerned, all these differences among African migrants and within the composition of the African diaspora in Guangzhou become blurred when they equate "Africans" with "black people" regardless of their national citizenship, lumping together not only citizens from various African nations but also African Americans, Caribbeans and Europeans without being aware of white Africans or those of Arab origin (Bodomo, 2012:3). Thus, the heterogeneity of the African diaspora in Guangzhou is often overlooked from a Chinese perspective, not only in popular imagination but also in official propaganda (Lan, 2015:293). However, as Lan Shanshan has argued, this does not mean that the racialisation of black Africans in China can simply be interpreted in a traditional black-and-white binary; it must be situated in the wider context of a triangular power relationship between China, Africa and the West (Lan, 2017:5). Against the background of a model of South–South racialisation, Lan highlights the different gazes by elite and non-elite Chinese on persons with black skin, which may or may not involve racialisation in the Western sense (Lan, 2017:9). Lan identifies different sources from which the Chinese knowledge of blacks is drawn: traditional Chinese aesthetic values that favour light over dark skin (associated with working in the fields, low social status); racialised images of blacks in Western literature and media; Chinese state propaganda such as the discourse on Sino-African friendship; Chinese-language media; and personal experience and hearsay (Lan, 2017:190). She argues that because of these different sources of racial learning, there is no overarching discourse of anti-black racism in China. Instead, she sees the representation of blackness as a highly contested issue that may or may not reinforce hegemonic discourses of racism originating from the West and at the same time may challenge them "in creative and unexpected ways" (Lan, 2017:191).

In addition to different academic definitions and everyday perceptions of African migrants in Chinese society, there is also an ongoing debate on the number of African traders/migrants in Guangzhou. The lack of official data has led to speculation and discussion on how to gather and verify such figures (Li and Du, 2016:005; Bodomo and Pajancic, 2015). The most frequent estimate for the period after 2008 has been 15,000–20,000 long-term African migrants in Guangzhou (Zhou, 2016:132; Mathews, 2015:118). Other estimates suggest 30,000 Africans operating in Guangzhou (Pieke, 2012:51). According to data published by the Entry and Exit Administration of the Guangzhou Public Security Bureau, the number of all (registered) foreign residents in Guangzhou increased from 18,000 in 2006 (Li and Du, 2016:005) to nearly 80,000 in March 2017, while the number of (registered) African residents in Guangzhou increased from 1,080 persons (or 6% of foreign residents in Guangzhou) in 2006 (Li and Du, 2016:005) to 11,000 (or 14% of foreign residents in Guangzhou) in 2017, including around 5,000 permanent and 6,000 temporary African residents.[4] While the number of Africans in 2020 fell to around a third of its level in 2019 following the outbreak of the pandemic, their share of the total number of foreign residents still in Guangzhou remained roughly the same as in previous years, at 15% (see Table 1).

Although they do not make up a large percentage of all foreigners in Guangzhou, the "Africans" are the only group of international migrants in Guangzhou to have created visible settlements. They have attracted more attention from academia and the media than any other group of foreigners. They are also the only group of international migrants to be described in the context of "illegal stays," "drugs" and "crimes" (Niu, 2016:156).

While it is not possible to chart a detailed trajectory, it is clear that the absolute number of African residents in Guangzhou has declined significantly in recent years. As we will discuss in more detail later, new immigration legislation at provincial and national levels plus strict visa

---

[4]According to public security statistics, the number of foreigners in Guangzhou subsequently peaked in 2014 at 118,000, including 57,000 (48%) from Asia, 22,000 (19%) from Europe, 16,000 from Africa (14%), 14,000 (12%) from North America, 5,000 (4%) from South America and 4,000 (3%) from Oceania.

Table 1. Number of African residents in Guangzhou (selected years, 2006–2020).

Year	Number of foreign residents in Guangzhou	Number of African residents in Guangzhou	Percentage of Africans among all foreign residents in Guangzhou
2006	18,000[a]	1,080[a]	6
2014	118,000[b]	16,000[b]	14
2017	80,000[c]	11,000[c]	14
2019	86,475[d]	13,652[d]	16
2020 (April)	30,768[d]	4,553[d]	15

Source: [a]Li and Du, 2016:005; [b]Niu, 2016:156; [c]Xinhua, 5 December 2017. See also www.xinhuanet.com/english/2018-01/29/c_136933673.htm and [d]Guangzhou's Mayor Wen Guohui at a Press Conference, *Nanfang ribao* 13 April 2020, http://leaders.people.com.cn/n1/2020/0413/c58278-31671189.html (accessed March 31, 2024, own compilation).

regulations from the local government combined with harsh enforcement campaigns in Guangzhou can be seen as the main reason for the decrease in the number of African migrants in Guangzhou. This trend was exacerbated during the COVID-19 pandemic.

African Traders in Guangzhou: Producing Transnational Urban Business Spaces

When an increasing number of African traders with various occupational experiences and different grades of familiarity with the region began arriving in Guangzhou in the early 2000s, they did not have the supportive infrastructure of an already existing African diaspora there. Attracted by the local business opportunities of the flourishing Chinese economy, particularly the advantage of cheap Chinese consumer goods, African traders concentrated on specific areas of the city. The emergence of African diaspora spaces in Guangzhou can be seen as part of the restructuring of Chinese cities that has produced new spatial forms such as glittering Central Business Districts, iconic architecture, forests of skyscrapers, development zones, gated communities, shopping malls, cultural clusters and university cities on the one hand but also urban villages and rundown areas such as some older residential districts and industrial areas on the other. Like many other Chinese cities (or even preceding them), Guangzhou has launched comprehensive entrepreneurial strategies to boost its role in intense intercity competition (Gransow, 2014:3). While this environment has advanced the economic interests of African traders in Guangzhou, both the Africans themselves and local Chinese residents view the traders as outsiders who are unfamiliar with local languages and customs and do not belong to the regulated urban system. Michal Lyons, Alison Brown and Li Zhigang have used the term *jianghu* to mark the urban environment the African traders encountered when arriving in Guangzhou (Lyons *et al.*, 2016:014).[5]

One of the early destinations of African traders in Guangzhou was Dengfeng Hotel in the Xiaobei area, constructed by local villagers. With the increase of real estate investments in the 1990s and mushrooming high-rise buildings, the landscape of Xiaobei changed completely. Local real estate agencies and Village Committees seeking to profit from their land promoted this development. Local shops targeting foreigners provided related services, e.g. visa applications, travel arrangements, packaging, international calls and medical services. With African food and an increasingly multi-lingual environment, an internationalised milieu was created (Li *et al.*, 2012:63).

The centre, or more accurately the centres, of the emerging African diaspora space in Guangzhou coalesced around hundreds of large wholesale shops that are clustered in the Xiaobei area (Yuexiu district) and Sanyuanli (Baiyun district). African-owned shops are prominent in several buildings in Xiaobei and Sanyuanli.

According to Li and Du (2016), there are five main areas of concentration for African residents and their business activities in Guangzhou and Foshan: Xiaobei, Sanyuanli, Panyu, Dongpu and Huangqi(zhen) (see Table 2).[6] A comparison of the main African business and residential centres in Guangzhou describes Xiaobei as accommodating traders of diverse backgrounds, including a significant French-speaking Muslim African population, and Sanyuanli as a slightly cheaper market with a high concentration of English-speaking Nigerian traders and Nigerian-owned shops (Han, 2013:85). Together, they form a huge year-round trading area specialising in Chinese-manufactured goods for lower-income countries, attracting businesspeople not only from many African countries but also

[5]For mega-urban *jianghu* (江湖) spaces, see also Chapters 3 and 4.

[6]For a slightly different distribution of African spaces in Guangzhou and Foshan and the changes between 2012 and 2016 (including maps), see Jin *et al.* (2021:5, 8).

Table 2. Distribution of African spaces in Guangzhou and Foshan.

Areas of concentration	Main streets	Main markets	Residential areas
Xiaobei	Xiaobeilu, Huanshi zhonglu, Taojinlu, Tongxin nanlu, Jianshe liumalu, Xiatang xilu, Henganlu, Baohan zhijie	Tianxiu Tower, Yueyang Trade City, Jinshanxiang Trade City, Yanhui International Trade Centre, Guolong Tower, Xiushanlou Chinese-African Trading City, Taoci Tower, Hengsheng Ceramics Tower	Tianxiu Tower, Dengfeng Hotel, Yueyang Business Building, Dengfeng Village, Tongxin Street, Xiatang Street West
Sanyuanli	Guangyuan xilu, Sanyuanli dadao	Tangqi Foreign Trade Clothing City, Jianan Foreign Trade Clothing Wholesale City, Tongtong Trade City, Parker Trade City, Tianen Clothing City, Aerospace Tower, Guozhan Clothing City, Yulong Clothing Market, Xiushan Building, 88 Foreign Trade Clothing Wholesale, Wantong Tower (besides Sanyuanli)	Shaoguan Tower, Longan Hotel, Huiyuan Hotel
Panyu	Lijiang Garden, Qifu New Village	Lijiang Garden, Qifu New Village	Lijiang Garden, Qifu New Village
Dongpu	Tianhe Square	Tianhe Square	Tianhe Square
Huangqi (Foshan)	Huangqi buxingjie	Huangqi buxingjie	Riverside Garden, Dasha Village, Michong village, Jiangbin Tower, etc.

Source: Li and Du (2016:004–005, Table 1-1).

from Pakistan, India, Turkey, Iran, Arab states and others (Müller and Wehrhahn, 2013:86/87).

In the vicinity of these wholesale markets, a broad range of services has arisen ranging from cheap hotels, cafés and restaurants specialising in various local African and other foreign cuisines to currency exchange and transfer offices, travel agencies and freight services (Müller and Wehrhahn, 2013:87). Here, the customers of established African businesspeople in Guangzhou can find establishments that convey a sense of home, including restaurants serving various national African cuisines, wholesale markets, hotels and cafés, hairdressers and home churches that serve as meeting points (Gilles, 2015:31). Also, some African migrants have become active in their communities' sports (soccer) and cultural (music) activities. While this indicates diversification of the African diaspora space, traders are by far the most dominant group among African migrants in Guangzhou. Their structure reflects their specific activities and functions in the African–Chinese trading business. With reference to Zhou *et al.* (2016a:147), we can distinguish three main subgroups of African businesspeople:

(1) **Expatriates working for African import/export or trading firms.** They are engaged in large-scale business with Chinese companies and manufacturers via formal channels. Generally, they are capital-rich with long-term business visas.
(2) **Independent merchants with prior experience in Hong Kong or Southeast Asian countries.** They have long-term business plans but travel on short-term business or tourist visas. Usually, they operate their own small or medium-sized firms and tend to rely on Chinese agents, trading partners and other intermediaries. Some of them deal directly with Chinese manufacturers. While they go back and forth between Hong Kong and Guangzhou, they maintain regular places of residence in Guangzhou.
(3) **The largest group consists of *petty entrepreneurs*.** This group shows the greatest diversity in terms of both socioeconomic background and business experience. Its members all strive to make quick money in China. "They tend to live among Chinese residents and trade face-to-face with Chinese merchants in local wholesale markets and street markets. They often carry large plastic bags or suitcases which is why Chinese refer to them as 'calculator merchants,' 'suitcase merchants'

or 'garbage-bag merchants'" (Zhou *et al.*, 2016a:147).[7] Some of them later succeed in becoming owners of small and medium-sized firms and move up to the second group.

Established African businesspeople generally speak Mandarin or Cantonese and are familiar with the business norms and practices of their Chinese partners (Gilles, 2015:32). African traders or customers who lack knowledge of the local business environment and come to Guangzhou on short-term visas may not be able to control the process of preparing goods for shipment or ensure that they are not cheated by Chinese business partners. They therefore turn to African intermediaries who function as guarantors and organisers of business deals between African customers and their Chinese counterparts (Gilles, 2015:33).

Using the example of African logistics agents, Gordon Mathews described the role of this special group of African traders and Guangzhou long-term residents in more detail: "Their job is to send their customers' goods by air or container ship from China to various African seaports and airports, e.g. Mombasa, Eldoret, Lagos or Matadi; they generally do not deal with logistics within Africa but only in getting the goods to African ports" (Mathews, 2015:126). The approximately 200 African logistics agents in Guangzhou, some of them with offices and signboards and others less obvious, normally work with Chinese logistics companies that book a large number of containers worldwide and can therefore get cheaper rates than if they worked on their own. African logistics agents may be involved in the inspection of goods (to ensure their quality for customers) and in ongoing customer care. Most of these agents work as partners or employees of logistics companies with offices in Lagos, Nairobi and Dubai. Some also work with Chinese companies that need African logistics agents for their contacts and dealings in Africa (Mathews, 2015:126). The goods transported are largely legal but very much underdeclared on customs forms (to minimise duties). This leads to a significant undervaluation of official Chinese–African trade figures (Mathews, 2015:127).

Middlemen between Chinese suppliers and African clients have included many undocumented traders who have generally entered China on valid business or tourist visas and then overstayed them. Some have

[7]On calculator communication, see also Bodomo *et al.* (2022).

combined their trade activities with unauthorised employment at, e.g. nightclubs, cargo companies or African restaurants (Lan, 2015:292/293). "These logistics agents/middlemen serve as cultural brokers because their business has made it necessary for them to help their customers practically and culturally adjust to China" (Mathews, 2015:139). But after the crackdown on visa infringements in 2013–2014, this became nearly impossible. In addition, these intermediaries seem to have a limited future in general because Chinese companies are seeking to supplant African middlemen in the PRD by placing their own factories and agents in African (and other) countries (Mathews, 2015:141).

National African Organisations: Providing Spaces of Care

Confronted with a foreign society and culture, African traders in Guangzhou moved closer together and strengthened their internal local networks by means of mutual assistance, shared information and mutual psychological security (Li and Du, 2016:10). African traders in Guangzhou have established various different organisations, although not a unified association for all African traders in Guangzhou (or China). Most of the organisations represent particular or national interests with, e.g. a Nigerian, Ghanaian or Cameroonian focus. Economic organisations include Chambers of Commerce, trade organisations and financial support groups. Social organisations are mainly family education groups for school children, childcare facilities and social support groups. Cultural and leisure organisations consist largely of church, sports and music groups. Other organisations have a political or other country-related focus, and participation in these organisations is generally described as not very high (Li and Du, 2016:11).

The African organisations in Guangzhou differ from the migrant organisations in immigration countries that focus on newcomers with a long-term perspective of settling down in the host society. This is because Africans arriving in Guangzhou usually come with the aim of trading goods between China and African countries and turning this into a profitable source of income. They do not have plans to settle down. Therefore, in order to highlight the transient nature of the Guangzhou environment, Niu (2015:140) suggests using the term "transient organisations" (*guoke shetuan*)[8] instead of migrant organisations. According to him, the African

[8] 过客社团.

organisations fulfil three main functions by providing representation and services to their members and advocating for their legal rights:

(1) **Mutual assistance to members:** Mutual assistance among members of the organisation consists largely of material and psychological support in the event of, e.g. major illness or deaths of family members.
(2) **Guidance on practical questions:** Most of these organisations provide guidance on matters such as apartment rentals, medical treatment, the Guangzhou public transport system, visa issues and accommodation registration. Visa and registration issues are the most important because it can be very expensive to obtain and prolong visas. Many Africans in Guangzhou try to overstay their visas in order to reduce their travel costs. Africans who are detected without valid visas and accommodation registration can be fined or even jailed and repatriated. The municipal government of Guangzhou has not (yet) set up a budget to repatriate foreigners. If Africans in Guangzhou go bankrupt or encounter other economic difficulties, they are often unable to pay the high repatriation-related fines or costs for return tickets.[9]
(3) **Representation of national African populations:** The African organisations in Guangzhou represent the people of their respective countries. Usually, these organisations have connections with other such organisations and with their respective embassies or general consulates. Members are often interviewed in the event of state visits or visits by leading government representatives to Guangzhou. But because of the visa difficulties faced by many Africans, the most basic function of these organisations is to communicate with relevant local government offices, particularly the Guangdong police. This is done primarily in the form of direct communication by the organisations' leaders (Niu, 2015a:132/133).

In response to an ever-greater perception of legal vulnerability, Africans in Guangzhou have established national community offices. Nearly thirty of these offices had been founded by around 2010. Their main missions include promoting understanding and ties among Chinese and Africans and generating an atmosphere of a home away from home

[9]The organisations normally decline to assist individual members if repatriation is caused by personal reasons, but they do not miss any opportunity to raise awareness among members about the high risks of visa and registration violations.

(Castillo, 2016:298). Their services and activities include legal representation, local-level diplomacy, financial aid, cultural and sporting events, family forums and marriage counselling, and aid to individuals in trouble (primarily those who have been cheated or who have overstayed their visas).

The Nigerian community office is one of the most visible with 3,000 registered members. As Castillo (2016) explains, their leader, Ojukwu Emma, is renowned for having united several Nigerian factions and also for seeking to unite Guangzhou's diverse community offices based on the experience that national distinctions among African offices count little when dealing with Chinese authorities.[10] Before Emma took office, the Nigerians in Guangzhou were fragmented along ethnic and religious lines. In addition, in the mid-2000s, some Nigerian newcomers engaged in criminal activities such as drug peddling, extortion and abduction of other Nigerians. These activities, particularly drug dealing, damaged the reputation of the entire African community in Guangzhou. When Emma became president of the Nigerian community, he established a group of vigilantes called "the peacemakers." They warned those engaging in criminal behaviour to stop doing so; if the latter did not comply, they apprehended them and handed them over to local authorities. Following Emma's consolidation efforts, the need for vigilantes faded away. While acknowledging the positive effects of Emma's approach, some people complained that he and his group used their position to combat rival groups. Not everyone therefore feels represented by the community offices (Castillo, 2016:298–300).

Even if not formalised, organised representation has brought major advantages in dealing with local authorities. It has signalled a strengthening of the African presence, and since the 2012 demonstrations, the local Public Security Bureau has begun to take the community offices seriously. After the COVID-19 outbreak, when Guangzhou city officials imposed mandatory testing on Africans in the spring of 2020, they turned to African community leaders like Emma and asked for their help. With undocumented Africans in Guangzhou at risk of deportation, African community leaders sought guarantees from the Chinese side that those registering for the test would not be arrested or evicted from their homes (Adebayo, 2023a; 2023b:169). Nevertheless, these offices still lack a formal, legal

[10]Ojukwu Emma passed away in February 2021 in Guangzhou.

framework to strengthen their representational activities (Castillo, 2016:300).

Intersection of International African Migrants and Chinese Internal Migrants: Spaces of Communication and Collaboration

The emergence of an African diaspora in Guangzhou increased the opportunities for African traders and ordinary Chinese people to interact with each other in everyday life. As Sino-African trade activities are concentrated in the informal economy, Africans have come mainly into contact with Chinese migrant petty entrepreneurs or other internal migrant workers (Lan, 2017:193). A range of encounters between African traders and Chinese people can be identified such as the relations between Chinese rental agents as providers of housing and African tenants,[11] Chinese transportation providers and African clients, Chinese and African neighbours, and Chinese authorities and African traders/migrants (Zhou *et al.*, 2016b).

Strong emotional relationships such as cross-cultural marriages, romantic ties and friendships have evolved and increased over time, but they are still rare. Most often, these relationships are between Nigerian Igbo men with a Christian background and Chinese women without Guangzhou *hukou*. While it is legally possible for Africans to obtain permanent residency, the requirements are very high and cannot be met simply by marrying a Chinese citizen (Mathews, 2017:196/197). Nevertheless, romantic relationships may be beneficial to both sides by bringing together African and Chinese connections and networks, or in the case of Africans who overstay their visas, the Chinese partner could represent the business to the outside (Mathews, 2017:201, 208).

Relationships more commonly take various economic forms such as business cooperation, employment or service relations. Three specific kinds of cooperation have been identified between African and Chinese business partners: (a) a Chinese trader and an African trader jointly open

[11] One problem in particular may arise for Africans who wish to reduce costs for housing. In practical terms, some accommodations can be cheap because the landlord/landlady does not pay income tax. As a consequence, they are not able to complete the registration process for their tenants smoothly and legally. Africans found to lack valid visa and accommodation registration can be penalised or even jailed and repatriated (Niu, 2015a:132/133).

a shop; (b) A Chinese trader could make a profit by being hired to register a business in a shopping centre for an African trader, while the African trader benefits by avoiding the paperwork of registration. (c) after a Chinese citizen has rented a storefront, he/she rents it out secondhand to an African trader and earns the differential rent (profit) (Li and Du, 2016:11). All three types of economic cooperation provide a win-win situation for both partners, but they all represent more or less informal arrangements. In addition, cooperation between Chinese migrants and African business partners can also take the form of transnational business partnerships, where the Chinese partner is responsible for sourcing goods in China and shipping them to, say, Lagos, while the Nigerian counterpart (who was previously in Guangzhou illegally) is responsible for clearing customs and selling the goods to customers in African countries (Lan, 2016:17).

The structural marginalisation of African traders in Guangzhou is comparable to that of internal Chinese migrants called the "floating population" (*liudong renkou*).[12] Both groups of migrants have moved to Guangzhou because they were attracted by the prosperous economic situation of the city. Neither group has the status of local citizens: the Africans because they are foreign passport holders and the internal Chinese migrants because they only have a rural and not an urban household registration. Both groups are therefore excluded from the formal support system of the Chinese city. Compared with Guangzhou permanent residents, both are second-class citizens, often disadvantaged in terms of employment, access to affordable housing and healthcare. For example, both groups have limited access to health insurance and suffer psychological effects due to social exclusion and insecurity regarding their legal status (Bork-Hüffer, 2015:69). Most members of both groups therefore work and live under primarily informal conditions. Despite all these similarities, it nevertheless came as a surprise when the Guangzhou municipal government announced in 2008 that foreigners would be included in the "floating population" category and be subject to the regulations of its management (Lan, 2015:294/295).

Collaboration in everyday life and economic win-win situations in the informal sector have enabled African traders – at least to a certain extent – to bypass some of the constraints imposed by local authorities. In contrast to the Chinese state and depending on personal trust, internal

[12]流动人口.

migrants seem to differentiate between good and bad economic partners and not between legal and illegal migrants (Lan, 2015:291, 298). In their efforts to survive outside the formal system, collaboration with internal migrants has helped African traders stay in Guangzhou and continue doing business. For example, despite the fact that foreign currency exchange is an illegal business, some Chinese migrants provide such services to African traders. If they are undocumented, African traders cannot open a bank account by themselves and are dependent on other Africans or Chinese to handle their transnational cash flows (Lan, 2015:298). In Yuexiu district, which had been home to Muslim migrants from Xinjiang and Ningxia, most money changers are Muslim migrants from Northwestern China. The *halal* restaurants in the Xiaobei area have become places of intersection for Chinese and African Muslims. The many Muslim restaurants and shops in Guangzhou were seen as very convenient by African Muslims. Interactions between internal Chinese migrants and African traders, particularly those from different Muslim communities, might have attracted the particular attention of public security organs in Guangzhou (Zhou, 2016:132). Tight surveillance of African small-scale traders in Guangzhou has pushed them even deeper into informal spaces and shadow economies, with the result that obtaining visas, housing and employment have increasingly turned into illegal activities.

Inventing the "Triple-Illegal" Foreigner (*sanfei waiguoren*)[13]

While the internal migrants had been the main target of the public security organs, after being included in the "floating population," small African traders became a new and additional target as a particularly mobile group of foreigners that interacts in different ways with internal migrants (see Niu, 2016:163). In the eyes of public security authorities, both groups were seen as possible troublemakers, but African small traders were additionally seen as making the management of internal migrants in Guangzhou even more challenging (Niu, 2016:163).

In 2007, the local press in Guangzhou began to associate crimes such as drugs, underground markets and illegal immigration, as well as several

13 三非外国人.

cases of HIV/AIDS, with the African diaspora, and its coverage took on a more negative tone, labelling African migrants in Guangzhou as 'problematic' (Li *et al.*, 2012:65). This marked the beginning of increased surveillance and control of foreigners in Guangzhou, particularly of black people. That same year, the municipality started to construct a networked informational system to collect information on foreign visitors from hotels, and the city's 219 police stations established a foreigner management system. In addition, the local government encouraged foreigners to live concentrated in commodity housing in formal residential areas instead of urban villages or other informal spaces. In Xiaobei and Sanyuanli, the local police established specific foreigner-related patrol zones and conducted formal and informal patrols and visa inspections. In addition, restaurants, hotels, shops and markets where African people gathered became the target of regular and intensive inspections. Despite these measures, in 2008, the Chinese People's Consultative Conference (CPCC) criticised the migration governance of Guangzhou city for unreliable statistics, lax enforcement of tenancy registration, loss of control over the housing market for foreigners, a lack of cooperation between government bodies and insufficient law enforcement resources (Li *et al.*, 2012:66). Legitimised by two mega-events, namely, the Beijing Olympics in the same year and the Asian Games in Guangzhou in 2010, the municipal government launched more radical reforms. Since 2008, when preparations for the Beijing Olympics became the focus of increasingly critical human rights coverage in the Western media, the situation for foreigners in China in general, and for Africans in Guangzhou in particular, has become more and more tense.

The Guangzhou municipal government then began to target the so-called "triple-illegal" foreigners, i.e. foreigners arriving illegally, staying illegally and/or working illegally in China (Li *et al.*, 2012:66). This policy exhibits strong similarities with earlier policies that had targeted the "triple-without" population, i.e. internal rural-to-urban migrants without temporary residence permits, housing and/or employment in their migration destination. Until 2004, the "triple-without" migrant population could be detained on the streets, and friends or relatives had to pay for their release or the detainees themselves had to work to finance their period of detention (Gransow, 2011:71). Now, included as part of the "floating population" or even the "triple-illegal" population, Africans in Guangzhou were informally inserted into China's complex systems of population control and management and were especially subject to the surveillance dynamics of the public security apparatus (Castillo, 2016:291).[14]

A "triple-illegal" management team was set up including officials from different administrative departments, such as the police, urban management and tax bureau (which later became more formalised), and related measures were undertaken. These management measures became more elaborate with the Guangdong regulations on the management of foreigners in 2011 and the national entry-and-exit administration law in 2013.

Immigration and Law Enforcement Targeting African Small Traders

Before the "PRC Entry and Exit Administration Law" (*Zhonghua renmin gongheguo rujing chujing guanlifa*)[15] came into force in July 2013, a basic set of laws and regulations governing international migration in and immigration to China had been established step by step with the development of China's reform and opening-up policy.[16] It included the "PRC Foreigners Entry and Exit Administration Law" (*Zhonghua renmin gongheguo waiguoren rujing chujing guanlifa*)[17] (adopted in 1985 and implemented in 1986), "Rules for the Implementation of the Law on the Entry and Exit of Foreigners" (*Zhonghua renmin gongheguo waiguoren rujing chujing guanlifa shishi xize*) (1994)[18] and "Regulations on the Examination and Approval of Permanent Residence of Foreigners in China" (*Waiguoren zai Zhongguo yongjiu juliu shenpi guanli banfa* 2004).[19] These laws and regulations were implemented by various institutions, including the Ministry of Public Security and the Ministry of Foreign Affairs (Lan, 2015:293).

[14] According to reports, there was a fine of 5,000 yuan for expired visas up to 2012, then a 10,000-yuan fine, and in 2014 a 12,000-yuan fine plus a five-year ban on returning to China (Mathews, 2017:122).

[15] 中华人民共和国入境出境管理法， http://english.gov.cn/archive/laws_regulations/2014/09/22/content_281474988553532.htm (accessed August 11, 2018).

[16] During the Mao era, from the 1950s to the 1970s, the number of foreigners in China decreased rapidly and was very limited.

[17] 中华人民共和国外国人入境出境管理法.

[18] 中华人民共和国外国人入境出境管理法实施细则.

[19] 外国人在中国永久居留审批管理办法.

On the local level, the Guangdong Provincial Government (Order 155) adopted "Provisional Regulations of Guangdong Province on the Administration of and Services to Foreigners" (*Guangdong sheng waiguoren guanli fuwu zanxin guiding*)[20] on January 1, 2011, which came into effect on May 1, 2011. This was the first local-level legislation concerning the administration of foreigners in the PRC. The Regulations officially combined measures to strengthen the control of foreigners with measures to provide community-based services for them. The Guangdong Regulations de facto targeted the so-called "triple-illegal" population. According to Guangzhou public security statistics, there were 3,179 "triple-illegal" foreigners in 2011, an increase of 12.5% from the previous year. It has been argued that an insufficient existing legal framework could enable foreigners to easily bypass laws and regulations and come to Guangzhou through various channels. For example, some foreigners registered a "one-yuan company" in Hong Kong and then established a branch office in Guangzhou. They could therefore hire personnel and relocate family members to Guangzhou. Theoretically, in this way, an African company could bring a whole village to Guangzhou. To close such loopholes, the public security organs in Guangzhou pursue the aim of "low and transparent numbers, management of housing, good services, fewer criminal cases involved" (Xu, 2016:74). For example, if hotels fail to verify passports, visa and other identity certificates or fail to report the discovery of expired passports or visas of foreigners (to the public security organs), they can be fined 5,000 to 10,000 yuan (Article 55). Similar penalties can be imposed on schools and training institutions, landlords, property service enterprises, real estate intermediary agencies, investors or management bodies, and units employing foreigners (Article 56–62).

The Guangdong Regulations have led to the following[21]:

- shifted the burden of immigration control to employers, hotels, educational institutions, landlords, property management offices and ordinary local residents;
- set up high penalties for institutions and individuals who withhold information on foreigners violating Chinese laws and regulations;
- expanded the authority of the police;

[20] 广东省外国人管理服务暂行规定.

[21] A detailed description of the "Regulations" can be found in Gransow, 2021.

- encouraged participation by foreigners in community affairs[22];
- represented a legal effort to restrict foreigners from certain urban spaces[23];
- sought to reduce the number of "triple-illegal" foreigners via integrated management and a combination of control and services.

Overall, the Guangdong Regulations stand for a pattern of immigration governance that spreads the responsibilities of the provincial government across a broad spectrum of local institutions and individuals. In order for this "cooperation" to function, the Regulations instituted high penalties for individuals and institutions who do not provide the requested information about international migrants. As discussed earlier, not everybody is motivated to cooperate in migration governance decreed from above. By combining strict controls on housing and providing a range of services to foreigners at the grassroots level, the Guangdong Regulations sought to reduce the number of "triple-illegal" foreigners. Based on these Regulations, Guangzhou was a pioneer in introducing a joint management mechanism under the head of public security that incorporates relevant institutions and covers the three administrative levels of municipality, district and street. To meet the challenge of implementing and coordinating such a complex system of managing foreigners, Guangzhou introduced an electronic information and management system.

Shortly after the implementation of the Guangdong Regulations, new national Chinese immigration legislation came into being. With an increasing number of foreigners entering China and finding employment

---

[22] In communities with relatively large concentrations of foreigners, the Regulations suggested establishing a comprehensive management service team. Also, foreigners who are interested in public affairs, enjoy some prestige among their communities and are able to speak and write Chinese may join the comprehensive community management and services team (Article 45). While the new model, known as "managing foreigners with foreigners" (*yiwai guanwai* 以外管外) sounds like a form of inclusive community participation, it also reminds one of the historical Chinese saying "let the barbarians fight it out among themselves" (*yiyi zhiyi* 以夷制夷) (Xu, 2016:78f).

[23] With regard to the city of Guangzhou, this has been interpreted as an effort to prevent the African community in the Xiaobei area from expanding southwards to where the Guangdong Provincial Government Building, the Guangzhou Municipal Government Building and the Guangzhou Municipal Party Committee Building are located (Lan, 2015:296).

there, formally or informally, the central government wanted to modernise the Foreigner Entry and Exit Law, enacted in 1985, to keep pace with changing migration patterns. According to the 2017 International Migration Report, the number of foreigners in China has nearly doubled from 2000 (508,000) to 2017 (1,000,000) (United Nations, 2017). However, this meant only an increase from 0.0 to 0.1% compared to the total population of China. The country's immigration record system was seen as outdated: While the Ministry of Foreign Affairs was responsible for issuing visas and the Ministry of Public Security was responsible for issuing residence certificates, information about the foreigners was archived based on the purpose of their visit (with files at the Departments of Human Resources, Foreign Experts, Commerce, Education, etc.). The new PRC Exit and Entry Administration Law (2013) was intended to tackle all these problems.

The new Law enables harsher punishment for foreigners who illegally enter, live or work in China, with inspections and enforcement of immigrant compliance under the responsibility of the public security administration. Foreigners suspected of immigration law violations may be detained (for up to 30 days) (Article 60). A guide defines the country's criteria for foreign workers and specifies which industries and occupations are prohibited or restricted from employing foreigners, and which are encouraged to employ them. The law allows visa and residence certificates to be granted to foreign experts. The "Regulations of the PRC on Administration of the Entry and Exit of Foreigners," which went into effect on September 1, 2013,[24] introduced the R visa as a new category for highly talented or specialised foreigners needed by the state (Article 6:9). The number of visa categories increased from eight to twelve.[25]

---

[24] http://english.www.gov.cn/archive/laws_regulations/2014/09/22/content_281474988553545.htm (accessed February 18, 2025).

[25] The eight previous visa categories (C, D, F, G, J, L, X, Z) were as follows: C: travel crew personnel; D: permanent residence; F: exchange, visits, study tours and research (an F visa no longer permits foreigners to conduct commercial activities); G: transit; J1: journalists at permanent foreign news agencies; J2: foreign journalists (short-term); L: tourists (individual and group travel); X1: long-term students; X2: short-term students; and Z: employment in China. The following new visa categories were added to the national regulations: R: long-term visa for high-level foreigners with specialised skills urgently needed by the state; M: temporary visits for business purposes (requires invitation); Q1: family members of Chinese or foreigners with permanent residence who are applying for residence permits

Illegal residency by foreigners in China is defined in the Administrative Regulations as holding an expired visa or travel document or conducting activities beyond the scope of the visa. Residence permits are divided by employment and non-employment purposes. Employment of foreign students has been restricted. Illegal employment of foreign students includes teaching foreign languages and engaging in illegal commercial activities. Work-related activities by students require permission from the educational institution and police confirmation of residence certification (Bork and Yuan, 2014:581). Measures to address foreigners guilty of "triple-illegal" activities were codified in the new law for the first time, including on-the-spot interrogation, continuous inspection, detention, restriction of movement and repatriation (Bork and Yuan, 2014:579).

The new Entry and Exit Law (2013) borrowed from the Guangdong Regulations (2011) in several areas: (1) the requirement for employers and ordinary people to report "triple-illegal" foreigners; (2) the promotion of a reward and penalty system by increasing the penalties for illegal entry, residence and employment of foreigners in China; and (3) subjecting hotels and other institutions that fail to report foreigners' residence or employment situations to high fines. Overall, strong similarities with the Guangdong Regulations can be identified and serve as evidence of the central government's affirmation of the Guangdong experiment (Lan, 2016:296, 297).

A difference between the national Entry and Exit Law and the Guangdong Regulations can be seen in the stronger emphasis the new Law puts on attracting highly qualified experts to China. It aims to attract foreign investors and highly qualified foreign nationals with talents needed in China while deterring those foreign nationals who do not meet these standards. After a while, Guangdong authorities adjusted the local regulations to the preferences of the national law. In August 2016, Guangdong province published details on applications by foreign nationals for residence permits in China that had been adjusted to the new visa categories. Similar to Shanghai and Beijing, for foreign nationals residing in the Guangdong Free Trade Zone, these changes meant a relaxation on requirements for Chinese permanent residence permits ("Chinese Green

for family unification purposes; Q2: visas for family members of Chinese or foreigners with permanent residence who are applying for short-term visits; and S: visas for foreign family members of Z visa holders (Regulations 2013, Article 6; see also Bork and Yuan, 2014:580).

Cards"). The greater flexibility and longer durations of Chinese residence permits for foreign nationals also benefit primarily those foreigners who can be expected to contribute to overall enhancement of the social structure and economic strength in Guangdong/China.[26]

In 2018, the Exit–Entry Administration and the Border Control Department were merged into a new National Immigration Administration (NIA) (*Guojia yimin guanliju*)[27] under the Ministry of Public Security. The creation of the NIA sparked a debate about the need for national-level immigration reform. Officially, China sees itself as a destination country (*mudiguo*)[28] for foreign migrants rather than a country of immigration (*yimin guojia*).[29] The timing of the establishment of the NIA has been interpreted as part of a government strategy to attract highly skilled professionals to China (including foreign nationals) by making it easier for them to obtain permanent residency in China (Speelman, 2020:9, 11; Meyer-Clement and Wang 2021:71).

After the COVID-19 pandemic, when many foreigners had left China, the NIA in early 2024 released a couple of measures to simplify business activities, studying and travelling for foreign nationals in China by facilitating visa formalities and use of the electronic information system.[30] As Niu Dong has argued, most African businesspeople or students would not fulfil the criteria of the "professional talents" the Chinese government seeks to attract. Government departments would therefore not offer preferential policies to African migrants in terms of housing or social support (Niu, 2018:93).

Effects of the New Immigration Legislation: Emerging Transnational Urban *jianghu* Spaces

Implementation of the new legislation in Guangzhou led to more complicated visa application procedures, higher penalties for violations and reports by African traders of being bullied by the police (Niu, 2016:162).

---

[26] http://english.www.gov.cn/state_council/ministries/2016/07/19/content_281475397170875.htm (accessed February 18, 2025).

[27] 国家移民管理局.

[28] 目的国.

[29] 移民国家.

[30] NIA Releases Five New Measures to Facilitate Entries of Foreigners, https://en.nia.gov.cn/n147413/c160935/content.html (accessed April 17, 2025).

On the local level, strict law enforcement required even higher mobility and coping strategies on the part of small-scale traders (Liu *et al.*, 2015; Zhou *et al.*, 2016a). Since around 2012, some of them, mainly Nigerians, have started to move their residency to Huangqi, which is administratively a part of Foshan but is well connected with Guangzhou by public transport. The relatively relaxed government involvement in Huangqi has enabled especially the poorer African traders to face less police harassment there while continuing their business activities in Guangzhou (Li *et al.*, 2012:68). Increased pressure from the local government on African traders in Guangzhou has apparently led to a more scattered pattern of African residence in the PRD. While this pattern (of a business centre in Xiaobei, Guangzhou, and residence in Foshan) has basically remained the same, the residences in or even outside Foshan in smaller towns have become more dispersed (Jin *et al.*, 2021:8, Figure 4).

With the new law and regulations, the African diaspora in Guangzhou experienced a variety of formal and informal changes in its daily life and business that particularly affected the petty traders. Since 2014,[31] the Xiaobei area had become the toughest environment for African traders and this situation continued. Even Africans with papers reported being detained for some time without any reason given. A climate of tension and intimidation spread from paperless Africans to those with papers to those doing business with them (Niu 2016:161/162). On the streets of Xiaobei, the police frequently checked foreigners' visa and residence permits. This happened not only in residential areas but also in places where Africans were concentrated for business. There were reports of nearly 100 policemen arriving at Tianxiu Building, Jinshanxiang trade city and other places, blocking the exits and conducting "building clean-ups" (*saolou*).[32] The mutual support system established by Africans began to suffer. Leaders of African organisations in Guangzhou criticised the Chinese police for acting against respectable citizens, but they also clearly stated that they supported efforts by the Chinese police to find drug dealers (Niu, 2016:161–162).

Rigid visa policies, or the "legal production of illegality" as Lan Shanshan put it, have led to an upswing in the trade in illegal or fake passports. Some voices attributed an increase in drug trafficking to the strict control measures of the Chinese police (Lan, 2015:291, 298). Rising numbers of people who for one reason or another could not or were not willing

[31] Africans in Guangzhou were quickly suspected of being a serious public health risk after the outbreak of Ebola in some West African countries (Giese and Liang, 2018: 143).

[32] 扫楼.

to leave the country and therefore overstayed their visas contributed to an expansion of informal spaces. Under the new legal conditions, they became even more dependent on informal arrangements for their papers, businesses, housing and everyday affairs. Their various needs gave rise to extended informal or illegal business niches that were filled by African social networks or by internal Chinese migrants who helped change money without asking for passports, rented shop floors or provided other services. Thus, small traders trying to muddle through were often driven to more informal and illegal – or "illegalised" – activities to avoid the strict visa, residence and work regulations. The whole situation of African traders in Guangzhou became even more precarious.

The conception of the African diaspora in Guangzhou as a *jianghu* space fits in well with Li Shiqiao's description of the Chinese urban landscape as divided into spaces of care and *jianghu spaces* (Li, 2014:98-116), at least with regard to the petty traders who are not perceived as part of the regulated urban system of care. They are in the *jianghu*, a space of uncare on the wild side of the city. With a strictly controlled NGO sector, there is not much room for civil society activities either, and African organisations cannot register formally as mutual aid organisations. The only "NGOs" working with Africans in Guangzhou seem to be those selected by local governments with the ultimate goal of ensuring that the Africans register within 24 hours of arrival and leave the country before their visas expire (Niu, 2018:93). As a consequence, Africans' spaces of care in the PRD are those they have produced themselves, especially by forming national African organisations, liaising with religious institutions, providing informal services within the diaspora (such as barber shops, restaurants, nightclubs, music and sports clubs) and using various informal services offered primarily by internal Chinese migrants in Guangzhou. While the *jianghu* of Chinese rural–urban migrants is determined by the *hukou* system, which excludes them from many of the privileges of local urban citizens in terms of education and health services, the *jianghu* of African migrants/traders is largely determined by their visas, or lack thereof.

The exclusionary attitude of the urban government at various levels fuels the expansion of informal spaces of care and business. Among African and Chinese migrants in a shared *jianghu* space, moral standards differ from legal standards: What counts is not whether someone has a valid visa or temporary local registration but whether they are seen as reliable (business) partners. Different African and Chinese actors who can benefit from each other are achieving various types of win-win situations at the low end of globalisation. Attempts to solve the problem of unwanted "immigrants" by means of strict visa policies plus extensive surveillance seem not only to mistake petty traders and businesspeople for immigrants but also fail to grasp the broader context of China's economic and international relations with the African continent and to correspond to the official national Chinese discourse of opening up and advancing South–South cooperation in a globalising world.

Conclusion

It has been shown that, despite the less than hospitable environment, it was economically attractive enough – at least for the less affluent African traders in Guangzhou – to buy cheaply produced goods in China, especially copies of well-known branded products, and transport them to Africa, where they were resold in local markets to customers who were eager to consume but had little money to spend. African traders were assisted in this business, which operates on the fringes of legality, by internal rural–urban migrants in Guangzhou, who, like their African partners, are seen as not belonging to the urban society and face material and social discrimination, and who are also part of Guangzhou's vast informal economy and part of urbanisation and globalisation from below.

The transnational urban spaces created or shaped by African migrants include first and foremost urban business locations and residential areas in Guangzhou, followed by residential areas in Foshan; secondly, spaces of care in the form of informal national African organisations (with leaders who act as contacts or intermediaries for their national communities in the city and the local authorities in Guangzhou); thirdly, spaces of communication and cooperation between African traders and internal rural–urban migrants in the city (who play a role in the provision of services, especially for undocumented African traders); and finally, spaces of uncare or *jianghu* spaces beyond the official order, with their own rules of trust and reliability.

These transnational urban spaces of African traders in both Guangzhou and Foshan can be identified as transient urban spaces for two main reasons: first, because of their professions as traders and small-scale entrepreneurs, which shape specific patterns of mobility and are not necessarily aimed at permanent immigration to China; and second, because of the strict visa policies of the local government, which have resulted in many undocumented African migrants in Guangzhou, driven by the constant fear of police checks, arrest and deportation. Another reason for considering the transnational urban spaces of African migrants as transient may be the expectation that e-commerce sellers such as Shein and Temu, who coordinate much of their supply chains from Guangzhou and are already increasing their sales in African countries, will create strong (and rapidly growing) competition that could pose a far greater challenge to African traders in Guangzhou than the strict visa policies at different levels of the Chinese government.

References

Adebayo, K. O. (2023a). Deportability, deportation and Nigerian "Deportspora" in China, *African Human Mobility Review* 9(2), 80–102.

Adebayo, K. O. (2023b). Pandemics and management of "dangerous communities": Ebola, COVID-19, and Africans in China, *The Professional Geographer* 75(1), 164–174.

Bodomo, A. (2010). The African trading community in Guangzhou: An emerging bridge for Africa-China relations, *China Quarterly* 203(September), 693–707.

Bodomo, A. (2012). *Africans in China. A Sociocultural Study and Its Implications for Africa-China Relations*, Amherst, New York: Cambria Press.

Bodomo, A., Che, D., and Dong, H. (2022). Calculator communication in the markets of Guangzhou and beyond, *Journal of Multilingual and Multicultural Development* 43(19), 981–992.

Bodomo, A. and Pajancic, C. (2015). Counting beans: Some empirical and methodological problems for calibrating the African presence in Greater China, *The Journal of Pan African Studies* 7(10), 126–143.

Bork-Hüffer, T. (2015). Health-care seeking practices of African and rural-to-urban migrants in Guangzhou, *Journal of Current Chinese Affairs* 4, 49–81.

Bork-Hüffer, T. and Yuan-Ihle, Y. (2014). The Management of foreigners in China: Changes to the migration law and regulations during the late Hu-Wen and early Xi-Li eras and their potential effects, *International Journal of China Studies* 5(3), pp. 571–597.

Castillo, R. (2015). Landscapes of aspiration in Guangzhou's African music scene: Beyond the trading narrative, *Journal of Current Chinese Affairs* 4, 83–115.

Castillo, R. (2016). 'Homing' Guangzhou: Emplacement, belonging and precarity among Africans in China, *International Journal of Cultural Studies* 19(3), 287–306.

Castillo, R. and Amoah, P. A. (2020). African in post-COVID-19 pandemic China: Is there a future for Chinas 'new minority'? *Asian Ethnicity* 21(4), 560–565.

Giese, K. and Liang, K. S. M. (2018). Shifting territorialities of an African Space in China, in Engel, U., Boeckler, M., and Müller-Mahn, D. (eds.), *Spatial Practises. Territory, Border and Infrastructure in Africa,* Leiden: Brill, pp. 129–149.

Gilles, A. (2015). The social construction of Guangzhou as a translocal trading place, *Journal of Current Chinese Affairs* 4, 17–47.

Glick Schiller, N. and Caglar, A. (eds.) (2011). Locality and globality. Building a comparative analytical framework in migration and urban studies, in *Locating Migration. Rescaling Cities and Migrants*, Ithaca: Cornell University Press, pp. 60–81.

Gransow, B. (2011). Migrant communities and social change in Chinese megacities: Slum formation or urban innovation? in Bade, K., Lorentz, B., and Pries, L. (eds.), *Rural-Urban Migrations in Mega Cities and 'Mega-Slums' Our Common Future, Essen*, Leipzig: CEP Europäische Verlagsanstalt, pp. 65–97.

Gransow, B. (2014). Contested urban spaces: Whose right to the city? (Editorial), *China Perspectives* 2, 3–6.

Gransow, B. (2021). Migrant actions and government responses: African traders in the Pearl River Delta, China, in Schubert, G., Plümmer, F., and Bayok, A. (eds.), *Immigration Governance in East Asia. Norm Diffusion, Politics of Identity, Citizenship,* London: Routledge, pp. 43–66.

Han, H. (2013). Individual grassroots multilingualism in Africa Town in Guangzhou: The role of states in globalization, *International Multilingual Research Journal* 7, 83–97.

Jin, X., Bolt, G., and Hooimeijer, P. (2021). Africans in Guangzhou: Is the ethnic enclave model applicable in the Chinese context? *Cities* 117, 1–11.

Lan, S. (2015). State regulation of undocumented African migrants in China: A multi-scalar analysis, *Journal of Asian and African Studies* 50(3), 289–304.

Lan, S. (2016). Between mobility and immobility: undocumented African migrants living in the shadow of the state, in Wang, D. and He, S. (eds.), *Mobility, Sociability and Well-Being of Urban Living*, Cham: Springer, pp. 3–21.

Lan, S. (2017). *Mapping the New African Diaspora in China. Race and the Cultural Politics of Belonging*, New York: Routledge.

Li, S. (2014). *Understanding the Chinese City*, Los Angeles: Sage.

Li, Z. 李志刚 and Du, F. 杜枫. (2016). Quanqiuhua, kuaguo shangmaozhuyi yu Zhongguo de feiyi shehui kongjian shengchan 全球化，跨国商贸主义与中国的非裔社会空间生产 (Globalization, transnational commercialism and the production of African social spaces in China), in Li *et al.* (eds.), 李志刚等编著, *Guangzhou guoji yiminqu de shehui kongjian jingguan* 广州国际移民区的社会空间景观 (*Socio-spatial landscape of Immigrant Enclaves in Guangzhou*), Nanjing: Southeast University Press, pp. 002–013.

Li, Z., Lyons, M., and Brown, A. (2012). China's 'chocolate city': An ethnic enclave in a changing landscape, *African Diaspora* 5, 51–72.

Li, Z., Ma, L. J. C., and Desheng, X. (2009). An African enclave in China: The making of a new transnational space, *Eurasian geography and Economics* 50(6), 699–719.

Liu, L. 柳林, Liang, Y., Song, G., and He, S. (2015). Zai Yue feizhouren de qianju zhuangkuang jiqi yingxiang yinsu fenxi 在粤非洲人的迁居状况及其影响因素分析 (Migration patterns and its influencing factors of African immigrants in Guangdong province: A survey from Guangzhou and Foshan cities, *Zhongguo renkou kexue* 中国人口科学 (*Chinese Population Studies*) 1, 115–122.

Lyons, M., Brown, A., and Li, Z. (2008). The 'third tier' of globalization. African traders in Guangzhou, *City* 12(2), 196–206.

Lyons, M., Brown, A., and Li, Z. (2016). Long tan hu xue: Guangzhou feizhou shangrende jianghu 龙潭虎穴: 广州非洲商人的江湖 (Dangerous Places [literally: In the dragon's pool and the tiger's den]: the *jianghu* of African Traders in Guangzhou), in Li *et al.* (eds.), *Guangzhou guoji yiminqu de shehui kongjian jingguan* 广州国际移民区的社会空间景观 (*Socio-Spatial Landscape of Immigrant Enclaves in Guangzhou*), Nanjing: Southeast University Press, pp. 014–031.

Mathews, G. (2015). African logistics agents and middlemen as cultural brokers in Guangzhou, *Journal of Current Chinese Affairs* 4, 117–144.

Mathews, G., Lin, L. D., and Yang, Y. (2017). *The World in Guangzhou. Africans and Other Foreigners in South China's Global Marketplace*, Chicago: The University of Chicago Press.

Mathews, G., Ribeiro, G. L., and Vega, C. A. (eds.) (2012). *Globalization from Below. The World's Other Economy*, London: Routledge.

McKeown, A. (1999). Conceptualizing Chinese diasporas, 1842 to 1949. *The Journal of Asian Studies*, 58(2), 306–337.

Meyer-Clement, E. and Wang, X. (2021). Global city competition and new hierarchies of urban citizenship in China's migration regime, in Schubert, G., Plümmer, F., and Bayok, A. (eds.), *Immigration Governance in East Asia. Norm Diffusion, Politics of Identity, Citizenship*, London: Routledge, pp. 67–90.

Müller, A. and Wehrhahn, R. (2013). Transnational business networks of African intermediaries in China: Practises of networking and the role of experiential knowledge, *Die Erde* 144(1), 82–97.

Niu, D. 牛冬 (2015a). 'Guoke shetuan': Guangzhou feizhouren de shehui zuzhi "过客社团": 广州非洲人的社会组织 ('Transient associations': Social organizations of Africans in Guangzhou), *Shehuixue yanjiu* 社会学研究 (*Sociological Studies*) 2, 124–148.

Niu, D. 牛冬 (2015b). Yimin haishi guoke? 移民还是过客? 广漂非洲人的现状观察 (Immigrant or transient? Observing the current situation of Africans in Guangzhou, *Wenhua zongheng* 文化纵横 (*Culture Review*) 3, 62–69.

Niu, D. 牛冬 (2016). Kunjing zhi min: Zhongguo 'xin yimin fa' yingxiang xia de Guangzhou feizhouren 困境之民: 中国'新移民法' 影响下的广州非洲人 (People's dilemma: Africans in Guangzhou under the impact of China's 'new immigration law', in Li *et al.* (eds.), *Guangzhou guoji yiminqu de shehui kongjian jingguan* 广州国际移民区的社会空间景观 (*Socio-Spatial Landscape of Immigrant Enclaves in Guangzhou*), Nanjing: Southeast University Press, pp. 156–167.

Niu, D. (2018). Transient: A descriptive concept for understanding Africans in Guangzhou, *African Studies Quarterly* 17(4), 85–100.

Niu, D., Lin, S., Chen, H., and Li, Z. (2020). A "transient neighborhood": Africans' spatial concentration in Guangzhou, *The China Review* 20(2), 211–234.

Pieke, F. (2012). Immigrant China, *Modern China* 38(1), 40–77.

Qu, J. 屈精瑞. (2016). Guangzhou shi feizhouren guanli wenti yanjiu 广州市非洲人管理问题研究 (Research on management problems with Africans in Guangzhou), *Fazhi yu shehui* 法制与社会 (*Legal System and Society*) 9, 203–204.

Speelman, T. (2020). Establishing the national immigration administration: Change and continuity in China's immigration reforms, *China Perspectives* 4, 7–16.

United Nations, Department of Economic and Social Affairs, Population Division. (2017). *International Migration Report 2017: Highlights* (ST/ESA/SER.A/404, New York, http://www.un.org/en/development/desa/population/migration/publications/migrationreport/docs/MigrationReport2017_Highlights.pdf (accessed August 10, 2018).

Xu, J. 许军珂. (2016). Beijing shijie chengshi jianshe zhong de waiguoren guanli yu fuwu jizhi yanjiu 北京世界城市建设中的外国人管理与服务机制研究 (Research on the management and service mechanism of foreigners in the process of developing Beijing into a world city, Beijing: Shijie zhishi chubanshe 世界知识出版社 (World Knowledge Press).

Zhou, B. 周博. (2016). Zai Hua Feizhouren guanli xin moshi: Guangzhou waiguoren guanli fuwu gongzuozhan 在华非洲人管理新模式: 广州外国人管理服务工作站 A new management model of Africans in China: Guangzhou station of foreigner management and service), *Guangxi minzu daxue xuebao* 广西民族大学学报 (*Journal of Guangxi University for Nationalities*) 38(4), 129–134.

Zhou, M., Xu, T., and Shenasi, S. (2016a). Chinese attitudes toward African migrants in Guangzhou, *International Journal of Sociology* 46, 141–161.

Zhou, M., Xu, T., and Shenasi, S. (2016b). Entrepreneurship and interracial dynamics: A case study of self-employed Africans and Chinese in Guangzhou, China, *Ethnic and Racial Studies* 39(9), 1566–1586.

Chapter 6

Forging Survival and Career Spaces: Rural Graduates in Guangzhou

"You have to rely on yourself."

"...after studying at a university for four years and earning a degree there's no difference to working as a street vendor."

Introduction

The college graduates in Guangzhou who are the subject of this chapter are a specific group of China's internal migrants. They are highly educated rural–urban migrants, like those found in other Chinese megacities, who seek to make a living in the city and possibly start a professional or business career there. Despite unemployment or job insecurity, they prefer to live in first-tier cities[1] rather than return to their home regions or try their luck in smaller second- or third-tier cities. The appeal of so-called first-tier cities such as Beijing, Shanghai, Guangzhou and Shenzhen has given rise to a phenomenon that has been in evidence at least since the global financial crisis of 2008–2009. Known by the term *Yizu* (ant tribe),[2] it has received widespread attention in Chinese media and academia.

[1] 一线城市 *yixian chengshi*, colloquially known as "Bei-Shang-Guang-Shen." In contrast to the country's administrative hierarchy of cities, the tier system is an informal yet popular ranking frequently referred to in the mass media. It includes only cities in mainland China.

[2] 蚁族.

The Chinese discourse contains competing definitions of the situation of young rural graduates in big cities. In addition to the widely used "ant tribe" label, classifications include the designation of a vulnerable group,[3] the notion of drifters (from inside or even outside China),[4] and the terms small white-collar (workers) or white-collar (workers) from outside.[5] International migration studies also use the concept of high-skilled migration or student migration (Rajan, 2016). All these concepts, terms or labels overlap to some extent, but also have clear differences.

The "ant tribe" label focuses on the crowded living conditions of unemployed or low-paid graduates concentrated in the urban villages of megacities. The term was first used in 2009 by social scientist Lian Si (Lian, 2009, see also Lian, 2010; 2013), who concentrated on Beijing. These early works directed public attention to the group of rural graduates in megacities but did not cover the educational efforts and achievements of these low-income graduates, nor their potentially significant role in achieving the Chinese government's goal of creating a broad middle-class society.

Li (2011) describes the "ant tribe" as a settlement group, defining it as "an economically vulnerable group that lives concentrated in economically developed cities and has received higher education" (Li, 2011:7). Slightly differently, Chen (2019) describes them as a fourth vulnerable group (in addition to peasants, rural–urban migrants, and unemployed workers and employees), suggesting that they are not just another urban settlement group but rather a social group that needs more attention in Chinese society and politics, otherwise possibly causing social unrest. Other authors similarly portray the *Yizu* as a vulnerable group that, without societal attention, could become an epicentre of social conflict and threaten social stability (Hu, 2017; Li and Jing, 2019). Holbig and Neckel note that this and similar labels of highly educated but relatively poor migrants that focus on vulnerability can lead to negative classifications that could stigmatise, discriminate and discourage this group of ambitious young people (Holbig and Neckel, 2016:404).

---

[3] 弱势群体 *ruoshi qunti.*

[4] 漂者*piaozhe* – the suffix *piao* stands for "drifting" or "vagabond."

[5] 小白领 *xiao bailing*, 外来白领 *wailai bailing*. Characterisations of white-collar workers from outside or small white-collar workers refer mainly to their office work as opposed to the physical labour of blue-collar workers (Li, 2009; Guiheux and Zalio, 2010).

The term *Guangpiao* or *Suipiao* for Guangzhou drifters came into use following similar terms for "drifters" in Beijing, Hong Kong and Shanghai.[6] According to Tjia and Ho (2018), the term emerged in the post-reform period and refers to well-educated and ambitious young people who do not have local household registration but move to the megacities from other places in China – including Hong Kong – in search of promising business or career opportunities. The term *Beipiao* has also been applied to some (prominent) foreigners. It has been said to aptly convey the sense of uncertainty and temporary movement of young migrants who flock to Chinese megacities in search of opportunities (Tjia and Ho, 2018:144, 152, footnote 2). The term *Guangpiao* suggests a form of mobility and a desire for big cities, but is unclear about the rural or urban origins of migrants, their educational achievements and family backgrounds.

Neither of these definitions fits the purpose of this chapter, which is to analyse the efforts of rural graduates to overcome the boundaries of the *hukou* system and become spatially embedded in the city of Guangzhou and to consider these efforts in the context of the educational, housing and labour market policies that influence them. The key questions of this chapter are as follows: What kinds of urban spaces have been produced by the agency and spatial perceptions of highly educated rural migrants in their struggles for survival and promising careers in Guangzhou? Will the educational and migration biographies that brought them from villages to megacities translate into upward social mobility that will enable them to join the urban middle class? Why are they reluctant to move to smaller towns, instead clinging to first-tier cities despite tense employment conditions?

Highly educated rural–urban migrants are therefore defined here as a specific group of Chinese internal migrants who have crossed an administrative boundary at least at the county level and stayed in Guangzhou without a *hukou* for at least several months. This definition formed the basis for the stratified sampling of respondents.[7] This chapter is based on thirty in-depth interviews conducted in the second half of 2011 with rural–urban migrants, half of whom (15) graduated from colleges and universities in Guangzhou and the other half (15) from other Chinese colleges or

[6] 广漂 *Guangpiao*, 穗漂 *Suipiao*, 北漂 *Beipiao*, 港漂 *Gangpiao* and 沪漂 *Hupiao*.

[7] Throughout this chapter, unless otherwise indicated, "rural graduates" and "educated migrants" are used interchangeably to refer to highly educated migrants from rural areas who were living in Guangzhou at the time of the interviews.

universities.[8] Most started their first job or career in Guangzhou city between 2006 and 2011.

The analysis also draws on a range of literature including studies on the policies and practices of enrolment expansion since 1999 and educational justice (Chan, 2012; Zhao-Ziupak, 2016), the problem of student employability and related labour market policies (Guiheux and Zalio, 2010; Chen Yongjie, 2011; Mycos, 2012), the "ant tribe" (Lian, 2009, 2010, 2013; Liang, 2010; Li, 2011; Wang, 2019; Li and Jing, 2019; Suda, 2021), student housing and the redevelopment of urban village space in Guangzhou (Qian *et al.*, 2013; He, 2015; Gu *et al.*, 2015; Zacharias and Lei, 2016; Shao *et al.*, 2018), and the social formation of the Chinese middle class (Zhou, 2005, 2008; Li and Zhang, 2008; Zhang, 2010; Li, 2013; Lu, 2013; Goodman, 2014; Rocca, 2017a, 2017b; Miao, 2017; Liang and Zhang, 2020).

The remainder of the chapter is divided into five parts. The first looks at the educational and family backgrounds from which rural graduates began their migration up the spatial hierarchy from villages to a first-tier city such as Guangzhou. The second part is an analysis of their housing choices, often in urban villages close to campus spaces. The third part examines the production of spaces relevant to graduate employment, including recruitment, job search, wages, and government policies to address graduate unemployment. Parts four and five consider how highly educated migrants position themselves in relation to the urban middle class and how they see their future prospects.

Traversing Interconnected Hierarchies of Cities and Educational Institutions

These young graduates have left their "two nests" – family and university (Yu, 2017; Zhu and Feng, 2018) – and need to find their way in a

[8]The interviews were conducted as part of the research project "Patterns of migrant community formation in China's mega-urban Pearl River Delta – linking informal dynamics, governability and global change" (2011–2012). See interview list at the end of the chapter. More details on the project and its broader research programme framework can be found in the introductory Chapter 1. One of the results of this project was a doctoral thesis by Kimiko Suda on the *Yizu* phenomenon (Suda, 2021).

competitive job market to acquire financial independence and launch professional careers in the city of Guangzhou. Young college graduates from rural backgrounds face a challenging situation. While the enrolment expansion policy in 1999 opened new doors in tertiary education, the transition from college to careers in big cities with high concentrations of educational institutes and large companies is even more difficult for rural graduates than for their urban counterparts who benefit from their household registrations, the *Gaokao* (National College Entrance Examination system),[9] and the financial resources and social connections of their families.

College graduates from rural areas who arrive in Guangzhou normally already have a history of educational migration, from village primary schools to junior and senior middle schools in small towns or county seats and then to big(ger) cities for college education. Rural graduates' educational biographies are therefore intertwined with their paths up the administrative hierarchy of cities to major cities where the institutions of higher education are concentrated. Having made it to a first-tier city like Guangzhou is an achievement that should make them proud and foster self-confidence. But as shown by the interview material, this is not (or not always) the case, and seems related to the fact that from an early age, they faced the need to make a variety of decisions laden with risks and far-reaching implications.

The expansion of higher education provided new and broader access to college and even university education for an increasing number of students, particularly from rural areas. From 1999 to 2009, the number of higher educational institutions nearly doubled from 1,071 to 2,035. In the same period, the overall number of enrolled students rose from 4.1 to 21.4 million (Chan, 2012:92).[10] With the expansion of higher education, the number of female graduates grew faster than the number of male students. While in 1998 female students made up 38.31% of the student population, in 2009, they took 50.48% of places in higher education (Li, 2021:178). Graduate education at the master's and doctoral levels also underwent enormous expansion.[11] According to Yan Zhao-Ciupak, China

[9]高考.

[10]During this period (1999–2009), the number of newly enrolled students increased from 1.6 to 6.4 million, and the number of graduates increased from 848,000 to 5.3 million.

[11]The number of master's candidates increased from 180,000 in 1999 to 1.37 million in 2011, and the number of doctoral candidates rose from 50,000 to 270,000 during the same period (He and Mai, 2015:335).

is now running one of the largest and fastest-growing systems of higher education in the world. The extended enrolment is especially striking in science and engineering. Early in the 21st century, China announced "mass higher education" with an overall college attendance rate of 15%. The reasons behind the policies to expand higher education were to drive economic growth, stimulate domestic consumption and counteract the negative effects of the Asian financial crisis in the late 1990s (Zhao-Ciupak, 2016:31, 32, 37).

Family background and early decision-making

In contrast to urban middle-class children whose families view college as a virtually natural part of education and whose parents actively participate in the relevant preparations, children of rural families with lower educational levels and social status go through a much more complicated process because decisions often need to be made that entail economic risks for their families (Zhao-Ciupak, 2016:47). In addition, their families have only limited abilities to advise them in the selection of educational institutes. GR 15, who graduated from South China Agricultural University, a key university in Guangzhou, is from the south of Guangdong province where his father sells wood and his mother works in the fields. He expected no support from his parents in applying to college: "I decided all by myself; they didn't help. My parents don't understand it either. I enrolled myself in whatever I liked, and there was no pressure."

Even if rural students from low-income families have very good grades (and most of the interviewees were such students), their success is nevertheless contingent on family and institutional support. GR 9, who came from a peasant family in northern Guangdong, explained that her parents had high expectations for her education "because I was very famous in our village, from a very young age up through the acceptance (exam) at the university. Ever since I entered primary school at the age of 4, at the end of each school term, doing exams, whatever, each time I brought home awards. We had only a few of these, each class has only three awards: the first, second and third. At home, they were very proud of this because we are quite poor there." It can be assumed that the emotional support had an encouraging effect on the bright young girl even if her family and village couldn't provide any guidance with respect to her studies.

The experience of GR 1, a male student from Foshan whose parents were laid off with his father now repairing motorcycles and his mother working as a tailor, was completely different. After finishing compulsory schooling and graduating from junior middle school, rural students have to decide at the age of 16 whether to continue with senior middle school or attend a vocational school instead (and earn money early). As GR 1 recalls, "My second aunt took a far-sighted view. She said we should pay money and invest in senior middle school, and we should definitely select a key school … But my father pays a lot of attention to money, and going to a fancy school costs a lot.… Besides, my father thinks learning a lot is not necessarily beneficial; it would be better to get out and gather experience as early as possible. At that time, I also thought I would not necessarily have to go to a key middle school."

After finishing senior middle school, the students and their families who often lack knowledge of most majors' content or career prospects have to decide whether to start tertiary education and apply for college enrolment or immediately start looking for a job. In contrast to students from some senior high schools in big cities that offer career counselling and informational sessions with college recruiters, rural students reported that their high schools lacked the resources to guide them through the college application process. It is evident that rural students require institutional support to navigate the pathway to higher education. This support should encompass the provision of essential information and guidance from teachers, as well as a shift in perspective that views college degrees not merely as prerequisites for urban residency and social advancement, but also as a means of pursuing careers aligned with personal interests and specialised expertise (Zhao-Cuipak, 2016:115–116).

Choosing a university and a major

The lack of counselling from parents, teachers and schools in applying to universities and selecting majors can lead early on to failing to take important steps. GR 9, the excellent female student and pride of her family and village, applied to Guangdong University of Chinese Medicine to study her desired subject of chemistry but lacked competent advice. "I was the first university student in my village, and when it came time to apply, I really knew nothing at all.… I just chose the first university (Guangdong University of Chinese Medicine) and filled out everything else without any knowledge or intent." The result was that she entered Guangdong Pharmaceutical University/Zhongshan Campus with a major in Chinese Medicine Resource Development. She continues, "I applied for that because no one was advising me, nor did I know what I would be learning in this field."

Another problem in the educational and testing system is that pupils focus solely on success in the exams, without seeing how the selection of a major will affect their subsequent professional careers. GR 28 warns in retrospect, "The biggest hurdle [in the job search] is the subject area. By that I mean the major you select at the university is very important. When students like me take the entrance exam, only very few consider whether they like the subject or not. I think I spent four years of my studies blind." The universities themselves do little to guide the students in finding "their" majors. According to a report by He, the structure of the Chinese educational system generally leads to universities deciding on the number of places for each major and then recruiting students to fill them based on their entrance exam scores, rather than letting them choose the majors themselves. As a result, many universities offer only low-cost subjects such as finance and law instead of the engineering and science specialties that society urgently needs (He, 2013).

Continue studying or start working?

Some of the bachelor graduates who started work immediately after graduation had still set themselves the goal of continuing their studies. On the advice of his uncle who was working in the sticker and package industry, GR 3 earned a bachelor's degree in graphic and package engineering from the Beijing Institute of Graphic Communication. He wanted to continue studying but did not show clear interest in a specific subject, appearing instead to be attracted to campus life. He applied to study social insurance at the People's University in Beijing, but was not accepted. A classmate had suggested it in the belief that social insurance was an increasingly hot topic. "In fact, at the time of my graduation," said GR 3, "I wasn't sure I would enter this industry – what matters to me is the People's University, the environment." Overall, the chances for college graduates to enter a post-graduate programme are quite slim. For example, there were 6.3 million college graduates in 2010; of these, 1.4 million took the entrance exam for a post-graduate programme and 465,000 were admitted (Chen, 2011:82, 84).

Why Guangzhou?

Two main reasons brought the graduates interviewed in this study to Guangzhou. Half of the 30 interviewees came to Guangzhou because they had been accepted to a university in the city and decided to stay and work there after graduation. Most of them were from hometowns in Guangdong province. The other half had graduated from universities elsewhere in China and came to Guangzhou to find work and gain experience. Common to all members of both groups was the lack of a permanent Guangzhou *hukou* in conjunction with a background from a rural area, usually from a village.

In addition to these two basic routes to Guangzhou, the interviewees also expressed two personal motivations for moving to the city. The first was the desire to become part of the mega-urban social fabric with its academic institutions, occupational perspectives and cultural stimuli. GR 2, who earned a bachelor's degree from Jiaying University in Meizhou city, said, "I don't want to work in Meizhou, I think Meizhou is too quiet.… I myself like these rather bustling cities – even if my personal life is not very comfortable, but comparatively speaking, I prefer more lively cities." By 2020, Guangzhou had become the favourite city for college graduates in China due mainly to its stable housing prices and more open and inclusive culture than Beijing or Shanghai (Yang, 2020). At the time of the interviews, Guangzhou attracted half of the local graduates and 3.8 per cent of the national total (Chen and Xu, 2012). The second personal reason was the existence of social networks of family and friends, classmates and colleagues. Whether the young graduates came from other places in Guangdong or from other regions in China, the fact that relatives or friends were already living in Guangzhou or that classmates or colleagues were moving there had a clear impact on their decision to choose the city. Most explicit is GR 27, a female graduate from Meizhou/Guangdong who had studied at a vocational college in Guangzhou: "I came to Guangzhou for my studies, perhaps because I am quite familiar with the Guangzhou environment. Besides, many of my relatives and friends are here; well, this is the principle of closeness."

The Attractiveness of Campus Spaces and the Studentification of Urban Villages

Regardless of whether the interviewees came to Guangzhou to work after graduating elsewhere or remained in the city after graduating from its colleges and universities, most decided to rent an apartment or room in one of the 131 urban villages in its central districts (Li, 2011:100). Those residing at company dormitories or in middle-class neighbourhoods (*xiaoqu*)[12] were the exceptions. Two-thirds of the 30 interviewees lived in the two central districts of Tianhe (15) and Haizhu (5).[13]

Three main criteria were operative in deciding where to live. *Of greatest significance* was affordability. Those interviewees with monthly incomes of 2,000 to 3,500 yuan paid a rent of around 500 yuan. Four of the graduates earned more than 5,000 yuan a month and spent correspondingly more on rent. Half the interviewees lived alone, and the rest shared an apartment with usually one or two others.[14] Two of the six female graduates were living with family members such as siblings, two with their boyfriends and two as singles at company dorms.[15] None of the female graduates was living alone. Whether this was due to financial or safety concerns is unclear. The *second selection criterion* for housing in Guangzhou was access to public transportation. Commute times of up to an hour are not viewed as problematic. The proximity of housing to a subway station was however considered important. The *third selection criterion* typical of quite a few of these highly educated migrants was easy access to a university campus. This applied not only to those who had studied at Guangzhou colleges or universities but also to those who had come to Guangzhou after graduating elsewhere. Although all the interviewees had left a university, they had not yet cut ties with the university lifestyle. Access to a campus can offer practical benefits as well as a sense of belonging to an academic milieu with the attendant individual and emotional assurance. The practical value of campus proximity lies in the

---

[12] 小区.

[13] Four interviewees did not provide this information, two lived in company dormitories outside of urban villages, two in Panyu, and one each in Huangpu and Yuexiu. Altogether, nineteen urban villages in Guangzhou were mentioned in the interviews as current or former housing locations.

[14] The relationship status of two interviewees was unknown; three were married or planned to marry in the near future. Four of the six female interviewees had boyfriends and six of the remaining nineteen male interviewees had girlfriends.

[15] The two female graduates living in company dorms shared a room with eight or twelve employees. The only male graduate also staying at a company dormitory shared a room with seven colleagues.

ability to make continued use of a university's resources. Consumer costs in the vicinity of universities are relatively low. Urban villages located close to university campuses provide graduates with affordable consumer goods and services tailored to their needs such as opticians and shops with clothing suitable for work (Li, 2011:99). Other residents are attracted by cheap meals at university cafeterias or the opportunity to play, e.g. basketball, at campus sports facilities.

Four urban villages can serve as examples here of preferred residential sites for educated migrants: Xiadu village adjoining the campus of Sun Yat-sen University (SYSU); Nantingcun on Xiaguwei Island (site of University Town); Xiaozhou, an artists' village close to University Town and the Guangzhou Academy of Fine Arts; and Shipai, Guangzhou's largest urban village located right in its centre in Tianhe and close to Jinan University, South China Normal University and other educational institutions.

Xiadu Village: A sense of university identity

Located right to the north of the SYSU campus, Xiadu has long had a connection with the university. Besides offering cheap housing, this urban village has developed into a prosperous commercial district with fast-food stores, snack bars and restaurants. Drawing on Smith (2005), He Shenjing (2015) has analysed the development of Xiadu village as a typical case of studentification. She divides Xiadu's student population into three groups: a large number preparing for graduate school entrance exams, regular SYSU students seeking privacy (e.g. student couples) and SYSU graduates who have passed their exams within the past few years. In contrast to the first two groups, the graduates took rooms on a long-term basis because the rent was cheap and they wanted to be close to friends and the campus (He, 2015:2862).

Xiadu's student tenants prefer to live in the newer part while migrant workers who run small businesses there live in the older part. Many students left the campus for Xiadu village on account of the university's substandard accommodation and rigid dormitory rules. At the same time, students were attracted by the village's convenient supply of various cultural and commercial services. And student renters were popular with village landlords who perceived them as civilised, educated and punctual with rent payments. In early 2003, this situation led to a conflict with the university, and specifically between food service providers on campus and in the village. It intensified to a point where the university blocked the small gate between the campus and the village (He, 2015:2861) to stop the drain of student customers from cafeterias and dormitories. At the same time, Xiadu village was presented as posing a threat to students' health and safety. Supported by students, the villagers opposed the university's action and tore down the wall. Ultimately, the small gate was retained. The existing concentration of students in Xiadu attracted even more. Rents in the village rose as housing boomed in the surrounding area and villagers invested in the rental business (He, 2015:2864).

Xiadu is most attractive for educated migrants who desire to enter post-graduate programmes and therefore want proximity to the campus to prepare for further exams. GR 1, who studied history and was now working as a quality controller for a private firm, had lived in Xiadu for a few months while preparing for the entrance exam for a master's programme in anthropology. He describes his daily routine during his time in Xiadu: "I am not studying here [in Xiadu]. The air circulation is a bit better in the SYSU library but I didn't know anyone; it was quite gloomy (*kumen*).[16] Later I went to the Teaching Building No. 1; every year students from throughout China come here to prepare for the exams, really, teacher, you should go and have a look … it let me recall my university life."

Campus proximity is also attractive to graduates for practical reasons such as using sports facilities and maintaining contact with classmates in post-graduate programmes at SYSU. These graduates have developed a sense of belonging to the place and want to continue their pre-graduation lifestyles (He, 2015:2858, 2862). Driven by their needs and interests, they become involved in processes that reorient some of the urban villages and change their consumer patterns.

Nantingcun village: Attracting students and teachers from the University Town

Another example of how an influx of students can considerably affect an urban village can be observed in the establishment of University Town

[16] 苦闷.

(*daxuecheng*)[17] in Panyu district. Located between the campus of the Guangzhou Academy of Fine Arts and that of the Guangdong University of Technology, Nantingcun is one of four remaining villages on Xiaoguwei Island that were not demolished during the construction of University Town on the island. Nantingcun has attracted more students than the other three villages. This is mainly because the art students are more individualistic and want a more private and expressive lifestyle, and therefore prefer to live off campus. In addition, many provide art lessons at the approximately 50 training institutes that now attract quite a number of pupils. Because of these developments, Nantingcun has a well-established rental market as well as other student-related services and facilities such as small billiards clubs and art supply stores run by university students (He, 2015:2865).

Another reason for renting a room in Nantingcun was raised by GR 19, a former art student now working for the Academy of Fine Arts on the University Town campus. As a painter, he needs some space for his tools and drawing boards. He pays 450 yuan a month for a room of 15 m^2. "It costs 700 yuan to live on campus; we teachers living in University Town all have to spend money; our academy is relatively expensive, and quite good." The painter also observed that "Nantingcun has changed quite a lot, its appearance has changed, the older buildings were torn down and also five or six of the new ones." Compared to other urban villages in Guangzhou whose population consists largely of two social groups, rural-to-urban migrant workers and original villagers, the social compositions of Xiadu and Nantingcun are more mixed.

Xiaozhou Village: A famous artists' village turned tourist area

Located across the river west of Xiaoguwei Island, Xiaozhou village is also close to University Town. Xiaozhou is a typical Cantonese "water town" surrounded by winding canals feeding into the Pearl River. When construction of University Town started in the early 2000s, some of the artists who had founded Guangzhou's earliest "artist village" on the island in the mid-1990s were forced to leave and proceeded to set up new homes in Xiaozhou with its temples, stone bridges, oyster-shell houses and old

[17] 大学城.

trees, namely, in a tranquil and leisurely atmosphere so different from the bustling life in Guangzhou city. After University Town went into operation around 2007, more and more young art graduates converged on Xiaozhou. Art spaces sprang up overnight with events attracting visitors and tourists. In 2009, Xiaozhou Art Zone was built under an expressway with studios, large exhibition halls and art markets. Xiaozhou became a symbol for art colonies in the further development of cultural and creative industries in Guangzhou (Qin, 2010). The village was able to maintain its traditional flair, first because of its proximity to the "Ten-Thousand Acre Orchard" nature reserve and the consequent ban by the Guangzhou government on industrial development and second because it became a "historical and cultural protected area" in 2000 (Qian *et al.*, 2013:336).

As more students came to Xiaozhou, its idyllic scenery suffered and a process of studentification and gentrification began. GR 23, who is from Zhanjiang in Guangdong province, moved to Xiaozhou after earning his master's degree in art theory from South China Normal University in Guangzhou. He rented an apartment of $40m^2$ and an atelier of 20–30 m^2. Without the help of friends already living in Xiaozhou, he said he wouldn't have been able to get the apartment and work space he was looking for.

As Qian *et al.* observed, for most villagers, Xiaozhou is a space of economic production and everyday life, whereas for the artists, it is a space for the enactment of a particular cultural aesthetic. Hidden conflicts became evident with the large influx of students around 2007 and of professional artists who began establishing training institutes (80 in 2009–2011). From then on, student-related industries and services became the cornerstone of the village economy (Qian *et al.*, 2013:341). A divide emerged between villagers who added 2-3 floors to their houses to rent out to students and those who maintained their traditional one-floor homes and sought economic development by reviving traditional culture such as dragon boat racing, clan temple rituals, lion dances, Cantonese opera and Cantonese enamel production (Zacharias and Lei, 2016:653–654). Some of the villagers preferred to rent to artists who were there all the time, whereas students only attended classes for four months a year. Other villagers argued that students (often from middle-class families) could afford higher rents and had more cash in their pockets than the grassroots artists; for their part, the latter distanced themselves from the art teachers coming to Xiaozhou for economic reasons alone and complained that the students were driving up the rents. The grassroots artists were therefore the ones most vulnerable to displacement. But less vulnerable artists were also moving out of Xiaozhou in search of rural authenticity. In their place, urban artists with commercial galleries, businesspeople trading antiques and art, and tourists came to the village (Qian *et al.*, 2013:342).

Shipai Village: Central location, socially mixed and close to universities

With a population of 55,000, Shipai village is the largest urban village in Guangzhou (Zacharias *et al.*, 2013:5). It is located in Tianhe district in the centre of the city and is known for the nearby wholesale electronics market. After all of Shipai's arable land had been confiscated by 1994, a strong village community centred on clan families like the Chis, Pans and Dongs used its compensation money to build a strong economy based on real estate. Combining economic interests with social clan structures, its members strengthened the social cohesion of the former village community, renovated its ancestral halls and used their historical and cultural resources to consolidate local power within the new market environment. While formally under the municipal administration, they could retain the relative autonomy of a village organisation (Lan, 2005:34).

As of the mid-1990s, ever more rural migrants in search of cheap housing came to Shipai. While the village looks somewhat dirty, dark and crowded from the outside with many confusing alleys, its low-priced housing, central location and excellent transport links make it ideal in many ways. The inhabitants of Shipai seem more socially mixed than those of any other urban village in Guangzhou. There are people from all walks of life and a broad range of services such as restaurants, barber shops, saunas and clinics. GR 17, who graduated from Hunan Railway Professional Technology College and works in computer sales in Shipai village, enjoys living there. "Everyone lives in urban villages …, it's very convenient. Even late at night, at 2 or 3 in the morning, you can go out; you always can find something to eat – although one has to say it is somewhat chaotic here." For GR 12, the situation is different. Also from Hunan, he was recruited from his China University of Politics and Law campus in Beijing by a well-known bank which sent him to its branch in Guangzhou. Then, his employer provided him with an apartment of 15m^2 in Shipai. The light and air conditions were acceptable to him and he only had to pay 100 yuan a month in rent to the trade union office of the bank. This is very cheap compared to the 500–700 yuan other graduates in our sample had to pay in Shipai. GR 12's apartment was some kind of "arrival offer" for newcomers with the bank and was only for one year. As for his neighbours, he said he had no contact with them because "the place is used for business as well as housing; also, there are workers and employees of different social classes, people are frequently moving in and out, the mobility is very high." Some other interviewees similarly describe their "home" in a Guangzhou urban village as a place for spending the nights. They know neither their neighbours nor the history or traditions of the villages they live in. Their landlord/landlady is the only person they know in the village (GR 3).

Several educational institutes such as Jinan University and South China Normal University are located near the village. Shipai has also long housed teachers and graduates at early stages of their careers. But in contrast to places like Xiadu and Nantingcun, students and graduates are not its dominant group of renters. GR 3, who is from Guangxi province and had studied at the Beijing Institute of Graphic Communication, was searching restlessly for his place, torn between the desires to continue academic training and to further his professional skills (as a technical service provider for a company producing labels and stickers). He confessed that "[I came to Guangzhou] because my brother is here, to be honest. My younger brother is in a master's programme at Jinan University, so I have everything; for example, I can go to the library, eat at the cafeteria, everything can be handled well." GR 3 is far from an exception. Proximity to a campus provides precisely those graduates who as job starters are actually no longer directly involved with the university with a continuing sense of belonging to an academic milieu and the idea that they can continue to develop and extend their period of education somewhat (Li, 2011:44). The "English Corner" offers not only a chance to improve English but also to meet and exchange information with other young people in the university environment. Regardless of whether it is about practical considerations or emotional comfort, proximity to a university campus constitutes a third nodal point complementing the urban village where recent graduates can find affordable housing and workplace(s) where they earn money and perhaps launch a professional career.

Redevelopment policies and shrinking living space

The existing challenges of finding affordable housing that meets transport and location requirements, especially regarding proximity to their workplace and eventually to a university campus, became even more difficult for graduates over the years. Their numbers were increasing every year. In addition, in 2009, the Guangzhou municipal government started a comprehensive programme to redevelop all of (at that time) the city's 131 urban villages within a period of about ten years. In 2011, when the redevelopment of seven villages in Tianhe district in the centre of the city had been completed, the impact of shrinking settlement space was already noticeable. As redevelopment work intensified, graduates started moving from a broader variety of settlements to a smaller number of villages. This tendency was accompanied by some graduates choosing to move to more remote urban villages at the periphery with more moderate prices. As the real estate market heated up, prices in Guangzhou's rental market also rose and even more graduates started to rent housing in urban villages (Li, 2011:40).

In 2011, the Guangzhou government did not include educated migrants in its affordable housing system. According to the "Guangzhou housing construction plan (2008–2012)," affordable housing policies were aimed only at local Guangzhou low-income families, and the authorities did not introduce corresponding policies for graduates.[18] Even if graduates had been included in the Guangzhou affordable housing programme, the location would not have satisfied their needs because it was too far from the city centre (Li, 2011:41). It was only in 2019 that Guangzhou launched a housing policy for new citizens without a Guangzhou *hukou* to create 150,000 new rental units for 300,000 new citizens, especially long-term residents without a *hukou* and newly settled and employed students. The policy is based on combined efforts by the government, financial institutions and enterprises to provide loans to finance implementation.[19] In January 2024, the Guangzhou municipal government unveiled a new long-term programme to redevelop 272 urban

---

[18] Other cities in China started to address graduates' housing problems with two types of measures. Cities such as Dalian, Chengdu and Ganzhou provided revolving student apartments, while others like Fuzhou, Xiamen and Hangzhou included graduates in their affordable housing systems.

[19] 广州将为"广漂"新市民提供15万套租赁住房 *Guangzhou jiangwei 'Guangpiao' xin shimin tigong 15 wan tao zulin zhufang* (Guangzhou will provide 150,000 rental housing units for new urban *Guangpiao* citizens) https://finance.sina.com.cn/china/dfjj/2020-05-15/doc-iircuyvi3299141.shtml (accessed May 15, 2020).

villages, including 124 micro-redevelopments.[20] It remains to be seen whether the affordable housing that will be lost as a result can be replaced by appropriate housing programmes that take into account the needs of rural graduates.

Job Search and Employability in a First-Tier City

With the transition from college to professional life, the challenge of having to make independent decisions took on a new dimension for rural graduates. The impact of the global financial crisis (2008–2009) and the decline of the Chinese economy from double-digit growth rates meant that companies were hiring less. By the time of the interviews at the end of 2011, this, combined with the steady increase in the number of graduates had already led to significant unemployment and job search pressure among graduates. The unemployment rate for college graduates averaged 9.8% in 2011 (MyCos, 2012:74).[21] In the following decade, economic growth slowed significantly, while the number of college graduates continued to rise, from 6.3 million in 2010 (Chen, 2011a) to 11.79 million in 2024 (Zhao and Cheng, 2024).[22]

In general, the socioeconomic impact of the COVID-19 pandemic greatly exacerbated the employment difficulties of young graduates. In addition, the regulatory crackdown in the early 2020s on big tech firms and on private after-school tutoring, industries, that both heavily relied on fresh graduates, contributed to worsened job prospects for those newly entering the job market (McCartney, 2024). The increasing number of Chinese students returning from abroad further intensified domestic competition. The urban unemployment rate for people aged 16–24 in China had been rising for several years in a row, reaching 21.3% in June 2023. Subsequently, the National Bureau of Statistics (NBS) did not publish youth unemployment figures for several months. Then the NBS changed

---

[20] 广州市城中村改造专项规划 (2021–2035年) *Guangzhou shi chengzhongcun zhuanxiang guihua* (Special plan for urban village renovation 2021–2035), https://www.gz.gov.cn/zwfw/zxfw/gysy/content/post_9464878.html (accessed April 20, 2024).

[21] No data are available for the specific unemployment rate of college graduates from the countryside.

[22] 2021: 9.09 million college graduates ("China will have 9 million new college graduates this year": http://www.ecns.cn/news/2021-05-13/detail-ihametef9042473.shtml, accessed February 20, 2025.); 2022:10.76 million and 2023:11.58 million (Qu 2023).

the methodology for calculating the age-specific unemployment rate to exclude students in educational institutions (*fei zaixiao xuesheng*),[23] and it fell to 14.9% for people aged 16-24 (December 2023).[24] In July 2024, almost 12 million additional college graduates entered the labour market, pushing youth unemployment up again to 17.1%.[25] A brief report by the Asian Development Bank (Feng *et al.*, 2023: 3,4) identifies the main factors behind China's rising youth unemployment as (1) weak job creation due to the economic downturn; (2) sectors with more young people such as services, private enterprises and gig work,[26] were hit hard by pandemic-related restrictions; (3) regulatory interventions in technology firms, private tutoring and the property sector, all popular with young job seekers, reduced job opportunities for young people.

Job search and recruitment

After graduation, educated migrants focus on finding a job. Their ideas and aspirations often conflict with the interests and selection criteria of their potential employers. They may also conflict with labour market policies – and with migration policies. Job recruitment processes for college graduates can be divided into three general categories: (1) online processes whereby employers provide information on open sites and graduates upload their CVs onto specific platforms; (2) campus processes whereby companies or other employers visit the campuses of major universities to directly recruit new employees; and (3) job markets at which companies and other potential employers are represented (GR 13). In addition to these official channels, informal recommendations also play a role, for example, from relatives (GR 4's uncle), colleagues (GR 26) or

[23] 非在校学生.

[24] NBS, 17 January 2024: National Economy Witnessed Momentum of Recovery with Solid Progress in High-quality Development in 2023, available at https://www.stats.gov.cn/english/PressRelease/202401/t20240117_1946605.html (accessed April 24, 2024).

[25] NBS monthly data, July 2024, available at https://data.stats.gov.cn/english/easyquery.htm?cn=A01 (accessed August 10, 2024).

[26] The gig economy has three components: independent workers who are paid by the "gig" (an individual task or project), consumers who need a specific service, and businesses that connect workers directly to consumers, including through app-based technology platforms (Feng *et al.*, 2023:1, fn.1).

classmates (GR 24). All these means were addressed by the interviewees.

Multinational corporations are considered the most popular employers among Chinese graduates in general (Chen, 2011:85). Of relevance are the anticipated high incomes as well as the sense of belonging to a global enterprise (usually located in one of China's megacities), at least for those graduates for whom studying abroad is not an option. In reality, however, small and medium-sized enterprises (SMEs) have more jobs to offer. But these are not very attractive for the young graduates on account of both the rather low wages and the expectation of unfavourable working conditions. According to GR 9 who had studied TCM resources and development, "In my experience, the biggest problem in finding a job is that there is no market for my specialty." This female graduate who had been in Guangzhou for only two months at the time of the interview was under financial pressure to pay back a student loan. After graduation, she therefore accepted a job found online. "At first I thought the company belonged to Jiaotong Bank, but when I went to sign the contract, I realised I had been tricked and the company did not belong to Jiaotong Bank at all." Her work basically consisted of soliciting credit card contracts on the street: "… Then there was the 'laying out,' like the small street vendors do, which normally attracts the *chengguan*.[27] When they come, you gather up your things … When I laid out my materials for the first time, I thought after studying at a university for four years and earning a degree there's no difference to working as a street vendor." At the time of the interview, she had already applied for another job (as an English teacher) and planned to quit the credit card work the next day.

Gender-based discrimination seems to be particularly pronounced in the recruitment of new graduates (Dasgupta *et al.*, 2015:29). In addition to the systemic disadvantages faced by educated migrants (related to family backgrounds and asymmetries in the education and examination systems), female graduates are confronted with additional obstacles and unequal treatment in their choice of occupation, job search, work situation, wages and recruitment. Reports of employers favouring male candidates or giving preferential treatment to male applications are not

[27] *Chengguan* 城管 is short for *chengshi guanli* 城市管理, a public order agency that supports municipal law enforcement; such urban management officers crack down on, e.g. illegal street vendors.

uncommon, with patriarchal attitudes becoming more pronounced in recent years as the labour market has become more competitive.[28]

Job-hopping

After landing a job, most graduates faced the decision of whether to stay or find a new one. Job-hopping seemed to be the rule instead of the exception for rural graduates. Almost all the interviewees had already had two or three different jobs in the first few years. A high turnover rate has also been noted for college graduates in China in general.[29] According to a study by the MyCos research institute, in 2011, 41% of graduates had left their first jobs within half a year of earning their degrees. The rate went up to 52% for graduates of vocational colleges, but was only 19% for graduates of the "211" universities[30] (MyCos, 2012:122). The reasons given were not enough opportunities for individual development (30%), insufficient salary and benefits (21%), the desire to change location or sector (17%), inability to adapt to the company's management system or culture (8%), excessive work requirements and/or stress (5%), no sense of security (4%), readiness to study (3%), and others (12%) (MyCos, 2012:124).

The interviewees listed similar reasons. For example, GR 14 stated that the job did not offer any opportunities for development, and GR 7 said he had left because what he learned at college did not apply to his job requirements in practice. Conversely, some interviewees changed their jobs to pursue positive aims such as learning and gaining experience (GR 24) or self-optimisation (GR 2). Job changes are intended to increase employability, income levels and professional development. Job-hopping is not undertaken exclusively or even primarily to achieve higher wages and better working conditions but to compensate individually for an insufficient fit between college education and the subsequent occupation. Nevertheless, the young graduates interviewed in 2011 interpret their

[28] See also the subsection on *policy responses to graduate unemployment* in the following.

[29] The turnover rate refers to the percentage of graduates who had a job but stopped working within six months after graduation, compared to those have a job and are still at it.

[30] The "211" universities are the 100 universities that have received special investment from the Chinese government to become top-level institutions in the 21st century (21 for 21st century and 1 for 100 universities) (He and Mai, 2015:350, footnote 6).

career entry problems primarily as individual inadequacies requiring stronger subjective efforts at compensation on their part. Further research is required to investigate whether and how the behaviour of rural graduates with regard to job-hopping is changing in response to the tight labour market conditions that prevail during the 2020s. It may be assumed that job-hopping is still a widespread phenomenon, but that it is now occurring more frequently as a result of the pressure exerted by short-term and less satisfying job offers than as a result of educated migrants' own volition.

Employability and salaries

Large companies and government institutions have their own ideas and criteria for hiring graduates. They prefer to take graduates of the "211" and "985" universities.[31] Drawing on a study of the employability of Shanghai graduates, Chen Yongjie presents the following seven factors that influence the screening process applied by potential employers: (1) education, (2) major, (3) category of educational institute, (4) birthplace and mobility, (5) work experience before graduation, (6) gender, and (7) parental social status and occupation. Of these factors, the students themselves can influence only one, namely, work experience before graduation, whereas employers look primarily at the first three (Chen, 2011:86).

These selection criteria suggest employers assume that the hierarchy of universities is an accurate map of their graduates' individual performance. As such, students from key universities are seen as more competitive in the labour market, earning higher salaries and receiving jobs endowed with comfortable social welfare and other benefits. As Chen Yongjie has argued, the same human capital does not automatically translate into the same competitiveness and employability for graduates. Several external factors, such as their birthplace, the status and location of the institution from which they graduated, and the differences in admissions scores and quotas of universities in different regions, weaken the social mobility of graduates with rural family backgrounds. Chen

[31] The "985" universities were proposed by President Jiang Zemin on the occasion of the 100th anniversary of Peking University on May 4, 1998 (98 for the year, 5 for the month). The 985 universities are the 39 state universities which the government expects to attain world-class status (He and Mai, 2015:350, footnote 5).

therefore explains that graduate employability problems are due not only to subjective dimensions of education, training and self-cultivation but also to structural deficits in the educational system and labour market (see Chen, 2011:89).

The median monthly income of the interviewees was 3,000 yuan, which was higher than the average monthly income of 2,766 yuan for college graduates in China in general in 2011 (MyCos, 2012:092). But the interviewees' actual incomes ranged from 1,300 to 12,000 yuan. Of the 24 male and six female interviewees, four male and four female graduates were earning less than 2,000 per month. The remaining 20 male graduates earned between 2,000 and 5,000 yuan a month, with individual peak earnings of 8,000 and 12,000. The other two female graduates earned 2,400 and 2,800 yuan per month, both of whom had been assisted by family networks in finding a job. The interviewees hardly mention the gender gap in connection with employment and salaries, or if they do, then with a fatalistic tenor, as a statement of their own weakness.

No correlation can be seen between interviewee income level and identification with the *Yizu* label. However, in the lowest income category, five of the six female interviewees refused to be called *Yizu*. Moreover, those who agreed that the label *Yizu* fits their situation did so in very different tones, including a degree of shame, irony or defiance, or the qualification "yes, temporarily."

Civil servant examination: An option?

Motivation to take the national civil servant exam in order to land a secure job was not very high. Of the 23 interviewees who commented on this, 15 waved it off with a "no, thank you" and eight responded with a "yes" or "yes, but." However, of the eight respondents who responded positively, three had already failed the exam. Two female graduates wanted to take the exam, but one feared not having the necessary connections to do so (GR 2) and the other not having sufficient time to prepare (GR 20). The remaining three wanted to take the exam later at the local level (GR 22) or with the help of an uncle (GR 4 and GR 7). Similar concerns were expressed by some of those who did not want to take the exam: lack of personal connections (*guanxi*)[32] (GR 8, 17, 25), too much competition (GR 9), and the association of the exam with the elites (GR 11). Other

[32]关系.

answers given were "not interested" (GR 10, 24), "don't like the work" (GR 13), "too boring" (GR 29) and "don't like the predictability" (GR 28). GR 24, who was working as a private asset manager, felt that the civil service exams were de facto designed for local students, who would perceive the participation of outsiders as competitive pressure, which in turn could lead to forms of discrimination against educated migrants like himself. As he said, "As long as there is no competition between the local Guangzhou people and me, I do not feel discriminated against by them. But if I were to take the Guangzhou civil service exam with other students, for example, they would definitely feel pressured … Since I don't want to do this kind of work anyway, I don't feel it is discrimination. But I'm sure the Guangzhou fellow students in my class are more or less all taking the Guangzhou civil service exam." The overall rather low motivation of the interviewees to take the civil service exams may also reflect a more general trend at the time of the interviews.

While civil service jobs were seen as stable and attractive for their state-funded pensions, graduates seemed to have very different career aspirations and made decisions based on motives other than a stable income (Chen, 2011b). In addition, the likelihood of being hired was low and working conditions could be quite harsh in reality (Chen, 2012b).

With youth unemployment on the rise, the general interest in the national civil service exams has risen sharply in recent years. Although the number of vacancies in central government agencies and their directly affiliated institutions has increased significantly since 2011 (from 17,800 vacancies to 39,600 vacancies in 2023), the increase in the absolute number of applicants from 1.41 million to 3.03 million shows the growing priority of having a stable job. For young graduates (in general, not just those from rural areas) taking the exams, the threshold for academic qualifications has been raised. While the number of jobs for junior college graduates has been reduced to only 56 vacancies in 2023, there should be 2,045 jobs available for graduates with a master's degree or higher. However, the number of post-graduates has also increased significantly, from 1.5 million in 2011 to 4.74 million in 2023, so there is also considerable competitive pressure here (Du, 2023; Zhang and Zaharia, 2023). The implications of these developments are, firstly, that the civil service exam is even less likely to be a source of stable employment for rural graduates than it was in the past, and secondly, that the increased demand for jobs for graduates in general can only be met to a very limited extent by the increased number of government jobs on offer.

Policy responses to graduate unemployment

The problem of high and structural unemployment for college graduates prompted a discussion on structural problems in the labour market. The dilemma was seen as a combination of graduates having difficulties finding jobs and many businesses having problems finding qualified workers and technicians. It was therefore proposed that the graduates lower their standards and gain more work experience. In other words, it was suggested that graduates take blue-collar jobs to meet the needs of the labour market. It was argued that many companies were in the process of switching from traditional manufacturing to high-tech production and therefore had a great need for technicians. By raising the wages for workers and particularly for technicians, blue-collar jobs could be made more attractive for graduates. This proposal, however, was not taken up by the graduates in their search for work. The reason given is that the argument failed to distinguish between education and skills, and ignored the fact that unemployed graduates associated blue-collar jobs with low social status and difficult work (Chen, 2012a).

As competition in the labour market has increased, so has discrimination against female graduates. In 2019, the Ministry of Human Resources and Social Security (MoHRSS) and the Ministry of Education (MoE) issued a circular to regulate recruitment behaviour and expand workplace protection for women, including prohibiting employers from asking women about their marital/family status and requiring women to agree not to have children (Circular, 2019). Another effect was that graduates began to lower their salary expectations (Fan, 2024).

Some of the new measures taken by the Chinese government to boost and sustain employment, especially for college graduates, include

- **Delaying entry into the labour market:** As mentioned above, the number of postgraduate students has increased significantly. From the perspective of job-seeking graduates, the most direct way to stand out from the competition is to become more educated. However, critics have argued that this is only a matter of exams and not a real investment in human capital, and ultimately leads to the problem of overqualification (Chen, 2011: 83).
- **Subsidising enterprises:** Following the outbreak of the pandemic, the government subsidised enterprises to encourage job retention and recruitment.

- **Skills training and employment:** The government supported training programmes and internships, organised job fairs and recruitment campaigns, and encouraged self-employment and flexible employment.
- **Provision of income support and temporary relief:** The government increased unemployment benefits and provided various forms of temporary assistance to people experiencing financial difficulties due to the pandemic (Feng *et al.*, 2023: 5,6).

At the Third Plenum of the 20th Party Congress in July 2024, the "employment-first policy" (*jiuye youxian zhengce*)[33] was enshrined in the plenary resolution on promoting Chinese-style modernisation in the second half of the 2020s. College graduates were among the three key groups (along with rural migrant workers and ex-servicemen) to be particularly supported by an improved employment system. Among other things, business start-ups should be encouraged, and the development of new forms of employment should be supported and regulated (Resolution, 2024).

Education: A Ticket to the Middle Class and First-Tier Cities?

Despite high housing and employment pressures, neither labour market policies aimed at attracting university graduates to (relatively well-paid) blue-collar work nor migration and urbanisation policies aimed at attracting them to smaller cities have been successful. To some extent, this can be explained by the desire of educated migrants for upward mobility and to belong to the middle class. But where do rural graduates position themselves in Chinese society and what are their channels for joining the urban middle class? Why do they want to stay in first-tier cities despite all the obstacles that stand in the way of their upward mobility? This section begins with a brief introduction to the sociological discourses on the Chinese middle class (society) as a background for presenting the respondents' views on where they see themselves in Chinese society. It discusses their expectations for the future, including the pros and cons of staying in Guangzhou rather than moving to a lower-tier city.

---

[33] 就业优先政策.

Conceptualisations of the Chinese middle class

The main debates in the research literature on the Chinese middle class since the early 2000s have focused on the difference between the middle class and middle-class society, the difference between middle-class society and consumer society, the relationship between the economic and political development of the middle class, and the question of what indicators can be used to determine who belongs to the middle class.

Some authors reject the search for objective and measurable indicators of the Chinese middle class altogether, juxtaposing it with subjective aspects such as self-image, identity, attitudes and behaviour (Miao, 2017; Lu, 2013). Other authors focus on new patterns of consumption, including luxury goods, lifestyles in middle-class neighbourhoods, gentrification, the popularisation of art and new urban design (Zhang, 2010; Cartier, 2013). As cultural sociological approaches, these need to be distinguished from stereotypical images in public opinion. The image of the middle class created by the media and advertising, Li Chunling argues, focuses on a very small segment of the upper middle class and primarily on their consumption habits and lifestyles. This image suggests that the middle class lives in large apartments, drives expensive cars, wears designer clothes and takes frequent holidays. Its members are seen as high-income, high-consumption entrepreneurs, professional managers or elite intellectuals (Li, 2013:396). Furthermore, and especially in Western literature, the question has arisen as to whether the expansion of the Chinese middle class would lead to a democratisation of Chinese society and even a "regime change," or whether the links with the Chinese party-state are so strong that such a development is inconceivable (Goodman, 2014). Rocca goes even further, arguing that the development of the Chinese middle class should be seen primarily as a political strategy (Rocca, 2017a, 2017b).

Zhou Xiaohong has explored the difference between the terms "middle class" (as a theoretical – or ideological – debate on whether contemporary Chinese society should be analysed in terms of the Marxist concept of class or as part of a stratified society, as in mainstream sociology) and "middle-class society" (as a strategic orientation for the development of Chinese society, where a broad middle class – an olive-shaped image of society – is seen as a guarantor of stability) (Zhou, 2008, 2005). It was in this latter sense that the then General Secretary Jiang Zemin proposed the "expansion of the middle-income group" as a policy goal in 2002 (Li, 2013:397). However, Li and other sociologists have been critical of the government's approach of using an income threshold to define the middle class. She argues that it is difficult to define a threshold income for the middle class, with proposals ranging from US$5,000 to US$30,000 or more per year. In particular, the large gap between rural and urban incomes would make it difficult to formulate a uniform standard for the middle class (Li, 2013:397). Deborah Davis and Jianying Wang emphasise the analysis of major occupational groups and their internal divisions (Wang and Davis 2010). Particularly relevant in our context are the studies by Li Peilin and Zhang Yi (2008), which include higher education in their criteria for who should be considered middle class. Li and Zhang have tried to develop a definition of the Chinese middle class that is, as they say, as realistic and measurable as possible. To this end, they use the three indicators of income, occupation and education. They also divide the middle class into three strata: a core middle class, to which all three indicators apply; a semi-core middle class, to which two of the three indicators apply; and a peripheral middle class, to which only one of the three indicators applies. We will return to these indicators later.

The self-positioning of rural graduates in Chinese society

When asked where they see themselves in society, the respondents used the following criteria (which overlap to some extent with the sociological approaches discussed earlier): income level, power/management, entitlement to social security, lifestyle, values, sophistication, development potential, family background and the distinction between rulers and ruled. GR 11, who works as an assistant engineer, positions himself within a model of five social strata. "The first is the highest layer, the government officials; the second is the one that has money; the third is the middle class, which includes white-collar and blue-collar workers, as well as lower management and technical staff; the fourth layer is people like us who are still struggling to make a living (*wenbao fangmian*).[34] These layers are divided according to income. At the bottom are families who are in trouble because they have no money to go to the doctor, for example." GR 12, who works as an account manager, highlights consumer behaviour and lifestyles to characterise social stratification. "Above me are those who go to cocktail parties, hold a glass in their hand, play golf and so on ..., in fact, the higher the class, the higher the sophistication of the

[34] 温饱 food and clothing.

people ... I belong to the upper class spiritually and to the lower middle class materially."[35]

For GR 19, an art academy graduate from a peasant family with 5 siblings, the two criteria that determine one's societal position are family background and education. "I think the most important thing is family background; the second generation of officials, the second generation of rich people, they stand out quite a bit, sometimes they do a lot of things that are different ... That is, if people haven't studied conscientiously, then they don't have a good education. If they don't have a good family background either, then they can only earn money by selling their labour." The desire for upward mobility is expressed in different ways. GR 4 simply says, "Now I belong to the layer of peasants, struggling; I want to jump from this layer to the middle class." GR 8 envies the middle class and hopes that "... in the future, I could be part of the middle class." When asked how this upward mobility should be achieved, support from relatives is mentioned as a means (GR 13), as well as seizing opportunities (GR 17), recognising their (social) skills (GR 20), and above all, the idea that "all must rely on themselves (*kao ziji*)" (GR 21, GR 9).[36] Only very rarely did graduates identify the education and examination system or labour market asymmetries as structural problems beyond their control. Further research is needed to gain a deeper understanding of the more recent attitudes of educated migrants towards their employment status, opportunities and perceptions of fairness in the labour market.[37]

If we use the three indicators (income, occupation and education) and three strata (a core, a semi-core and a peripheral middle class) highlighted

---

[35] It should be mentioned that GR 12 is the only homeowner among the interviewees, with a middle-class family background and comparatively high income but living in an apartment in Shipai village provided by the employer.

[36] 靠自己.

[37] In July 2024, Ilaria Mazzocco and Scott Kennedy (2024) presented survey data collected by Martin K. Whyte (who has been observing China's "social volcano" for decades) and Scott Rozelle that suggested changing assessments of inequality in China, highlighting that respondents in 2023, compared to survey results in 2004 and 2014, were less willing to attribute success or failure to their individual shoulders and had less confidence in China's economic system and institutions in China than in previous decades. Unfortunately, without information about the 2023 sample, such as the demographic characteristics of the respondents, it is almost impossible to interpret these data, which have been widely reported in the international media.

by Li and Zhang (2008) to categorise middle-class belonging and make a rough assessment of the group of respondents, the following picture emerges: In terms of educational attainment, all respondents would be classified as belonging to the educated middle class. Some of the respondents who meet only this criterion would then be considered as belonging to the peripheral middle class. In terms of their occupation, some respondents can be classified as white-collar workers in the professional middle class and would therefore meet the criteria of the semi-core middle class. The income middle class (whose threshold is 5,000 yuan per month according to Li and Zhang, 2008) includes very few respondents. These exceptions could be counted as "core middle class" by meeting all three criteria. Comparing the sociologists' criteria with the respondents' self-positioning, it seems that the respondents underestimate the value of education (perhaps out of frustration that it hasn't paid off as expected) and tend to compare themselves with the expensive consumption and lifestyle habits of the upper middle class as propagated by the media and advertising. In particular, the social pressure to buy an apartment in the city seems to be a significant burden on respondents.

Expectations for the future

The graduates' visions of the future (which generally cover a period of about 5 years) provide an even clearer picture of how upward mobility is to be achieved. Three aspects stand out in the interviews: (1) future expectations in terms of a normative life versus self-realisation; (2) gender differences in evaluating future career and family options; and (3) attempts to stay in Guangzhou or move to lower-tier cities.

Becoming self-employed and/or taking up a managerial position are seen as opportunities to move up into the urban middle class. GR 4, who comes from a peasant family and now works as an architect, says, "I believe that a life's dream is closely linked to work. In this respect, I think I have two paths to choose from. As far as the subject is concerned, I could always go on like this, or I could go into administration/management.... If I joined a real estate company, I would no longer have to make design drawings, I would just manage." GR 8, who works as a sales engineer for water treatment plants, plans to start his own company in 5–10 years. His role model is the CEO of his company, who himself started out as an electrician. "Because I'm living on a salary now, I can't buy an apartment and it's very difficult to raise children. Only when I become self-employed, when I have saved something, will I be able to buy an apartment, get married and have children. Education is much too expensive now, and without the right savings, it is not possible."

The interviewees' expectations for the future are based either on a "normal" life, in which all the associated professional and family demands are fulfilled as far as possible, or on a life plan centred on individual self-realisation. While GR 6 and GR 8 struggle financially to achieve a "normal life," GR 23 rejects this path. He is an artist living and working in Xiaozhou village, whose interest lies in expressing himself through his paintings rather than living a "normal life." But he would rather live in Beijing, mainly because a friend told him that "in Beijing, people still see you as a human being, they still respect you, but in Guangdong, if you don't have money, people don't see you as a human being, for them art means nothing, especially in relation to those like us who don't work traditionally... ."

Male and female graduates show a clear difference in their prioritisation between earning money/having a career and family commitments/starting a family. GR 2, who is 24 years old, says that she will not start a family until she is 27: "I think if you get married at 24, right after graduation, then you won't have time to earn money to give to your own parents, and after you get married, you will have to take care of another family." GR 7 describes the life she wants to live as follows: "... I don't think it's really necessary to earn so much money. If I achieve that, I will be very happy, because I think it's true that if you don't have to worry about survival, your life is relatively good. If I work normally and go on holiday, I can enrich myself and then I will see my family again, go out and have fun, take part in some activities. I like that kind of life.... If I prepare well, I might try to become self-employed ... I have to rely on my own experience, I have to constantly develop and improve myself... My child should take part in some activities, practical ones, to improve its abilities. I hope it will have a happy life; it doesn't necessarily have to have the best grades." GR 6, who graduated from Guangzhou Sports University and now earns a living promoting credit cards, is not very optimistic about his future life: "Do you think you can buy an apartment with this salary (he earns 3,000 yuan a month)? If you can't buy an apartment, will anyone want you? I don't think so; an apartment is so important. If you want to start a family, everyone attaches importance to an apartment. When I think about this apartment, it scares me."

Stay in Guangzhou or move to a lower-tier city?

The respondents, who have generally not yet started their own families, are in a period of transition, both professionally and personally, which does not allow for definitive answers to the question of whether they want to stay in Guangzhou in the future. However, they clearly articulate their wishes, motives and feelings, including that they have developed a sense of belonging to the city of Guangzhou. Of the 28 respondents asked whether they could imagine moving to a second-tier city, seven said yes, eleven said no and the remaining ten were undecided. Of the seven respondents who could imagine a future in a second-tier city, four limited their answer to "later." The reasons for possibly leaving Guangzhou included environmental problems, climate and high population density, too much stress, and personal networks and family relationships.

The attractive features of Guangzhou mentioned by interviewees included its vibrant urban life (GR 2), career opportunities (GR 28), income levels and the feeling that "when you're here, it's like standing a little higher, having moved up to a higher place, like this" (GR 19). Guangzhou is often termed "tolerant"[38] (GR 16, 26, 29). As GR 29 describes it, "Guangzhou doesn't make you arrogant like other cities, all kinds of people can find their place in Guangzhou." GR 28 compares Guangzhou to Beijing and Shanghai: "Beijing is like a gentleman, Shanghai is like a noble young woman and Guangzhou is like a youth." GR 6, who studied in Guangzhou, says, "I've thought about going back to my hometown [in Guangdong], but I've lived here [in Guangzhou] for so long, my brothers and sisters are here, many of my family have come here, so I don't want to go back." What bothered him about Guangzhou were the high property prices and the high stress, "but in small cities, the cost of living is also very high. Of course, if you want to live a modest life, you can go back to a small place. But if you want more opportunities, it's better to live here.... If I leave, I'll have to start all over again. That's why I think it's not an option now." GR 24 focuses only on first-tier cities: "The advantage of first-tier cities and big cities is that there is more emphasis on one's own abilities. In small towns, you are completely dependent on *guanxi*. And compared to big cities, I think a place like Shanghai or especially Hong Kong could actually be better; a city made up entirely of

[38] 包容.

foreigners could be better. In this respect, Guangzhou still has a lot of local people." GR 24 indicated that he was considering moving to Shenzhen.

What ideas did political decision-makers rely on to provide answers to the situation of educated migrants? With college graduates already in great need of jobs in 2010, Lian, whose books on the *Yizu* had attracted considerable attention, suggested that the government should focus on second- and third-tier cities to create more job opportunities for graduates.[39] This recommendation was also linked to the idea of easing population pressure in fast-growing megacities. Subsequent media attention focused on the advantages of smaller cities in terms of lower living costs and more space for personal development (Wang, 2010). The media discourse indicated that some graduates at the time were influenced by these promises, but as it turned out, they quickly became returnees to the first-tier cities. Reasons given included a lack of social ties and networks in the smaller cities, insufficient job opportunities and lower social status (Chen and Xu, 2012). Based on the location preferences of rural graduates in Guangzhou, as presented above using some urban villages as examples, it can be assumed that another reason for the low attractiveness of smaller cities may be their lack of high-quality higher education institutions, including their socio-cultural environment.

In recent years, it has become clear that second- and third-tier cities, despite their lower housing costs, do not offer adequate attractions for graduates. This has led to the idea of the "new first-tier cities" *xin yixian chengshi*, i.e. other first-tier cities besides Beijing, Shanghai, Guangzhou and Shenzhen (*Bei-Shang-Guang-Shen*).[40] As part of its New Urbanisation Plan (2014–2020), the central government called on local governments to reform their *hukou* systems to make migrants eligible for social benefits. Cities then began to compete for qualified workers, including college graduates. Guangdong province expanded its point-based *hukou* policy introduced in 2010 (see Wang, 2020:281; Gransow, 2012:23, 24).

More recently, policies to attract highly skilled manpower have focused not only on the needs of companies and industrial estates but also

---

[39] Graduates, migrants are failing to bridge the skill gap, in *China Daily*, March 5, 2010.

[40] 新一线城市. Mainly for commercial reasons, the Chinese financial media outlet Yicai is publishing a yearly ranking of 15 "new first-tier cities," including Chengdu at the top, followed by Hangzhou or Chongqing, Wuhan, Nanjing, Xi'an and other cities; this list is not to be confused with the official administrative ranking of Chinese cities.

on attracting young people to balance the ageing population in larger cities. City authorities expect that an influx of young people will increase the demand for housing and thus push up property prices. This, in turn, would mean higher revenues for local governments, which derive 60–70% of their income from land revenue, enabling them to afford social services for their elderly residents (Li and Pei, 2020). While these new policies aim to ease the flow of talent across the country, it is questionable whether they will actually attract graduates to second- and third-tier cities. Some of the new talent policies in Guangdong province aim to provide more housing for graduates. In addition to smaller cities such as Zhuhai, Guangzhou's inner-city district governments, such as the Huangpu district government, appear to be involved in this race to attract talented young people without local household registration, who would be allowed to buy apartments after working in the district for six months (Qiu, 2020). With economic policies focusing on information technology and the development of artificial intelligence, competition and related policy initiatives among local governments in the PRD are expected to continue.

Conclusion

The real estate-driven growth of Guangzhou as an entrepreneurial city is leading not only to a decrease in affordable housing due to ongoing redevelopment of the urban villages but also to rising rents in the remaining villages. Nevertheless, urban villages in Guangzhou continue to provide affordable housing for both blue-collar and highly educated migrants. But the latter differ from the former in their clear preference for urban villages in the vicinity of a university campus. Based on practical, educational, recreational, cultural, lifestyle and/or emotional reasons, this preference is a characteristic of the rural graduates' agency and perspectives, in short, their production of urban spaces. The subjective meaning of housing in an urban village can be quite different for individual rural graduates. While for many it is simply a place to sleep at night, without any social relations within the neighbourhood except perhaps with the landlord, for others such as young artists, an urban village like Xiaozhou is not only a popular art space but also a place to build social networks and careers.

Rural graduates' upwardly mobile expectations along their paths from village and primary school to megacity and university are marked by the experience of making decisions early on and relying on themselves in the process. In the interviews, this is repeatedly expressed as "you have to rely on yourself" (*ni yinggai kao ziji*).[41] The interviewees also interpret the obstacles they face in the job search and at work primarily as deficiencies in their own qualifications and experience. The assumption is widespread that these obstacles can be overcome by gathering more experience and by self-optimisation. Respondents seem reluctant or unwilling to attribute individual success or failure to a higher education system that offers limited opportunities for individual choice in subject combinations or professional fulfilment in the subjects studied. However, such structural factors may contribute to hindering their upward social mobility into the urban middle class. The strict hierarchy of educational institutes, for example, which is closely linked to the hierarchy of cities, is reflected in employers' recruitment criteria, which in turn put talented young people and especially female graduates from rural backgrounds at a disadvantage. The societal imperative to own an apartment before starting a family gives not a few highly educated male migrants sleepless nights. In sum, the threshold to the middle class becomes ever higher and can be crossed only by a small number of rural graduates.

Despite the increasingly tough employment prospects, high property prices and growing shortage of affordable housing, Guangzhou is a popular city for highly educated migrants. The willingness of highly educated migrants to move to smaller towns and cities is generally low. An exception is the return to their place of origin. Precisely for those who wish to "move up" to the major cities (as GR 19 put it), these cities have many attractions: not only higher wages but also factors such as professional opportunities, professional peers, cultural offerings, opportunities for personal development and comparatively tolerant atmospheres. Urbanisation and migration policies that seek to spread highly educated migrants across smaller cities have been unsuccessful for years. Whether the creative construction of a category of "new first-tier cities" can provide a way forward here remains to be seen. In its favour at least is the fact that nearly all the candidate cities are also the sites of leading institutes of higher education.

---

[41] 你应该靠自己.

Appendix

List of in-depth interviews with rural–urban graduates in Guangzhou (August–December, 2011)

Graduate interview no.	Sex	Age	Hometown	Type of company	Study/ profession
GR 1	Male	24	Foshan, Guangdong	Private company	History/office work
GR 2	Female	24	Heyuan, Guangdong	Private company	Accountant
GR 3	Male	28	Guangxi	Foreign company producing stickers	Technical customer service
GR 4	Male	26	Meizhou, Guangdong	Private company	Architect
GR 5	Male	27	Zhanjiang, Guangdong	Private company	Financial business
GR 6	Male	28	Shanwei, Guangdong	Joint venture	Credit card promotion
GR 7	Female	24	Zhaoqing, Guangdong	Private company	Sales and marketing
GR 8	Male	26	Heyuan, Guangdong	Private company	Technical engineer
GR 9	Female	22	Shaoguan, Guangdong	Joint venture	Credit card promotion
GR 10	Male	24	Anhui	Private company	ATM sales
GR 11	Male	24	Chuzhou, Anhui	Private company	Assistant engineer
GR 12	Male	26	Henan	Joint venture	Sales manager
GR 13	Male	23	Jiangsu	Unemployed	Human resources
GR 14	Male	24	Guilin, Guangxi	Private	Veterinarian
GR 15	Male	24	Hengyang, Hunan	Private	Computer sales

GR 16	Male	27	Yangjiang, Guangdong	Joint venture	Stock market sales
GR 17	Male	24	Zhanjiang, Guangdong	University	Administrative staff
GR 18	Male	–	Chaozhou, Guangdong	Newspaper	Sales
GR 19	Male	–	Yangjiang, Guangdong	Private company	Welding
GR 20	Female	23	Jiamusi, Helongjiang	Private company	Customer service
GR 21	Male	23	Jinan, Shandong	Private company	Customer service
GR 22	Female	23	Xingning, Guangdong	Private company	Customer service
GR 23	Male	28	Zhanjiang, Guangdong	Public institution	Exhibition coordinator
GR 24	Male	25	Yantai, Shandong	Private company	Private asset manager
GR 25	Male	–	Maoming, Guangdong	Private company	Human resources
GR 26	Male	24	Wuzhou, Guangxi	Private company	Architect
GR 27	Female	22	Meizhou, Guangzhou	Private company	Human resources
GR 28	Male	24	Jilin province	Private company	Architect
GR 29	Male	27	Huaihua, Hunan	Public institution	Architect
GR 30	Male	23	Shantou, Guangdong	Educational organisation	Training

References

Cabinet. (2020). Cabinet addresses job market pressure. Measures to expand postgraduate enrollment and employment channels for migrant workers, *China Daily*, March 3.

Cartier, C. (2013). Class, consumption and the economic restructuring of consumer space, in Chen, M. and Goodman, D. S. G. (eds.), *Middle-Class China. Identity and Behaviour*, Cheltenham: Edward Elgar, pp. 34–53.

Chan, W. K. 陈永杰 (2012). *Student Poverty in China: How to Assist Students from Disadvantaged Backgrounds*, Saarbrücken: Lambert Academic Publishing.

Chen, X. (2011a). Cities asked to help grads obtain Hukou, *China Daily*, June 3.

Chen, X. (2011b). Fewer grads taking test for government job. Stricter assessments and more career options cited as reasons, *China Daily*, October 26.

Chen, X. (2012a). Grads should take blue-collar work, *China Daily*, July 24.

Chen, X. (2012b). Civil service jobs harder than they look, *China Daily*, October 16.

Chen, X. and Xu, J. (2012). Graduates find first-tier cities still appealing, *China Daily*, September 18.

Chen, Y. 陈永杰 (2011). 大学生就业能力与社会不流动 Daxuesheng jiuye nengli yu shehui bu liudong (Employment capacity and social immobility of college students), 武汉大学学报 Wuhan daxue xuebao (*Wuhan University Journal*) 64(3), 081–089.

Chen, Z. 陈智钰 (2019). 突破边缘: "蚁族" 的现状及路径分析Tupo bianyuan: "Yizu" de xianzhuang ji lujing fenxi (Break the edge: Analysis of the situation and path of the "Ant tribe", 智库时代 Zhiku Shidai (*Think Tank Era*) 27, 9–10.

Circular. (2019). Circular of Ministry of Human Resources and Social Security, the Ministry of Education and nine other Departments on further regulating recruitment behavior to promote women's employment 中华人民共和国人力资源和社会保障部, 教育部等九部门关于进一步规范招聘行为促进妇女就业的通知, February 21, 2019.

Dasgupta, S., Matsumoto, M., and Xia, C. (2015). *Women in the Labour Market in China*. ILO Asia-Pacific Working Paper Series, May.

Du, Q. (2023). China's 2024 national civil servant exams begin with candidates, vacancies hitting record high, *Global Times*, 26 November.

Fan, F. (2014), Recent graduates lower expectations in tight job market, *China Daily*, July 3.

Feng, S., Lu, J., Terada-Hagiwara, A. and Qi, W. (2023). A closer look at causes of youth unemployment in the People's Republic of China. *ADB Briefs* 247 (June).

Goodman, D. S. G. (2014). Middle class China: Dreams and aspirations, *Journal of Chinese Political Science* 19, 49–67.

Gransow, B. (2012), Contested urbanization in China: Exploring informal spaces of migrants-in-the-city, *Harvard Asia Quarterly* XIV(1&2), 12–24.

Gu, C., Sheng, M., and Hu, L. (2015). Spatial characteristics and new changes of the "Ant tribe" urban village in Beijing: Case studies of Tangjialing and Shigezhuang, in Wong, T.-C., Han, S. S., and Zhang, H. (eds.), *Population Mobility, Urban Planning and Management in China*, Cham: Springer International Publishing.

Guiheux, G. and Zalio, P.-P. (2010). White-collar migrants in coastal Chinese cities. Entrepreneurs of their professional careers, *China Perspectives* 4, 48–58.

He, N. (2013). Graduates face grim hunt for work. Jobs: Graduates face high degree of hardship, *China Daily*, July 3.

He, S. (2015). Consuming urban living in 'villages in the city': Studentification in Guangzhou, China, *Urban Studies* 52(5), 2849–2873.

He, Y. and Mai, Y. (2015). Higher education expansion in China and the 'Ant Tribe' problem, in *Higher Education Policy* 28, 333–352.

Holbig, H. and Neckel, S. (2016). Negative classifications and the symbolic order of social inequality: evidence from East Asia, *Critical Asian Studies* 48(3), 400–421.

Hu, C. 胡春明 (2017). 大学生"蚁族"现象的教育社会学探析 Daxuesheng "Yizu" xianxiang de jiaoyu shehuixue tanxi (The phenomenon of college students "Ant tribe" from the perspective of sociology of education), 陕西师范大学学报 (*Journal of Shaanxi Normal University*) 46(1), 163–170.

Jiang, C. (2018). Jobs grow at steady pace during Q1-3, *China Daily*, October 26.

Lan, Y. (2005). Urban village community: A case study concerning the mode of urbanization of peasants and their lifestyles, *Social Sciences in China* (Autumn), 27–40.

Li, C. (2013). The heterogeneous composition and multiple identities of China's middle class, in Li, P., Gorshkov, M. K., and Scalon, M. (eds.), *Handbook on Social Stratification in the BRIC Countries: Change and Perspective*, Singapore: World Scientific, pp. 395–417.

Li, C. (ed.) (2021). The reversal of gender balance in education, and its challenges, in *China's Youth. Increasing Diversity amid Persistent Inequality*, Washington, DC: The Brookings Institution, pp. 177–190.

Li, P. 李培林and Zhang, Y. 张翼 (2008). 中国中产阶级的规模,认同和社会态度 Zhongguo zhongchan jieji de guimo, renting he shehui taidu (The scope, identity and social attitudes of the Chinese middle class), 社会 (*Society*) 28(2), 1–19.

Li, R. 李若建 (2009). 广州市外来白领群体现状分析 Guangzhou shi wailai bailing qunti xianzhuang fenxi ("Urban white-collar group": Analysis on Guangzhou population data), 中国人口科学 Zhongguo renkou kexue (*Chinese Population Science*) 2, 84–92.

Li, X. 李霞 (2011). 广州 „蚁族" 聚居区分布与规划对策研究 - 以天河区棠下村 "蚁族" 聚居区为例 Guangzhou "Yizu" jujuqu fenbu yu guihua duice yanjiu – yi Tianhe qu Tangxia cun jujuqu wei li (*Research on Distribution and Planning Strategies of Concentrated "Ant Tribe" Communities in Guangzhou – A Case Study of Tangxia Village in Tianhe District*). MA Thesis, Department of Geography and Planning, Sun Yat-Sen University.

Li, X. 李曦 and Jing, G. 井国兰 (2019). 浅析大学生 "蚁族" 群体思政教育现状 Qianxi daxuesheng "Yizu" qunti sizheng jiaoyu xianzhuang (Analysis of the status quo of ideological and political education of the "Ant tribe" students), 锦州医科大学学报 Jinzhou yike daxue xuebao (*Journal of Jinzhou Medical University*) 17(5), 98–101.

Li, Y. and Pei, P. (2020). Dream cities versus urban legends, *China Daily*, June 26.

Lian, S. 廉思 (ed.) (2009). 蚁族. 大学毕业生聚居村实录Yizu. *Daxue biyesheng jujucun shilu* (*Ant Tribe. Records of College Graduates Inhabiting a Village*), Guilin: Guangxi Normal University Press.

Lian, S. 廉思 (2010). 蚁族 II. 谁的时代? Yizu II. *Shui de shidai?* (*Ant Tribe II. Whose Era?*), Beijing: CITIC Publishing Group.

Lian, S. 廉思 (ed.) (2013). 中国青年发展报告Zhongguo qingnian fazhan baogao (The development report on Chinese youth 2013) 1, 城市新移民的崛起*Chengshi xin yimin de jueqi* (*The Rise of New Urban Immigrants*). Blue Book of Youth, Beijing: Social Sciences Academic Press.

Liang, S. Y. (2010). Property-driven urban change in post-socialist Shanghai: Reading the television series *Woju*, *Journal of Current Chinese Affairs* 4, 3–28.

Liang, Y. and Zhang, H. (2020). Survey report on the social middle class in Beijing, Shanghai and Guangzhou, in Li, P., Chen, G., and Zhang, Y. (eds.), *Chinese Research Perspectives on Society: Analysis and Forecast of China's Social Conditions (2016) (5)*, Leiden: Brill, pp. 231–265.

Lu, C. (2013). China's middle class: Unified or fragmented? *Japanese Journal of Political Science* 14(1), 127–150.

Mazzocco, I. and Kennedy, S. (2024). Is it me or the economic system? Changing evaluations of inequality in China, available at https://bigdatachina.csis.org/is-it-me-or-the-economic-system-changing-evaluations-of-inequality-in-china/ (accessed August 12, 2024).

McCartney, M. (2024). China's economic woes deepen with sky-high youth unemployment. *Newsweek*, August 21.

Miao, Y. (2017). *Being Middle Class in China. Identity, Attitudes and Behavior*, London: Routledge.

Mycos Research Institute. 麦可思研究院 (2012). 2012 年中国大学生就业报告 2012 nian Zhongguo daxuesheng jiuye baogao (*Chinese College Graduates Employment Annual Report* (2012). Blue Book of Employment, Beijing: Social Sciences Academic Press.

Qian, J., He, S., and Lin, L. (2013). Aestheticisation, rent-seeking, and rural gentrification amidst China's rapid urbanization: The case of Xiaozhou village, Guangzhou, *Journal of Rural Studies* 32, 331–345.

Qin, S. (2010). Creative country. The booming art scene in Guangzhou's Xiaozhou village, *That's PRD* 2010, 14–15.

Qiu, Q. (2020). Guangdong offers more housing to help graduates, *China Daily*, December 16.

Qu, Y. (2023). Down-to-earth approach vital for job-seeking graduates, *China Daily*, 7 March.

Rajan, I. (2016). High-skilled migration, in Triandafyllidou, A. (ed.), *Routledge Handbook of Immigration and Refugee Studies*, London: Routledge, pp. 88–95.

Resolution (2024). *Resolution of the Central Committee of the Communist Party of China on Further Deepening Reform Comprehensively to Advance Chinese Modernization* (Adopted at the third plenary session of the 20th Central Committee of the Communist Party of China on July 18, 2024), available at https://english.www.gov.cn/policies/latestreleases/202407/21/content_WS669d0255c6d0868f4e8e94f8.html (accessed September 5, 2024)

Rocca, J.-L. (2017a). *The Making of the Chinese Middle Class. Small Comfort and Great Expectation*, New York: Palgrave Macmillan.

Rocca, J.-L. (2017b). Governing from the middle? Understanding the making of China's middle classes, in Shue, V. and Thornton, P. M. (eds.), *To Govern China. Evolving Practices of Power*, Cambridge: Cambridge University Press, pp. 231–255.

Shao, R. 邵任薇, Zhang, Y. 张俨, and Wu, Y. 吴映霖 (2018). 城市更新中的文化保护与整合再生 – 以广州市恩宁路和小洲村改造为例 Chengshi gengxin zhong de wenhua baohu yu zhenghe zaisheng – yi Guangzhou shi Enninglu he Xiaozhou cun gaizao wei li (Cultural protection and integrated regeneration in urban renewal – taking Enninglu Road and Xiaozhou Villages as examples in Guangzhou), 广州公共管理评论 Guangzhou gonggong guanli pinglun (*Guangzhou Public Administration Review*) 6, 203–216.

Smith, D. (2005). 'Studentification': the gentrification factory? In Rowland, A. and Bridge, G. (eds.), *Gentrification in a Global Context: The New Urban Colonialism,* London: Routledge, pp. 73–90.

Suda, K. (2021). *Das Phänomen ‚Yizu' (蚁族): Migrantische Hochschulabsolvent*innen als Chinas Wendepunktgeneration? Eine ethnografische und wissenssoziologische Fallstudie*, Berlin: Transkript.

Tjia, L. Y.-N. and Ho, W.-C. (2018). *Beipiao* and *gangpiao*: Young Chinese migrants' drifting experiences in Beijing and Hong Kong, in Chan, Y. W. and Koh, S. Y. (eds.), *New Chinese Migrations. Mobility, Home and Inspirations*, London: Routledge, pp. 144–155.

Wang, H. (2010). "Ant tribe" should try luck in smaller cities, *China Daily*, August 19.

Wang, J. and Davis, D. (2010). China's new upper middle classes: the importance of occupational disaggregation, in Li, C. (ed.), *China's Emerging Middle Class. Beyond Economic Transformation*, Washington, D.C.: Brookings Institution Press.

Wang, Q. (2019). Civil service exam highlights political quality, moral conduct, *Global Times*, October 15.

Wang, Q. (2020). China revises policy on curbing 'gaokao migration' to make higher education fairer, *Global Times*, June 10.

Wang, X. 王晓霞 (2019). 大学生职业生涯规划目标可实现性研究 – 基于大学生"蚁族"产生原因分析 Daxuesheng zhiye shengya guihua mubiao ke shixianxing yanjiu – jiyu daxuesheng "Yizu" chansheng yuanyin fenxi (Research on the achievability of college students' career planning goals – based on an analysis of the causes that generated college students' "Ant Tribe"). 现代商贸工业 Xiandai shangmao gongye (*Modern Business Trade Industry*) 5, 66–67.

Wang, X. (2020). Permits, points, and permanent household registration: Recalibrating Hukou policy under "Top-level design", in Alpermann, B. (ed.), Special Issue: China's rural–urban transformation: New forms of inclusion and exclusion, *Journal of Current Chinese Affairs* 49(3), 269–290.

Yang, Y. (2020). Guangzhou most favorite city for college grads in China, *China Daily*, July 5.

Yu, A. 于安龙 (2017). "空巢青年" 现象：表现、成因与认知态度 "Kongchao qingnian" xianxiang: biaoxian, chengyin yu renzhi taidu (The "empty nest youth" phenomenon: performance, causes and cognitive attitudes), 前沿 *Qianyan Forward Position* 7, 78–82.

Zacharias, J., Hu, Y., and Huang, Q. (2013). Morphology and spatial dynamics of urban villages in Guangzhou's CBD, *Urban Studies Research*, http://dx.doi.org/10.1155/2013/958738.

Zacharias, J. and Lei, Y. (2016). Villages at the urban fringe – The social dynamics of Xiaozhou, *Journal of Rural Studies* 47, 650–656.

Zhang, E. and Zaharia, M. (2023). Chinese graduates hold off career dreams, take temporary government jobs, *Reuters*, 14 November, https://www.reuters.com/world/china/chinese-graduates-hold-off-career-dreams-take-temporary-government-jobs-2023-11-14/ (accessed April 21, 2024).

Zhang, L. (2010). *In Search of Paradise. Middle Class Living in a Chinese Metropolis*, Ithaca: Cornell University Press.

Zhao, Y. and Cheng, S. (2024). Youth employment to get further boost, *China Daily*, March 11.

Zhao-Ciupak, Y. (2016). *On the Nexus of Local and Global: Chinese Higher Education and College Students in the Era of Globalization* (*Issues in Globalization and Social Justice*), Norwalk: AMS Press.

Zhou, W. (2019). Recruiters more likely to view resumes from male job seekers, *China Daily*, August 26.

Zhou, X. 周晓虹 (2005).中国中产阶级调查 *Zhongguo zhongchan jieji diaocha* (*Survey of the Chinese Middle Classes*), Beijing: Social sciences Academic Press.

Zhou, X. (2008). Chinese middle class: Reality or illusion? In Veer, P. and Jaffrelot, C. (eds.), *Patterns of Middle Class Consumption in India and China*, London: Sage Publication, pp. 110–126.

Zhu, H. 朱慧劼 and Feng, X. 风笑天 (2018). 网络形象与概念反思: 对 „空巢青年"的再审视 Wangluo xingxiang yu gainian fansi: dui „kongchao qingnian" de zaishenshi (Internet image and conceptual reflections: Revisiting the "Empty nest youth". 青年探索 *Qingnian tansuo (Youth Exploration)* 2, 77–84.

Chapter 7

Responding to Resettlement Space in Unexpected Ways: A Relocated "Village" from the Three Gorges Area in Foshan City

"You think you're being resettled to a metropolis, and then you see that there's a lot of garbage lying around and you yourself have to take care of removing it."

"It's still the same. Ten years have passed but you only know the people in the village."

Introduction

As part of the resettlement waves from the Three Gorges Dam project (TGP) area, forty households comprising 134 people arrived at Foshan in the Pearl River Delta (PRD) in August 2001. Two rows of newly built houses were waiting for them. On their way down to South China, they had been accompanied by leading cadres of various ranks and regions. Along with media coverage and state propaganda, this gave the group being displaced from the Three Gorges to a distant location the sense of being special and of being heroes who were sacrificing their small personal homes for their big national homeland (*she xiaojia, wei dajia*).[1] The discourse that constructed the displaced persons as both heroes

[1] 舍小家，为大家.

and victims was shared by the local government on the receiving end, which felt not only an administrative obligation but also compassion and commitment for the newcomers.

In contrast to voluntary migrant workers, the resettlers were entitled to support from local host societies. The rationale behind the government's distant resettlement scheme was the following: Displaced people should be moved to the regions in the middle and downstream catchments of the Yangtze River benefitting from the TGP and to economically developed provinces such as Guangdong (Tan, 2008:87, 97; State Council, 2001:5, §17). The resettlers were considered to deserve their share of the local host society's resources. Soon after arriving at their final destination in South China's Foshan city in the PRD, at a place called Baicun Resettlement Village,[2] the newcomers were given a piece of land, newly built houses and other resources to compensate for their losses. But as it turned out, the resettlers did not simply absorb the designations ascribed to them by the local host government but responded in unanticipated ways (see Watters, 2013:105).

Given that the PRD is a rapidly developing region that could provide significant economic opportunities for people displaced by the TGP, and given that the local Baizhen[3] government has made a concerted effort to manage the risks and address the needs of project-affected people, the focus of this chapter is on the question of why the Baicun Resettlement Village has nevertheless become a "problem space." In order to answer this question, it will be examined how the group of people resettled from the TGP area, who became the Baicun villagers, contextualised and appropriated the resettlement space provided to them over a period of more than ten years. The chapter looks at the coping strategies developed by the villagers, the contestation of space that resulted from their agency, the urban spaces they produced and more generally the informal dynamics set in motion at the micro level by this newly established resettlement village in Foshan city.

While research on dam resettlement in China in general and on the TGP in particular[4] has increased over the years, there are very few

[2]The actual name of the village has been altered to Baicun in this chapter to preserve the privacy of the residents.

[3]Baizhen is not the real name of the local town.

[4]Heggelund (2004), Li (2000), Ying (2011, 2013, 2016), Tan (2008), Padovani (2016), Habich-Sobiegalla (2016) and on distant relocation Zhou *et al.* (2011), Liu and Wu (2016).

longitudinal studies on the impact of displacement.[5] Of special note is the anthropological research by Cheng on life in Baicun Village during the early years of resettlement (Cheng, 2006; Cheng and He, 2006). It provided the background for this chapter and a rich baseline for preparing, understanding and interpreting the 26 in-depth interviews conducted in August and September 2012 with members of Baicun Village, this time as part of a broader research programme on rural-to-urban migrant communities and the informal dynamics of megacity development in the PRD.[6]

The analysis here is informed by relational sociological approaches to the production of social space, as presented in the introductory Chapter 1. It seeks to understand how a group of persons displaced from the TGP shared, created, used and negotiated the resettlement space they received from the local host government. The focus is on the perception, appropriation and use of resettlement space. While a use-centred view of the sociology of space as suggested by Herbert Gans (2002) has been criticised for its limitations,[7] when combined with the classical study by Henri Lefebvre on the production of space (1991), it seems to be an adequate and fruitful approach to a deeper understanding of resettlement space. As a springboard for the analysis of the interview material, it reveals that the respective perceptions and normative frameworks of the resettlement space differed widely between the group of displaced people and the local host government and society.

To better contextualise the understanding and agency of these main actors and their different perceptions of the resettlement space, this analysis also uses the concept of moral economy. In essence, this concept stands for economic modes that are based on moral values and reciprocal support in peasant communities. It has been elaborated by E.P. Thompson in the context of food riots in the eighteenth-century English countryside where peasants saw a traditional "fair" price as more legitimate than the market price and as justification for bread rebellions (Thompson, 1971).

---

[5]Exceptions are studies by Wilmsen (2016), Wilmsen and van Hulten (2017), Gransow (2021) and Rousseau (2021).

[6]The interviews were conducted as part of the research project "Patterns of migrant community formation in China's mega-urban PRD – linking informal dynamics, governability and global change" (2011–2012). See interview list at the end of the chapter. More details on the project and its broader research programme framework can be found in the introductory Chapter 1.

[7]See replies to Gans in *City and Community* 1(4), 2002.

Later, James Scott took up the concept (Scott, 1976) with regard to Southeast Asian peasant society and emphasised the role of shared moral values, group solidarity and collective practices in avoiding subsistence crises for all villagers. This perspective was challenged by Samuel Popkin who presented the Asian peasant as an economically rational agent motivated by private interest (Little, 1989:29).

Following these classical studies, the concept of moral economy was taken up in China studies by scholars of contentious politics. O'Brien and Li highlight both overlapping (sincerity in acting out of conviction) and diverging (from policy-based resistance) elements with their influential concept of "rightful resistance" in the context of rural contention in China (O'Brien and Li, 2006:XII,23). Tilt (2015) used the concept of moral economy with a focus on water management decisions in China's Yunnan province. He analyses the strategies of social interest groups and the normative choices that must be made when various economic, environmental and social objectives come into conflict, and how these groups advance different moral visions about how water resources should be managed (Tilt, 2015:XII). Ying Xing, who has done extensive empirical research on petitioning and collective actions in the TGP area, discusses the idea of moral economy in relation to the Chinese concept of vigour (*qi*),[8] which he sees as suited to bridge the opposition between sense and sensitivity, and rights and emotions, in the study of contentious politics (Ying 2013:12–13). Most stimulating for this chapter was also a paper by Watters (2013), who built on Thompson's work on mediaeval notions of the "deserving" poor in England and thereby broadened the understanding of moral economy as inherently linked to ideas of "deserving" and "undeserving." Watters applied the concept of moral economy to the field of forced migration, particularly to the figures of the refugee, the asylum seeker and the voluntary migrant as well as to the associated narratives of "deserving" and "undeserving" (Watters, 2013:104–105).

This chapter has three parts and a conclusion. Part 1 examines the experience of displacement of a group of resettled people from the Three Gorges area and their first encounters, bodily perceptions and impressions of the resettlement site with its unfamiliar environment. Part 2 analyses the perception and uses of resettlement space by the newcomers from the Three Gorges (based on the village, their houses, the land, and social

[8] 气.

spaces and social networks beyond their resettlement village and former hometowns). Part 3 starts with an introduction to the government-organised distant resettlement scheme as a specific approach in the TGP based on a broader legal, political and administrative framework. It then zooms in on the relevant policies of the local governments of Foshan city (including lower administrative levels), their efforts to act as responsible and effective hosts, and their subsequent disappointment at grassroots (administrative) responses by the host village and at the "ungratefulness" and dissatisfaction on the part of the resettlement villagers – all of which highlight the moral economy of the official resettlement policy and its administrative implementation. The conclusion reflects on the enduring isolation of Baicun Resettlement Village, the shattered promise of an urban lifestyle, and the loss of social status and identity, undermining the slight increase in living standards.

"Voluntary" Resettlement from the Three Gorges Area: Encountering the Unknown

The group of Baicun resettlers from Wushan's mountainous regions came from urban and peri-urban areas. Although their household registrations listed them as rural, they lived in the vicinity of the Wushan county seat on the banks of Yangtze. Tourism had risen strongly in Wushan with the advent of reform policies. Many Baicun resettlers had lived right next to the county seat and the tourism industry was their main source of income. The families generally set up stands in front of their homes or opened small shops with local specialties or souvenirs. If they had the right education, some worked as guides, which could earn them several thousand yuan a month. Hardly anyone worked in the fields. Some grew a few vegetables and sold them in the city. But they had very little land per capita on steep slopes that were hard to cultivate and in an area of otherwise high population density. Regardless of what they actually did, however, in formal terms they were considered peasants (Cheng, 2006:98).

Two types of rural settings have been identified in the TGP: purely rural agrarian areas and mixed peri-urban agricultural zones. According to Tan Yan and Wang Yiqian, this implies significant differences in agricultural production, income sources, land-use types and the perception of displacement and resettlement. But people living in the peri-urban zones of a city or town were compensated and resettled like other rural residents (Tan and Wang, 2003:35–36). The criterion was the rural household registration of these families and not their occupation, sources of income or lifestyles.

Leaving the Three Gorges Dam Area, Chongqing

RS 2, a 35-year-old resettlement villager, told us about her previous situation in Wushan county, Chongqing municipality: "I used to live in the county seat. I had a rural *hukou*, no work and no land. We were called peasants, but we weren't peasants. We were city dwellers even though we weren't called city dwellers." RS 7, a 52-year-old resettler, said, "We used to live in a district of the city .... Since I left school, I was always in the city - life, work, everything was comfortable." RS 20, a 49-year-old resettler who works as a security coordinator, described the situation in similar terms: "Our house was in the city centre even though we had a rural *hukou*. We were [on] the banks of the Yangtze, very close. The urban people were moved to the back [to new development areas behind the city], while the rural people were moved far away. I didn't want to leave either."

The interviewees generally stated that they had come voluntarily to Foshan, especially because it is in an economically developed region. Some of them already had experience as migrant workers in the PRD; others simply hoped for higher income levels or better educational opportunities for their children. They had also gotten the chance to visit their future location beforehand. They would not have been required to move there, but the voluntary aspect of the choice had to do with the location of resettlement and not with the fact of resettlement itself. RS 11, a 34-year-old resettlement villager, said, "We came voluntarily to Guangdong [province]; we also could have chosen not to come. At that time, we thought it's the same everywhere, you have to rely on yourself. And the state had this policy, everything would have become hard for us, the water would have covered everything a few years later. A new city was built, but we weren't able to buy an apartment then. Those considerations were what led us to decide to come here." This explains why the Baicun resettlers repeatedly confirmed that they came to South China voluntarily, yet at the same time said that they didn't want to leave their homes at all and would have greatly preferred to stay there.

These conflicting points of view were reinforced by intensive persuasive efforts by local resettlement cadres in Wushan, which generated a certain pressure, especially on party members, to make the commitment voluntarily. RS 14, a 45-year-old female resettler, remembered, "At the time I didn't want to come here at all, no one did. But then there was this resettlement office, which was responsible for resettlement, and they kept trying to convince us with ideological arguments. [They said that] if they tried to convince us three times without a result, then they would take measures. No idea what measures they wanted to take, but at any rate it wasn't possible not to come here (*feilai buke*).[9] People had lived there so long, they basically also didn't want to go; everything was so familiar, everyone had grown up there, people didn't want to go, to a strange place, people didn't want to go, that's what they thought."

Arrival in Foshan: Bodily perceptions

A new space is first perceived by means of one's body. "When 'Ego' arrives in an unknown country or city, he first experiences it through every part of his body – through his senses of smell and taste, as (…) through his legs and feet. His hearing picks up the noises and the quality of the voices, his eyes are assailed by new impressions. For it is by means of the body that space is perceived, lived – and produced" (Lefebvre, 1991:162). The first thing to be perceived is the immediate environment and how it differs from familiar space. For the resettlers from the mountainous areas on the Yangtze, this first meant the unfamiliar climate, the food, physical reactions and tense moods. Above all, they did not understand Cantonese, and it was not always possible to communicate with locals in Standard Chinese.

To avoid having to eat non-spicy Guangdong cuisine, the resettlers brought sufficient ingredients to make their own Sichuan dishes. Because they did their own cooking, this should not have been a problem. But the climate in subtropical Guangdong is very different from that in their mountainous home region of Wushan. That not only required bodily adaptations but also had an effect on their nutritional habits because they could not necessarily tolerate their usual food like they had at home. RS 14

[9] 非来不可.

remembered, "I've become used to the food, and I no longer eat as much chili. At home it didn't matter how much chili we ate, we never got pustules from it. Here you just have to eat chili once and you'll get them."

Stomach troubles, particularly in the male population and probably often due to psychological factors, were one of the main illnesses in Baicun. RS 4 said, "My husband just went to the hospital to have his stomach examined. His stomach is not doing very well. You know, the things we eat here are all chemical products. What we eat is not good for the body." Whether the increased incidence of stomach problems had psychological reasons or was due to unsuitable food does not change the fact that the body, in its organs or on its skin, was reacting to the new environment. Simply going out and eating at the nearest small restaurant, as they had done at home, was no longer an option around Baicun. This all served to strengthen the resettlers' impression that they had exchanged their vibrant urban environment for a rural area, where they were now supposed to live in a village community. Everything was mixed up – especially when one considers that in formal terms, they were supposed to be farmers who had been relocated to an economically developed urban region like the PRD.

There were also an increasing number of injuries due especially to motorcycle accidents. Nearly every resettler household had brought a motorcycle to Guangdong or had purchased a new one upon arrival. Accustomed to mountain roads back at home, they had less experience with traffic lights and rules. It was difficult for them to get used to traffic conditions in the PRD, which led to an ongoing series of accidents. That in turn prompted a number of misunderstandings. The locals thought the resettlers could not be poor if they could afford motorcycles. They also assumed the newcomers had rather low levels of education if they couldn't even learn the traffic regulations. As for the resettlers, some of them thought that the locals involved them deliberately in accidents in order to make their lives more difficult (Peng and Feng, 2015:37, 38).

RS 14 talks about her husband, who had multiple accidents. "My husband had several motorcycle accidents here; it wouldn't have taken much for him to be dead … It was always other people who bumped into him, or hit him and then ran away, and no one ended up finding them. For his first accident, he had to go to the hospital and we had to pay more than 60,000 yuan, that was in the second half of 2001. At that time, the government provided jobs for us in factories and my husband started to work in a ceramic factory then, … the accident happened that year, and since then, his body has not been in good shape." The resettlers were clearly more vulnerable both physically and psychologically. Their self-confidence, which had risen with the move to Guangdong and the associated official recognition and praise for their contribution to the success of this major and prestigious national project, increasingly began to wane.

In retrospect, the first 1–2 years after arriving in Guangdong are described by the resettlers as the most difficult period, in which they experienced multiple situations of shock. RS 20 said, "The first step was very hard. You think you're being resettled to a metropolis, and then you see that there's a lot of garbage lying around and you yourself have to take care of removing it." The new location was considered remote, and the county seat was 10 kilometres away. RS 15, a 45-year-old housewife, explained, "At the beginning everything outside was full of fish ponds, there wasn't a single factory. Now things are better." Although the original land-for-land idea consisted of giving displaced farmers a basis for their lives again, social security and a source of income commensurate with their previous activities and qualifications, land-for-land resettlement for people from the peri-urban areas in Wushan meant moving to a desolate, newly founded resettlement village surrounded by fish ponds, which from their perspective was more of an urban-to-rural resettlement than the anticipated move to an economically more developed region.

The host(ile) village and the experience of being rejected

Immediately after arrival, the Baicun resettlers were visited by members of the local Baizhen government. According to Cheng Yu, on behalf of the Guangdong provincial government, the representatives wanted to welcome the newcomers and give them a welcome gift of 100 yuan per person. This was not part of the compensation payment, but rather a friendly gesture by the provincial government and an expression of solidarity with the resettlers (Cheng, 2006:51). What the resettlers did not notice on this day was the absence of a representative from Chen Village,[10] i.e. the administrative village (*xingzhengcun*)[11] to which they were to be assigned as a village work group (*cunmin xiaozu*)[12] according to the plan

[10]Not the real name of the village.

[11]行政村.

[12]村民小组.

of the Baizhen government. But the leaders of Chen Village did not want to take the new Baicun Resettlement Village under its wing because this would have posed too many problems for them. First and foremost, they argued, the collective economy of Chen Village was very strong, whereas Baicun had essentially no collective economy. Virtually all of the affiliated natural villages distributed a dividend (*fenhong*)[13] from the jointly earned surplus at the end of the year. Because the resettlement village had no collective economic resources and could not contribute anything to the collective contract, it would have to receive dividends without having made its own contribution. But this would necessarily be dissatisfactory to the other work groups of Chen Village. Under pressure from the mayor (*zhenchang*)[14] of Baizhen, the leaders of Chen Village ultimately agreed to accept Baicun at least on formal terms and to sign some documents from the Baizhen government. However, they made it clear that the resettled people would not be able to share in the dividends (Cheng, 2006:50, 51).

Various types of discrimination and exclusion posed a second hurdle to the Baicun villagers in their attempts to explore the new physical and social spaces in their immediate vicinity. Baicun is very close to Chen Village. However, it is at a higher elevation and visually very different from Chen Village. Its walls reinforce the impression of a separate place. The people of Chen Village were leery of the newcomers whom they called the "new Hakka" (*xin kejia*),[15] a label with somewhat enigmatic connotations.[16]

If the resettlers saw the need, they defended themselves physically against hostilities. In the beginning, Cheng reports, there were many disputes, including actual fights, both within the resettler village and with outside locals. Chen villagers characterised the Three Gorges resettlers as people spoiling for a fight, and therefore saw themselves justified in their wish to avoid them (Cheng, 2006:150, 153). In their eyes, the Baicun

[13] 分红.

[14] 镇长.

[15] 新客家.

[16] The Mandarin term for "Hakka" is *kejia*, which literally means "guests." Historically, the Hakka were a group of Han Chinese from northern China with their own language who migrated south in several waves and reached Guangdong in the late 9th and early 10th centuries. During the 19th century, conflicts between Hakka and Yue (abbreviation for Guangdong) increased and the Hakka–Yue confrontations were particularly fierce in and around the PRD. Since the early 20th century, "Hakka" has been used as an ethnic label.

villagers left the land to its own devices and sat around on their doorsteps during the day (the resettlers didn't have jobs in the beginning), while they, the members of Chen Village, tilled their fields and appreciated the value of agriculture. The Baicun villagers had loud and shrill voices, they said, and marital difficulties and other disputes, about card games or with officials, were only too evident. They described Baicun as dirty and the newly built houses as making a messy impression (Cheng, 2006:152 f., 181).

Chen Village, in contrast, was seen as a peaceful, clean and quiet place. With their critical and demeaning view of Baicun villagers, Chen villagers also underscored their self-image as an economically and socially intact community and justified their disdain. The gap between Chen and Baicun was widened by actions such as a basketball tournament organised for all the natural villages that were part of Chen Village except for Baicun – despite the fact that Baicun belonged at least formally to Chen Village (Cheng, 2006:155). Baicun villagers felt discriminated against by this attitude. In the eyes of one Baicun villager, the relationship between the two villages underwent some changes over the long term. Looking back, RS 8, a 40-year-old resettler, said, "It was unpleasant at first, when people were condescending toward you; it was as if you were somehow being discriminated against or even shoved to the side. Now the attitude is that you don't owe me anything and I don't owe you anything." This statement may be interpreted as the emerging urban indifference of the metropolitan person (in the sense of Georg Simmel). With Chen Village's refusal to serve as the host organisation for the new resettlement village, the local Baizhen government became the direct contact for the resettlers. The Baicun newcomers first had to become acclimatised to their new location and new life. How they perceived and used the resettlement space will be the object of analysis in the next part of this chapter.

The Appropriation and Uses of Resettlement Space

Confronted with a completely new situation in unfamiliar surroundings, the resettlers tried to appropriate the resettlement space provided by the host government. The analysis of the ways they perceived, used and produced the resettlement space starts with their perception and uses of the village space and the social spaces beyond the resettlement village (including language, factory and school spaces); it then proceeds to their use of the compensation houses and the compensation land, and finally looks at the emerging transregional space between the resettlement village in Foshan and the former hometown in Chongqing.

Perception and use of village space

Baicun Village is neither a natural village nor an administrative village; it is a special resettlement village (*yimin cun*)[17] under the administration of the Baizhen town government. It is therefore not represented by a village committee leader (*cunweihui zhuren*)[18] but rather by an elected representative called the village head (*cunzhang*)[19] (Cheng, 2006:49, n2). The resettlers who suddenly became Baicun villagers in mid-August 2001 had lived in four different villages in the Three Gorges area before relocation and therefore had a limited mutual sense of trust and security within Baicun Village (Cheng, 2006:181; Cheng and He, 2006:75). A decade later, RS 15 recalls, "When we arrived, I didn't know the other people, just three families who came from the nearby area; we knew them like neighbours. The other resettlers all came from the suburbs of the county town, and our area was more rural. We only got to know the other resettlers after we came here. Now the relations in the whole village are very good, like members of a family." Earlier in the same interview, RS 15 gave a less positive impression of relations with other people in the village: "They are all right. Anyway, we don't have any arguments or fights with people in the village."

About half of the Baicun villagers know each other very well or are even related to each other. RS 7, a 52-year-old resettler, describes the composition of the village as follows: "Overall one can say there are three systems: the biggest would be those who belong to the Li family. A lot of people have the Zhou family name, then their relatives on both sides, those who are connected to them, close relations.[20] The others are like us, individual households, without relatives or with only a few." The fact that the village was made up of different groups of resettlers and that there was a lack of mutual trust became evident shortly after the arrival of the resettlers in Foshan when the local government wanted to hold elections for the village head of the newly established Baicun Resettlement Village.

---

[17]移民村.

[18]村委会主任.

[19]村长.

[20]Li and Zhou are not the real names of the families.

In the beginning, the local town government displayed a type of "welcome culture" towards the new Baicun villagers. It sought to let Baicun assume more of the organisational work itself, which would increase social cohesion with the result that the government would be relieved of the burden of being approached on each and every topic by the Baicun villagers directly. As Cheng has described in detail, the first elected village head of Baicun, a young female villager who appeared fearless in front of higher officials and the media, stepped down after no more than six weeks on the job. While the local government wanted her to establish a collective Baicun fund to care for public issues of the village such as garbage disposal or working electric street lights and provided the village some revenue, the villagers who up to that point had literally only swept in front of their own house doors, preferred to have the money distributed to the households (Cheng, 2006:153). It was a complex situation with too many different expectations of the young village head who became increasingly isolated. Under pressure to prove to the villagers that she was not lining her pockets but rather standing up for their wishes, she got into an argument with the town mayor who had highlighted the generosity of the host village. Ultimately, the money was distributed to the individual Baicun households as requested, but after this snub of the Baizhen town mayor, the welcome culture phase came to a definitive end and a "phase of cold war" (*lengzhan qi*)[21] – as Cheng put it – began (Cheng, 2006:103, 104).

The local government then established an administrative office for the resettlers from Three Gorges – but one that lacked special staff and designated office space and therefore only made the local government anonymous and difficult to approach. After 2002, cadres from the local government avoided visiting Baicun Village and only came for special occasions such as the tenth-anniversary celebrations in 2011. About this time, the village got a new wall – for both protection and surveillance. RS 24, a 51-year-old female resettler, explained, "[The wall is] for security. Each village has to build one, to install the cameras. The government provides 30,000 yuan, the rest should be paid by us."

Attempts by the local government to foster a common sense of responsibility for Baicun Village among the resettlers met with little response. Shared projects or investments did not move beyond the initial consideration phase, even after years. The meeting hall and even the office of the village head remained unused except for some attempts to

---

[21] 冷战期.

use the former as a privately run drugstore (which was not approved by the local government) and as an informal restaurant. The only community space that was created in the village was a game hall with special mahjong tables and space for playing (Sichuanese) cards. In the long run, the resettlement space provided by the government did not lead to a process of increased social cohesion among the Baicun villagers but led to individual families trying to make the best of the situation.

The use of compensation houses

Most of the resettler families received one- or two-storey houses in compensation for the apartments or houses they had lost. The objective was to prevent them from becoming homeless as a result of the resettlement and to give them new homes. As it turned out, the resettlers were interested not only in the practical value of living in the houses themselves but also saw them as resources, or possible sources of additional income, especially by renting out rooms or apartments. In contrast to the bungalows in other resettlement villages in the region, the houses had such good foundations that one or two additional storeys could easily be added to them. RS 5 explains, "Generally, everyone rents out, and lives above with their families. They rent to migrant workers, who come from everywhere. Some of them are from near here, and some from further away, and they all rent rooms from us, ... they all live here with us. It costs 120–150 yuan a month to rent a room." That was not the case in the beginning. The resettler families lived on the ground floor then, and it was easier to engage in conversation with passersby. RS 1 regrets, "I don't go out very often. I used to live below, and everything was better, everyone came to the door. Now everyone lives on the upper floors, so you can't just stop by, or generally very infrequently." But rentals are essentially never the sole source of income. Instead, they are seen as additional financial security in the event of unemployment or old age, or when one needs to pay school fees for children. RS 11 explains, "We rent out, but that doesn't bring in much. We rent out four rooms on the second floor, and two rooms on the first floor, for a total of six, which brings in 700–800 yuan a month, which is better than nothing, ha ha." One of the effects of the financial crisis in 2008–2009, however, was a decrease in the number of migrant workers in the PRD and therefore a decrease in the number of real or potential tenants. That shows the instability of this source of income.

But it wasn't easy for every family in Baicun to come up with the money needed to enlarge their houses. One example would be the family of the man who had several motorcycle accidents. RS 14 says, "In the beginning it was hard, and we didn't manage to do the extensions on the house ... we still had debts from the accident; finally, our relatives saw that we were having difficulties and they said to us that everyone else had built onto their houses, and if we didn't do that too, where would we get the money later for school fees? Then some of our relatives lent us a little money, which enabled us to build onto the house." The wife borrowed money for the house from her sisters, who had remained in Chongqing. But because of the husband's accidents, this family still had debts of 70–80,000 yuan. After enlarging the house, the wife described the situation as follows: "We live on the third floor, the other one is rented out, and also some of our relatives still live here. Relatives of my husband, who work here. They aren't resettlers, they just work here; they helped us enlarge the house, so now they don't need to pay rent."

The somewhat more prosperous families in Baicun, or those whose families had grown, faced other problems. For example, if they wanted to purchase a second residence, they could not use their special status as TGP resettlers to get more favourable conditions to finance their purchase, or even the same conditions as the local Guangdong people. A former Baicun village head, RS 10, describes the situation as follows: "Now the policy has changed, and housing purchases are limited.[22] Actually our houses are not commercial housing … but when we buy housing a second time … the bank asks for a mortgage, [normally] several tens of thousands, not that much money, [but] they want 60 per cent because you are a second-time buyer, the deed tax may also be doubled." She continues, "These people don't care about you … The provincial government also said that our houses are resettlement houses and not commercial housing, and that everyone owns a house here for stability, families have their own houses, and so everyone receives a title deed. [But] the bank … just looks at your title deed and doesn't care about anything else." According to her, there is no support from politicians either: "To address this problem, the provincial government, or the one in Foshan, would first have to send down a document, but the provincial government doesn't send us anything … It's

[22] Since 2010, the Chinese government has introduced various policies at central and local levels to cool the property market. Measures include restrictions for second-time buyers of apartments and higher transaction taxes.

very unfair to us. The villagers went there, they're not that patient, they went there once or twice, the Standing Committee of the People's Congress has its office there. They complained to the People's Congress and lost their tempers [there], which gave the People's Congress a bad impression; they said what we told them didn't make sense, our arguments were unfounded."

Other families ran into difficulties if they had to list their houses as security to take out a loan so as to buy a motorcycle or a car. RS 26 complains, "When we wanted to take out a loan, they said we had no fixed assets, they totally ignored us. We turned to the government, but in vain, they said they couldn't do anything about it. Local people may get 180,000 (yuan) without any mortgage. I said we also have a local household registration, then they said, you are different – one sentence and they sent us out. It's not that we don't integrate into this society, it's the local government, ah, and institutions which simply don't take us as one of their members. Real integration is not an easy thing, the local people here are too xenophobic. This becomes most obvious when they don't treat us as people from here."

More than ten years after arriving in Guangdong province, the inhabitants of Baicun Resettlement Village were not associating their compensation houses with the idea of "belonging" or "home" in the PRD. Their understanding of deserving would give them the same entitlements as the local population, such as the ability to take out a loan on their home. This was very different from the local government's understanding of deserving, which was to provide solid housing that would prevent evictees from becoming homeless.

The use of compensation land

A similar difference in the understanding of deservingness between the resettlers and the local government can be seen with regard to land compensation. The local host governments wanted to implement the resettlement policy of the local government and fulfil their contractual obligations to the Baicun villagers. This meant they had to provide the "peasants" from the TGP with 0.6 Mu arable land and 10 m^2 homestead land per capita (in addition to the per capita 20 m^2 housing area). This was not an easy task for them – arable land was a scarce and precious resource, and the idea of passing their responsibility down to the administrative Chen

Village was not met with any kind of appreciation on the part of Chen Village. The only concession the Baizhen government was able to negotiate with Chen Village (without taking compulsory measures) was 0.2 Mu arable land plus 0.4 Mu fish ponds per capita for the 134 residents of Baicun.

Because most of the resettlers from the Wushan area had no background in agricultural production, they did not really care about the compensation land, at least not in the beginning. RS 19 says, "Many people in the village don't know how to farm the fields. Because many people from the county seat didn't work in the fields, in Chongqing they did not farm. When they decided to come here, it was definitely not to work in the fields; moreover, that field was quite far away." But as mentioned earlier, the Baicun resettlers were wondering why they received only 0.6 Mu per capita compensation land (which was more than they had had in Wushan before resettlement) while their neighbours from Chen Village had 2.6 Mu arable land per capita. Here, one should note that the Chen villagers have much more farmland per capita than the average in Guangdong, which (in 2004) was also just 0.6 Mu (Tan, 2008:2010).

The 0.6 Mu per capita compensation land consisted of 0.4 Mu fish ponds and 0.2 Mu arable land, which in fact also was a former fish pond that had been filled with mud from other ponds and lay well below the surrounding area. This piece of land had a much poorer appearance than the land belonging to Chen Village. The impression was strengthened by piles of ash lying around from a nearby coal plant (Cheng, 2006:100, 101). Usage rights for the land were subsequently sold to the coal plant to use as a stockyard. RS 15, a 39-year-old housewife, says, "The land has been sold, but the problems remain. I think we sold the land too cheaply. We sold 1 Mu for 36,000 yuan.... The coal plant back there leased it." She also considers how the 10 m^2 of homestead land (*zhaijidi*)[23] could be used in a lucrative way: "Homestead land is 10 m^2 per person; for our family, this would mean 50 m^2. We could build housing and rent it out. When we get older and don't work anymore, then we'd still have the rental income – but we don't have the money now to build." Here, too, more than ten years after the resettlers arrived, the question of the homestead land and its use had still not been cleared up with the local government. On the one hand, there was always the option of building on this land, but only under certain financial conditions. On the other hand, the

[23] 宅基地.

land-for-land compensation idea was that the land should be used to grow food which the resettlers could use themselves or sell on a small scale.

Over the years, as more factories were built around Baicun, the villagers not only benefited from renting out rooms and apartments to migrant workers but they also found factory jobs in the vicinity of Baicun. In particular, a newly built ceramics factory (2003) had a positive impact on the income situation of many Baicun villagers by providing jobs and increasing the number of migrant workers renting rooms. In addition, 0.4 Mu land was requisitioned for the factory, which generated an income of over 10,000 yuan for the village. But because it was distributed on a per capita basis, there was not much money for each family, RS 2 says. A bit of money could also be made by selling, e.g. drinks to the factory workers – at least until the factory installed a self-service machine with drinks.

Similar to housing, the compensation land turned into a resource with exchange value, i.e. a resource by which the resettlers could generate income. Whereas in the beginning the Baicun villagers didn't show much interest in the land for agricultural purposes, they later perceived it as a precious resource and spent many years negotiating with the local government about the use of the homestead land.

Social spaces beyond the resettlement village and their limitations

Various factors hindered the resettlers in experiencing the mega-urban spaces beyond the boundaries of Baicun Village and in establishing links with the local society of which they had formally become a part. RS 2 remembers, "The worst part when we came here was that you knew nobody, no one at all in the society. Now it is not much different. People in the society such as officials, you don't know them at all. You have no contact with them whatsoever. Very different from home, there you have relatives, there you have friends, right? If something happens, what do you do? … It's still the same. Ten years have passed but you only know the people in the village. [I] deal [primarily] with people from the village."

- Language spaces

A major initial barrier was language. While the local dialect spoken in the new environment was Cantonese, the resettlers talked to each other in

Sichuanese. Sometimes, it was possible to use Mandarin, but this did not always work. RS 7 recalls, "In the beginning, the first one or two years, what created the most problems was the language. When we spoke, we stood there like idiots." RS 5 describes the situation as follows: "When you go shopping in the morning, you go outside. How should I put it, the old women from here, so, you say something they don't understand and they say something you don't understand. But the young people, you can communicate with them very well, they all speak Mandarin."

As expected, the children at school and pre-school could adapt comparatively quickly to their new language environment. A 15-year-old schoolgirl who came to Baicun in 2001 at the age of 4, recalls, "I learned Cantonese at pre-school, and after the first school period could speak it. The teachers spoke to me constantly in it, so very quickly, in two months, it worked" (RS 13). For the older resettlers, Cantonese language skills generally stayed at a level sufficient to meet everyday needs. Chongqing dialect remains the major language in the life of the Baicun villagers.

- Factory spaces

Virtually the only way out of the isolation of the resettlement village and into the local community was through employment for the adult villagers and schooling for the children. Except for the position of village head, only a few jobs required intensive contact with the local population. An exception is described by RS 7: "In 1990, I started to do business up there (in Chongqing), to be my own small boss. Now, I am working for other people at a construction firm. Every day, I have contact with people from here, because of the work and the projects I am doing. Because I am managing projects, and especially because it's the construction sector, the people are mainly from here, outsiders are rarely seen ... communication arises, we have to be in contact with each other, exchange information about whether things should be done or not."

But the usual factory jobs in production, warehouses or lower administration that the resettlers were looking for did not provide many opportunities for more intensive contact with local people because most of their co-workers were migrant workers from other provinces. There was not really much opportunity for friendships to emerge between resettlers and local people at the workplace. However, in one interview, a 40-year-old Baicun female villager argues that connections with local people were a precondition for landing a factory job: "When the new factory had just been established, I went there four times. But they never took me. She said I was too old. But if you have connections, for example, if a family has connections, for instance, has ties to a cadre who can open doors for you ... For them everything's fine, they get into the factory with the help of a cadre. When we were there, we had no idea" (RS 5). For the younger Baicun females, it was easier to find a factory job, but long working hours and low pay (only a few hundred yuan a month while the male villagers' wages were normally around 1,000 yuan) made these jobs less attractive. In addition, the younger women sometimes had small children and if the work meant they had to pay for childcare, not much money would be left. It appears that limited employment opportunities, poor working conditions, low pay at most of the factories, childcare costs and the difficulties for "elderly" women to get a job meant that more women remained housewives at Baicun Village the entire time.

- School spaces

The children were those most likely to meet teachers and pupils from Guangdong at school. They could attend primary and middle school near Baicun Village. While it was easier for schoolchildren to communicate verbally with local people, Baicun mothers (RS 5, RS 14) reported that their sons had been threatened and their daughters insulted. RS 14 says, "When he attended the higher middle school in Foshan, there were some boys from here who wanted to beat him up. They had no special reason. They said they didn't like him. They only said that he should wait for them there after school, then they wanted to beat him up. Then my son also got some classmates together and chased them away. They never came again." For the Baicun girls, it didn't seem to matter whether their classmates had a resettlement, migrant worker or local background; the most important factor was gender – girls hang out with girls, and boys with boys. A 13-year-old school girl says, "I find the students from outside normal. I talk with the schoolgirls from outside. I can't talk with boys. It's the same with the local ones." But the girl also complains, "Sometimes students from here give outside students a hard time. The ones from here say things like 'kids from outside are really dirty,' or something like that. When the outside kids get on their nerves, the local kids sometimes insult them by calling them 'hill boys' or 'hill girls'" (RS 17).

Whereas the adult generation indicates that they have more contact with migrant workers than with the local Guangdong population, this difference plays a much smaller role among the Baicun youth. Parents in Baicun hope that their children can benefit from going to school in Guangdong and possibly also make the leap to university, and there are some examples of this. The schools in Guangdong are considered better than those back home in Chongqing. Any hopes for social advance rest on the younger generation.

Overall, social relations and networks extending beyond the resettlement village are very rare. With the exception of schoolchildren, friendships with people from Guangdong have remained exceptions. There is also hardly any contact with other resettlement villages in the region, unless people knew each other before resettlement. Although the overall standard of living in Baicun has improved in recent years – ten out of forty families owned a car in 2012 – and tensions with Chen Village have eased, isolation and an uncertain status remain. Baicun villagers see themselves less as local migrants and more as a diaspora village of Three Gorges resettlers.

- Coming down and going up – A transregional space in limbo

Visits to their old home involve considerable costs and time. Villagers therefore need a special reason to go, or sufficient financial resources if they simply "feel like it," although these are rarely available. RS 5 says, "The first time I went back was because I had to take care of something, the second time because I was sick, and the third time because my husband's mother was sick ... I went by train and that takes 17 or 18 hours, and then a boat, so it takes a total of 26 or 27 hours."[24] RS 1 makes the following calculations: "It's not possible to visit our old homeland several times a year; that would be several thousand yuan a year, one return ticket already costs more than 600 yuan. There and back, several family members; you can't go back there, but who wouldn't want to go back? When you go back, you spend several tens of thousands of yuan, and you spend all your savings up there. You can't go back. It's painful just thinking about it." Some families in Baicun didn't go "back up" a single time from 2001 to 2012. In some cases, small trade is done with specialties from

[24] With a high-speed train, the travel time from Guangzhou to Chongqing has reduced considerably but is even more expensive.

Sichuan, which opens up a transregional space, but these remain exceptions.

Some families were already thinking before resettlement of using the compensation as a type of business whose revenue would put them in a financial position to go "back up." This normally didn't always work out because the resettlers' houses could not just be sold like commercial housing. RS 1 complains, "What really annoys me is the lack of decision-making power (*zizhuquan*).[25] I never thought that I would actually live here; instead, I thought I'd sell the house, [but] now there's no way you can sell your house. It's not possible because of the collective land; not to buy and not to sell." Other families tried to keep the option of returning open but in informal ways. RS 20, the security coordinator, considers, "At home, I still have housing. When we're old and everything is settled with our son, then maybe we will go back ..."

In the first years after arriving in Baicun, some families relocated entirely back to Chongqing. But compared to other resettlement villages in the region, Baicun Village is seen as rather stable. The following is said about another resettlement village by RS 8, a 40-year-old male resettler: "Conditions are really bad. There are now only 5 or 6 families left. [There used to be] more than 20 families, some went back many years ago, their *hukou* is still here." Nevertheless, more than ten years after resettlement, many families in Baicun are still thinking strongly of going back "up." Some of them still have relatives up there and see that as a possible way to return. RS 4 (whose parents are still in Chongqing) says, "This year the prices are incredibly high; for vegetables you have to pay several yuan, for the children you have to spend several thousand yuan. I want to go back and look around to see whether there is something I could do ... At home, the air and the environment are just somewhat better, it's not because of the money."

But several barriers stand in the way of returning to Chongqing. Some families find the idea of returning appealing but hesitate because of the administrative hurdles involved. This is also the case with RS 8: "It's hard to say [whether we'll return]. We moved away from up there; our connections with the government there are broken off, that is [now] very complicated. You can't go back to the factory, you can't work, everything is very complicated. Didn't the government say something about a new old-age pension scheme ... nothing has happened. Things are alright here, but

---

[25] 自主权.

there could be something better than this village." Others are undecided, too. They want to go back but they do not want to lose face by returning home without having achieved their objective of becoming rich. RS 19 expresses this feeling: "Now we are all changing into country people, we do not dare to go back, we all do not dare to see our classmates or others. Our male classmates look like bosses now, our female classmates like rich ladies, they are all well off, but we here, it's absolutely unacceptable, it's embarrassing for all of us to go back. Families that used to be much poorer than ours are now much better off than our families, really, up in Chongqing it is really very good, we would very much like to go back. This year (2012), we are planning to go back to Chongqing and have a look; we intend to go to Chongqing for New Year's. The plan is for our son to finish lower middle school first, then we'll see how his grades are. If they are good, then we'd stay here and continue to work, and he could attend the upper middle school here. If his grades are not so good, then we'll see; if they're not good, then maybe we'll go back to Chongqing. Because there aren't any prospects here, we only can go for work." Returning, it seems, is especially an option for older people who don't have to provide for their children anymore, and who either don't have other family obligations to keep them in Baicun or now live alone.

Legal and Policy Background of "Resettlement with Development" and the Three Gorges Dam Project

Resettlement from the TGP was shaped by legal, political and administrative guidelines. Despite a long history of resettlement actions that range from early dam projects to subsequent transport and urban infrastructure work with the involuntary relocation of many millions of people, the People's Republic of China has not yet enacted a comprehensive national resettlement law.

Legal regulations and policy guidelines

Reservoir displacement in China is guided on three levels: fundamental laws and regulations, sector regulations, and specific laws and regulations for large hydro projects. The fundamental laws underlying resettlement regulations are the Chinese Constitution and the Land Administration Law. Constitutional law stipulates that urban land belongs to the state, while land in rural and peri-urban areas belongs to collectives and is used by individuals, and that the state can requisition land for the national public good. The Land Administration Law set up compensation standards and relevant procedures for the requisition of agricultural land (Shi *et al.*, 2022; Tan, 2008:98f.) Of special importance for the TGP-displaced people were the revised Regulations on Resettlement in the Yangtze Three Gorges Project of 1 March 2001, which superseded those of 1993 (State Council, 2001). They continued to focus on accommodations and support for the resettlers, penalties for violations and administrative matters in both the source and destination locations.

According to the revised version of the Regulations, rural persons no longer needed to be resettled in the traditional agricultural sector, and the policy of local resettlement was replaced by a combination of near and distant resettlement. The central government's decision, backed by environmental reasons, that land with a gradient of more than 25 degrees should no longer be developed but rather used for forestry or grazing meant that such areas were no longer available for resettlement. The stronger emphasis on environmental protection contributed to an increase in distant resettlement.

The policy guideline for TGP resettlement was the idea of "developmental resettlement" (*kaifaxing yimin*).[26] Proposed by the Chinese government in the mid-1980s, this policy had two objectives: (1) solving the ongoing problems of reservoir resettlers from earlier dam projects such as large-scale impoverishment and (2) preparing for TGP resettlement (Tan, 2008:21, 44). Article 3 of the Regulations stated that to create conditions for economic and social development in the reservoir area, the TGP would implement a developmental resettlement guideline, coordinate use of resettlement funds, show reasonable development of resources, protect the environment, make proper arrangements for resettlers and enable resettlers' production and lives to achieve or exceed their original standard (State Council, 2001:1). This broad and rather vague formulation gave rise to questions and controversial interpretations of the concept of developmental resettlement. What exactly does it mean to say resettlers' production and lives should achieve or exceed the original level? Is this based on an understanding of development as economic growth or as sustainable development? Is it consequently just about restoring the income levels of displaced people or about achieving sustainable livelihoods? Regarding

[26] 开发性移民.

poor households, should they be left as poor as they were before? Recent evaluations of China's development-oriented resettlement policy seem to be impressed by the institutional apparatus for dealing with resettlement issues (Cernea, 2016; Habich-Sobiegalla, 2016). However, without a national resettlement law that can clarify, strengthen and protect the rights of citizens affected by involuntary resettlement, it may be difficult for them to achieve sustainable livelihoods after resettlement.

Interestingly, when the concept of developmental resettlement was taking shape in China during the 1980s and 1990s, the World Bank, a pioneer in drafting involuntary resettlement policies (and which refused to help fund the TGP because of the project's high risks), watered down its most progressive definition of development-oriented resettlement (OD 4.30, 1990) into its 2001 version, which allows borrowers the option of merely restoring income, which can end up in impoverishing the majority of resettlers (Tan, 2008:42).[27] The shift in rural household resettlement locations from higher-elevation sites within the immediate reservoir area to more distant sites, which began in 2000, was an important policy adjustment that also largely shifted the responsibility for restoring and developing resettlers' livelihoods to the distant host governments.

According to official statistics, 1.27 million people were displaced from the TGP from 1993 to 2009, of whom 196,000 were resettled to distant locations. The latter figure can be divided into 35,000 self-organised distant resettlers who moved to family or friends throughout the country and 161,000 government-organised distant resettlers who were sent to 11 provinces or province-level municipalities (Zhou *et al.*, 2011:1351, 52). There were two different kinds of receiving provinces: (1) downstream provinces benefiting from the dam construction such as Anhui, Hubei, Hunan, Jiangsu and Jiangxi and (2) comparatively developed provinces and municipalities (in terms of GDP) such as Fujian, Guangdong, Shandong, Shanghai and Zhejiang (Tan, 2008:87).[28]

---

[27]Reasons for potential impoverishment of resettled people include: lengthy pre-project planning processes that lower people's living standards; inaccurate baseline surveys of pre-project living standards; failure to provide development opportunities; lack of support from host governments after resettlement (Tan, 2008:44).

[28]An exception was Sichuan, which was assigned the resettlement task because people from the reservoir area share Sichuan's culture, language, lifestyle and agricultural production methods (Tan, 2008:87).

Implementation of the government-organised distant resettlement

In 2000, the government of Guangdong produced a document (No. 123) that specified the distribution of 7,006 distant resettlers among the four cities of Foshan, Huizhou, Zhaoqing and Jiangmen.[29] As part of these specifications, distribution was to be concentrated in municipalities[30] and scattered among individual villages. The distributing cities were to select 6–7 towns under their administration, and each town in turn was to select 3–5 suitable sites which were each to take 10 households or approximately 40 people (Guangdong, 2000). In the case of Baicun Resettlement Village, the decisional chain went from the Guangdong provincial government to a district of Foshan city, and the district government distributed its 1,202 resettlers to 10 resettlement stations (*anzhidian*)[31] (*China Digital Times*, 2011).

The town government on behalf of the district government selected Chen Village as the host for the new Baicun Resettlement Village – but here the top-down chain ran into problems. The towns, villages and village groups at the bottom, in this case the Baizhen town government and the Chen administrative village, were made responsible for requisitioning land from the local people and community, allocating land to the newcomers, and organising and inspecting housing construction. Based on the directives from the provincial government, the rural resettlers in Guangdong were to be accommodated in accordance with the principle of "moving out, steady housing, gradually getting rich" (*bandechu, wendezhu, zhubu neng zhifu*).[32] Land and agriculture were to form the basis for resettlement, and local governments were to ensure that the newcomers received contracted arable land, private plots and homesteads (*chengbao de gengdi, ziliudi, zhai jidi*),[33] of a quantity and quality not below the average level of local farmers. Based on the strategy of development-oriented resettlement, the newcomers were to contribute to farming, forestry, animal husbandry, fishing and associated rural industry in accordance with local conditions

---

[29] From 2000 to 2006, 9,007 rural residents from the TGP area were displaced to Guangdong: 7,005 from Wushan County and 2,002 from Wanzhou County (Tan, 2008:194).

[30] On the administrative level of township (乡) and town (镇).

[31] 安置点.

[32] 搬得出，稳得住，逐步能致富.

[33] 承包的耕地, 自留地, 宅基地.

and encouraged to engage in the production and service sectors in order to increase their incomes on a step-by-step basis. Counties and cities considered suitable for resettlers possessed good natural conditions, sufficient land, strong leadership and the ability to provide sufficient infrastructure (water, power, roads), as well as schools, hospitals and other public facilities. The resettlement locations were to be in the vicinity of market towns and were also to have convenient working, living and transportation conditions for the resettlers. The accommodation was to be based on the principle of "3 × 1" (*sange yi*),[34] i.e. each household was to have one piece of arable land, one house and one person joining the outside labour force (Guangdong, 2000).

In accordance with the requirements from the Guangdong government and on behalf of the district government within the city of Foshan, the Baizhen town government made an agreement with Baicun Resettlement Village that included the following ten points (Cheng, 2006:57, 58): (1) The resettlers receive 0.6 Mu arable land and 30 m^2 homestead land per capita. After the contract is signed, the location of the arable and homestead land can no longer be changed. (2) House construction is calculated at a cost of 480 RMB per m^2, of which the resettlers have to bear 250 RMB. Each resettler will get 20 m^2 of housing, which means a subsidy of 4,600 RMB. (3) The resettlement village will be provided with infrastructure (electricity, water, roads and postal service). (4) The government will bear the fees for the household registration booklet, the house title deed (*fangchan zheng*)[35] and the land document (*tudi zheng*).[36] (5) Resettlers will receive guidance and training for setting up production. (6) The government will provide each resettler with 3,875 RMB during the transitional period for a living allowance and for purchasing production materials. The living allowance will be paid for 18 months at 100 RMB per capita and per month. Households in economic difficulty will receive a subsidy based on procedures in the related document from the State Council. (7) Resettlers who meet the conditions will receive assistance in finding factory work. (8) After registration in Baizhen, school fees will be reduced by 50% for at least 3 of the 9 years of compulsory schooling and for upper middle school students. (9) After settling in Baizhen and becoming legal members of the village, resettlers will have the same rights and

[34] 三个一.

[35] 房产证.

[36] 土地证.

obligations as local villagers. (10) Based on national and Guangdong regulations for resettlers in Baizhen and starting from the year of resettlement, income from non-wasteland agriculture and from special local agricultural products will be tax free for 3 years.

Compensation and accommodation costs were shared between the Wushan county government in the TGP area, which sent the resettlers, and the designated district government in Foshan, which received them. The Wushan county government provided compensation for housing and related facilities (according to the 1991 Yangtze Water Resources Commission standards for submerged materials), subsidies for relocation losses and loss of working days (558 yuan/person); subsidies for distant relocation of housing and attached facilities (2,480 yuan/person), and compensation for fruit trees (485 yuan/person). The district government in Foshan was responsible for the transitional living allowance (1,800 yuan/person for 18 months), the purchase of production materials (2,075 yuan/person), and the purchase of farmland and homestead land for distribution to the Baicun resettlers (Cheng 2006: 81).

The compensation standards for the Three Gorges resettlers were higher than those for any previous reservoir resettlement project in China. But as is well known from resettlement research, the losses are much broader than income alone (Price, 2009:273). According to the Impoverishment Risk and Reconstruction Model developed by Cernea (Cernea, 2000), involuntary resettlement may cause eight kinds of risks, which have economic and social dimensions. The model has two main functions: a diagnostic and predictive function, and a problem resolution and planning function. Despite some criticism for not addressing the education or gender dimensions of resettlement impact, the model provides guidance for avoiding the social risks of resettlement and suggests measures to achieve more sustainable livelihood results after relocation. The model will be used as a checklist to review the set of measures taken in the resettlement of the Baicun people.

Resettlement measures undertaken by the local town government: A preliminary assessment

In his concluding analysis of the Baicun villagers' first years after relocation, Cheng (2006:175–182) used Cernea's model to evaluate safeguarding measures taken by the local government. What follows is a brief summary of the measures taken by the Baizhen government and Cheng's comments on whether the problems identified in the model were consistent with the situation in Baicun village and could be resolved accordingly.

Risk 1: Landlessness; reconstruction measure: Land-based resettlement. The resettlers in Baicun Village received 0.6 Mu arable land per capita – which was more than they had had before. Based on the principle of land-for-land compensation, the local government followed the measure to avoid landlessness as the first risk of impoverishment after resettlement. But the peri-urban residents from Wushan County, Chongqing, had not previously worked in the fields. They were rural residents but not peasants in the strict sense. According to Cheng, they viewed land compensation more as a symbol of their status as land-owning Guangdong residents. Because local residents had 2.6 Mu land, the resettlers perceived this as an injustice and complained.

Risk 2: Joblessness; reconstruction measure: Reemployment. The Baicun resettlers saw joblessness as a much greater problem than landlessness. Because most had worked in the service sector of the tourism industry, they generally lost their business and clients. The new environment devalued their labour qualifications and experience; skilled workers only found unskilled jobs and they were not used to the higher intensity of labour at factories. The local government provided jobs in factories but on a low-income basis, with long working hours and often only at distant locations. For this and similar reasons, 19 people left Baicun Village before 2003 and went back "up."

Risk 3: Homelessness; reconstruction measure: House construction. Housing funded by both the sending and receiving governments was an important measure completely in accordance with Cernea's Risk and Reconstruction Model. Moreover, compared to other resettlement villages in the same district of Foshan city, Baicun's houses were praised for their solid foundations. Nevertheless, Cheng points out that the loss of housing means losing not only the material structure but also a cultural space. In keeping with this observation, there was a strong feeling of "placelessness" (*shiweigan*)[37] in Baicun Village which Cheng links to the fact that

[37] 失位感.

the resettlers were not from a single village community but instead came from different natural villages and had not known each other before arriving in Baicun.

Risk 4: Marginalisation; reconstruction measure: Social inclusion. Economic and psychological marginalisation had a negative impact on the relationship between the Baicun villagers and local residents. The attitude of rejection on the part of Chen Village as the formal grassroots host unit of Baicun Village exacerbated the lack of inclusion shown to the Baicun villagers. The resettlers experienced alienation, a loss of agency and anxiety, which had a devastating impact on their self-esteem.

Risk 5: Food insecurity; reconstruction measure: Adequate nutrition. The various compensation measures undertaken by the local government meant that food insecurity was not a problem in Baicun Village.

Risk 6: Increased morbidity and mortality; reconstruction measure: Increased healthcare. As is well known from involuntary resettlement projects worldwide, morbidity and mortality may easily increase during this stressful period. Two kinds of illnesses predominated in Baicun: stomach problems, particularly among men and probably often caused by psychological issues, and tuberculosis. Hygiene conditions in Baicun were not very good. There was a lack of concern for public health, heaps of smelly garbage were not removed, the climate was relatively hot and flies swarmed everywhere. Traffic accidents increased the accident and mortality rates in Baicun Village. Motorcyclists from Baicun in particular were involved in traffic accidents with light and severe injuries. In addition, high labour intensity levels in three shifts with only one day off a month contributed to fatigue and a lack of concentration in traffic.

Risk 7: Loss of access to common property resources; reconstruction measure: Restore community assets and services. Loss of access to common property resources is often seen as a particular problem for poor people, who can no longer use woods, water or community institutions to live on after resettlement. Although the Baicun resettlers had not used these resources directly while in Wushan County, the breathtaking Three Gorges landscape right outside their doors offered the opportunity to work in the local tourism industry or make a living from related small businesses and services. There was no substitute for this loss in the new environment, and the local Baizhen government had no type of adequate replacement to offer.

Risk 8: Social disarticulation; reconstruction measure: Network building and community rebuilding. While the Baizhen government quickly realised the necessity of holding elections in Baicun after the arrival of the resettlers and encouraged the election of a village head, the officials were motivated primarily by the wish to have a contact person and possibly a Communist party village authority, which would facilitate handling all the upcoming questions and problems – particularly given the fact that Chen Village consistently refused to include Baicun Resettlement Village in any of its economic or social activities. But the political and administrative interests of the Baizhen town government did not match the internal social relations within the resettlement village. The Baicun resettlers came from four different villages and their relations were not based on networks of reciprocal trust and security. Social disarticulation and lack of cohesion among Baicun villagers manifested in frequent and noisy quarrels that arose from minor everyday issues and quickly turned into conflicts. This confirmed the poor image in the eyes of Chen villagers who saw Baicun as a loud, dirty and chaotic place. Thus, a vicious cycle of estrangement between the resettlers and the residents of Chen Village emerged. The attitude of the Baizhen government, which visited Baicun less frequently over the years, also reinforced the problem of social disarticulation. No compensation was available because the resettlers had irretrievably lost their familiar environment and substantial parts of their social networks.

Overall, the Baizhen government did not have an easy task. On the one hand they had to meet the demands of higher levels of government (district, city, provincial), and on the other hand, they had to deal with the stubborn leaders of Chen Village, who refused to accept responsibility for Baicun Resettlement Village, which the Baizhen town government had assigned to Chen Village. As a result, Baizhen officials have had to deal directly with a number of issues relating to the resettlement village. Although the Baizhen government has demonstrated a commitment to addressing most of the risks associated with resettlement as outlined in Michael Cernea's Impoverishment Risk and Reconstruction Model, in the eyes of officials, even after a decade of post-resettlement development, the resettled people were still neither satisfied nor grateful, and the Baicun resettlement village had become a 'problem space'.

Conclusion

The people displaced from the Three Gorges area who have turned into the Baicun resettlement villagers in Foshan city perceived the resettlement area mainly as an individual resource for each of the smaller and larger families, and did not want to generate or share collective village income.

They used the houses, the land and the village space to cope with the challenges in the new environment but only on an individual family basis. The Baicun villagers had their own understanding of "resettlement with development." As people agreed to the displacement for the national good, they saw themselves as deserving of material as well as social recognition and as entitled to enhance their own life opportunities as new but equal local Guangdong citizens. However, despite their new local household registration and their home ownership, the Baicun villagers felt more on an equal footing with the migrant workers from Central China's provinces than with the local Guangdong citizens with whom they had very limited social interaction. Their emerging identity became shaped more by their status as Three Gorges resettlers than by their new formal status as Guangdong citizens.

The local government saw the resettlement space provided for the Three Gorges resettlers as a place where they could stay and eventually feel at home, in what the government envisioned as a self-organising village that would soon take care of its own community issues and public spaces. From a perspective of moral economy, the Baizhen local government had a different understanding of the "deserving" and the "undeserving" resettlers than the Baicun villagers themselves. The local officials saw it as their duty to provide solid houses, compensation land, jobs, and basic material and social infrastructure for the newcomers, and in return they expected a grateful and quiet resettlement village to emerge. At the beginning, they showed compassion for the "deserving" resettlers, but this attitude changed when the resettlers did not respond in ways they had expected but turned into what they saw as a disorganised group of noisy and demanding villagers who even insulted them. Instead of searching for the root problems of such behaviour (deriving from discrepancies between the resettlers' new "rural" status and the urban lifestyles they were accustomed to, devaluation of their former sources of income, etc.), the local government retreated from the resettlement village. They saw their obligations towards Baicun Village as largely fulfilled. In addition, they had to balance their administrative duties with the upper-level local governments as well as with Baicun's formal host village, which did not change its negative attitude towards the resettlement village over the years.

Contestation over the resettlement space arose from different respective contextualisations of this space by the local governments, the Baicun villagers and the Chen villagers. The local government wanted to see Baicun Village as an internally integrated community with some sense of belonging on the part of its inhabitants so that the officials could be acknowledged for having carried out their task successfully. The Chen administrative village saw the resettlers as "the others" who might infringe on their resources; they wanted the resettlement space to be limited, separated from Chen Village and as invisible as possible. The Baicun villagers themselves used the resettlement space as a resource; they generated additional income by renting out rooms and some hoped to sell the houses and eventually go back "up" to Chongqing. Taken together, this has produced a transient peri-urban space in an arrested state without decay but without a clear development perspective either. The spatial and social positioning of the Baicun resettlement village contributes to the socio-spatial mosaic of the PRD's expanding mega-urban area, adding a unique peri-urban and trans-regional dimension.

Appendix

List of interviews with residents of a Three Gorges resettlement village in the Pearl River Delta (August–September 2012)

Resettler interview number	Gender	Age	Relationship to the resettlement village
RS 1	Male	43	Resident of the Three Gorges resettlement village
RS 2	Female	35	Resident of the Three Gorges resettlement village
RS 3	Male	35	Resident of the Three Gorges resettlement village
RS 4	Female	34	Resident of the Three Gorges resettlement village

RS 5	Female	40	Resident of the Three Gorges resettlement village
RS 6	Female	26	Got married in the resettlement village
RS 7	Male	52	Resident of the Three Gorges resettlement village
RS 8	Male	40	Resident of the Three Gorges resettlement village
RS 9	Male	43	One of the representatives of the residents of the Three Gorges resettlement village
RS 10	Female	–	Resident of the Three Gorges resettlement village
RS 11	Female	34	Resident of the Three Gorges resettlement village
RS 12	Female	57	Resident of the Three Gorges resettlement village
RS 13	Female	15	Resident of the Three Gorges resettlement village; student
RS 14	Female	45	Resident of the Three Gorges resettlement village
RS 15	Female	45	Resident of the Three Gorges resettlement village, housewife
RS 16	Female	35	Village Head of the Three Gorges resettlement village
RS 17	Female	13	Resident of the Three Gorges resettlement village; student
RS 18	Female	58	Not resettled, visiting relatives in the Three Gorges resettlement village
RS 19	Male	–	Resettler from Huizhou, currently working at New Pearl Group Ceramics
RS 20	Male	49	Resident of the Three Gorges resettlement village; security coordinator
RS 21	Male	54	Resident of the Three Gorges resettlement village
RS 22	Female	32	Resident of the Three Gorges resettlement village
RS 23	Male	40	Resident of the Three Gorges resettlement village

RS 24	Female	51	Resident of the Three Gorges resettlement village
RS 25	Female	74	Resident of the Three Gorges resettlement village
RS 26	Female	32	Resident of the Three Gorges resettlement village

References

Cernea, M. (2000). Risks, safeguards and reconstruction. A model for population displacement and resettlement, in Cernea, M. and McDowell, C. (eds.), *Risks and Reconstruction. Experiences of Resettlers and Refugees*, Washington: The World Bank, pp. 11–55.

Cernea, M. (2016). Foreword: State legislation facing involuntary resettlement: Comparing the thinking in China and India on development-displacement, in Padovani, F. (ed.), *Development-induced Displacement in India and China. A Comparative Look at the Burdens of Growth*, Lanham: Lexington Books, pp. vii-li.

Cheng, Y. 程瑜 (2006). 白村生活。广东三峡移民适应性的人类学研究 Baicun shenghuo. Guangdong Sanxia yimin shiyingxing de renleixue yanjiu (*Life in White Village. An Anthropological Study of the Adaptability of Three Gorges Resettlers in Guangdong Province*), Beijing: Minzu Press.

Cheng, Y. and He, X. (2006). Power games and migrant adaptability in migration villages. The case of White Village, a settlement in Guangdong Province for migrants displaced by the Three Gorges Dam Project, *Chinese Sociology and Anthropology* 38(3), 71–89.

China Digital Times. (2011). 嗨！历史-三峡移民十年：两头无根 想回迁却回不去 Hai! Lishi – Sanxia yimin shi nian: liangtou wugen, xiang huiqian que huibuqu (Hi! History – Ten years after resettlement from the Three Gorges area: no roots at both ends, want to move back but can't), https://chinadigitaltimes.net/chinese/173742.html (accessed July 14, 2024).

Gans, H. (2002). The sociology of space: A use-centered approach, *City and Community* 1(4), 329–339.

Gransow, B. (2021). Contestation over moral economy: distant resettlement from the Three Gorges area to the Pearl River Delta, in Habich-Sobiegalla, S. and Rousseau, J.-F. (eds.), *The Political Economy of Hydropower in Southwest China and Beyond*, Cham: Palgrave Macmillan, pp. 69–87.

Guangdong (2000). 广东省人民政府办公厅文件 123 Guangdong sheng renmin zhengfu bangongting wenjian 123 (Document No.123 of the Office of the People's Government of Guangdong Province), 印发广东省安置三峡库区

外迁农村移民实施方案的通知 Yinfa Guangdong sheng anzhi Sanxia kuqu waiqian nongcun yimin shishi fangan de tongzhi (Notice on issuing the implementation plan for accommodating rural resettlers outside the Three Gorges reservoir area in Guangdong Province) http://www.gd.gov.cn/zwgk/gongbao/2001/1/content/post_3360273.html (accessed March 2, 2025).

Habich-Sobiegalla, S. (2016). *Dams, Migration and Authoritarianism in China. The local state in Yunnan*, London: Routledge.

Heggelund, G. (2004). *Environment and Resettlement Politics in China. The Three Gorges Project*, Aldershot: Ashgate.

Lefebvre, H. (1991). *The Production of Space*, Oxford: Blackwell Publishing.

Li, H. (2000). *Population Displacement and Resettlement in the Three Gorges Reservoir Area of the Yangtze River Central China*, PhD Thesis, University of Leeds.

Little, D. (1989). Chapter 2: The moral economy debate, in *Understanding Peasant China. Case Studies in the Philosophy of Social Science*, New Haven: Yale University Press.

Liu, J. and Wu, D. (2016). 刘晶，吴弟红, 三峡外迁移民社会适应分析 Sanxia waiqian yimin shehui shiying fenxi. (Analysis of Social Adaptability in the Three Gorges Distant Resettlement), 中国水运 (*China Water Transport*) 16(10), 60–62.

Löw, M. (2001). *Raumsoziologie*, Suhrkamp: Frankfurt am Main.

O'Brien, K. J. and Li, L. (2006). *Rightful Resistance in Rural China*, Cambridge: Cambridge University Press.

Padovani, F. (ed.) (2016). Analysis of the social implications of the Three Gorges Dam Project, in *Development-induced Displacement in India and China. A Comparative Look at the Burdens of Growth*, Lanham: Lexington Books, pp. 169–190.

Peng, H. and Feng, G. (2015). 彭豪祥，冯耕耘, 三峡移民社会适应性研究 Sanxia yimin shehui shiyingxing yanjiu (*Study on the Social Adaptability of Three Gorges Resettlers*), Wuhan: Wuhan University Press.

Price, S. (ed.) (2009). Prologue: Victims or partners? The social perspective in development induced displacement and resettlement, *The Asia Pacific Journal of Anthropology. Special Focus on Displacement and Resettlement* 10(4), 266–282.

Rousseau, J.-F. (2021). As time goes by … longitudinal analysis of dam impacts upon livelihood strategies in the Red River Valley, in Habich-Sobiegalla, S. and Rousseau, J.-F. (eds.), *The Political Economy of Hydropower in Southwest China and Beyond*, Cham: Palgrave Macmillan, pp. 171–189.

Scott, J. C. (1976). *The Moral Economy of the Peasant*, New Haven: Yale University Press.

Shi, G., Jiang, T., and Sun, Z. (2022). Evolution of land administration law and resettlement regulation in China. Setting new standards, in Zaman, M.,

Nair, R., and Shi, G. (eds.), *Resettlement in Asian Countries. Legislation, Administration and Struggles for Rights*, London: Routledge, pp. 56–70.

State Council. (2001). 长江三峡工程建设移民条例 Changjiang Sanxia gongcheng jianshe yimin tiaoli (*Regulations on Resettlement in the Yangtze Three Gorges Project*), Beijing: Chinese Legal Press.

Tan, Y. (2008). *Resettlement in the Three Gorges Project*, Hong Kong: Hong Kong University Press.

Tan, Y. and Wang, Y. (2003). Rural resettlement and land compensation in flooded areas: The case of the Three Gorges Project, China, *Asia Pacific Viewpoint* 22(1), 35–50.

Thompson, E. P. (1971). The moral economy of the English crowd in the eighteenth century, *Past and Present* 50(1), 76–136.

Tilt, B. (2015). *Dams and Development in China. The Moral Economy of Water and Power*, New York: Columbia University Press.

Watters, C. (2013). Forced migrants. From the politics of displacement to a moral economy of reception, in Gold, S. J. and Nawyn, S. J. (eds.), *The Routledge International Handbook of Migration Studies*, New York: Routledge, pp. 99–106.

Wilmsen, B. (2016). After the deluge: A longitudinal study of resettlement at the Three Gorges Dam, *World Development* 84, 41–54.

Wilmsen, B. and van Hulten, A. (2017). Following resettled people over time: The value of longitudinal data collection for understanding the livelihood impacts of the Three Gorges Dam, China, *Impact Assessment and Project Appraisal*, 35(1), 94–105, doi:10.1080/14615517.2016.1271542.

Ying, X. 应星 (2011). "气"与抗争政治。当代中国乡村社会稳定问题研究 'Qi' yu kangzheng zhengzhi. Dangdai Zhongguo xiangcun shehui wending wenti yanjiu (*"Vigour" and Contested Politics. A Study of the Problem of Stability in Contemporary Rural Chinese Society*), Beijing: Social Sciences Academic Press.

Ying, X. (2013). *A Study of the Stability of Contemporary Rural Chinese Society*, Berlin, Heidelberg: Springer Verlag.

Ying, X. (2016). Analysis of the interest expression mechanisms among Chinese Dam Resettlees: An account of the first case linked to the Three Gorges Resettlement, in F. Padovani (ed.), *Development-Induced Displacement in India and China. A Comparative Look at the Burdens of Growth*, Lanham: Lexington Books, pp. 191–206.

Zhou, Y., Zhou, Y., Hu, H., and Xiang, C. (2011). 周宜君，周银珍，胡红青，向长春，三峡工程农村外迁移民安置效果区域差异及其启示 Sanxia gongcheng nongcun waiqian yimin anzhi xiaoguo quyu chayi jiqi qishi (The regional differentiation of the Three Gorges rural emigrants adaptability and the revelation), 经济地理 (*Economic Geography*) 31(8), 1351–1357.

Chapter 8

Conclusion: The Enduring Promise of the Megacity

The PRD has increasingly evolved from a peri-urban to an urban and then to a mega-urban region. With the global financial crisis of 2008–2009, the export-led urbanisation that had characterised the PRD since the early 1980s came to an end. This type of urbanisation represented villages and towns in the PRD that were production sites for export-oriented manufacturing industries (Lin, 1997:5). They were directly linked to foreign investors and were very weakly connected to each other. In response to the crisis, local governments promoted industrial relocation and shifted to high-tech industrial parks rather than relying on scattered village economies (Wu, 2020:466). Individual cities began to compete with each other, resulting in uncoordinated development. According to Wu Fulong, the state responded by attempting to re-regulate the economy by changing the scale of governance, with the city-region as the appropriate scale for regulatory control (Wu, 2017:1148).

In 2017, a "Framework Agreement on Deepening Cooperation between Guangdong, Hong Kong and Macau and Promoting the Construction of a Greater Bay Area (Yue Gang Ao dawanqu)"[1] was signed, and in 2019, an "Outline Development Plan for the GBA" was released (a few months before the Hong Kong protests began). The GBA

[1] 粤港澳大湾区.

consists of nine cities in Guangdong province[2] and Hong Kong and Macau as two Special Administrative Regions (SARs). The authorities aim to make the GBA a world-class mega-urban region on a par with the elite economies of Tokyo, New York and the San Francisco Bay Area (Patchell, 2024:6). Interpreting the mega-urban city-region as a social product (Buser, 2012), the state-led spatial transformation of the PRD into the GBA can be interpreted (1) as an interventionist approach through the development of urban clusters (*chengshiqun*)[3] and regional economic integration across administrative boundaries; (2) as visions, design and planning used to justify high-level state intervention and an economic perspective beyond the "one country, two systems" formula; and (3) as regional institution building, interjurisdictional cooperation and the upscaling of governance to city-regions as part of broader processes of promoting state power.

Between 2010 and 2020, the permanent population of the nine cities in the PRD increased by 22 million people (from 56 million to 78 million).[4] During this period, there has been a shift in population distribution within the PRD. The megacities with more than 10 million inhabitants have grown the most. The provincial capital, Guangzhou, grew by 6 million to 18.67 million permanent residents (2020). Shenzhen actually grew by 7 million to 17.56 million, while Dongguan and Foshan grew to 10.48 million and 9.5 million respectively. As the long-term trend of people moving to economically developed urban centres continues, the driving force seems to have shifted from the purely economic motivation of the first generation of rural–urban migrants, namely, to earn more money for a while, to a more social motivation among the younger generations. For them, quality education conditions and development opportunities are key. The provision of inclusive and equitable services by city governments has become a core element of the attractiveness of large cities. For younger generations of rural–urban migrants, the prospect of settling in the city has become increasingly important. However, the

[2]Guangzhou, Shenzhen, Foshan, Dongguan, Zhuhai, Zhongshan, Jiangmen, Huizhou and Zhaoqing.

[3]城市群.

[4]The data from the 7th Census of 2020 in this paragraph are from https://m.21jingji.com/article/20210515/herald/ff7d5ea380301c269fb7bfc5d2205608_zaker.html (accessed June 10, 2024).

realisation of settlement intentions is closely linked to stable employment in the formal sector (Zhao, 2023:1969) or to other requirements set by the city governments, such as participation in social security or a certain level of education. The stepwise phasing-out of the *hukou* system is thus accompanied by the emergence of "softer" walls around and within megacities.

In response to the economic upgrading of the PRD, all nine cities in the region have developed policies to position themselves favourably in the competition for highly skilled workers (talents). Point systems are being used to regulate inflows into the very large megacities. In other words, the process of dismantling the *hukou* system, which has been going on for decades – albeit at a snail's pace – should not be understood as a linear process of gradual disappearance. Instead, the *hukou* system is increasingly being replaced by point systems that seem to fulfil the function of opening (to admit highly skilled workers) and closing (to limit the cost of social services) in a more individualised and flexible way. For the time being, it seems that the megacities of the PRD will continue to be places where the production of transient urban spaces by different types of self-incorporated residents becomes a permanent – or at least a long-term – phenomenon. A closer look at their risk situations could possibly be helpful in designing more adequate and targeted policies for people, not just for human resources.

This book started from the insight that there is no single path of integration or incorporation of migrants into the megacity. Subsequently, it has raised the question of what kinds of migrant pathways into the megacity might be discovered by studying migrants' own agency. The six micro-studies in this volume have shown how different groups of migrants connect with the megacity through their everyday routines and practices of constituting and appropriating space. It could be learned that this relationship with urban space often implies a relationship with one's own body – even when the body becomes a "disruptive factor" and causes an interruption in everyday routines.

The empirical-methodological contribution of this study is to unpack the generalised term of migrants in Chinese megacities. In order to represent as wide a range of different groups of migrants as possible, the study began with common binary categorisations, including internal and international migrants, voluntary and involuntary migrants, unqualified and highly educated migrants, and legal and "illegal" migrants.

While each of the micro-studies presented in this book can be assigned to one or more of these binary categories, these classifications are only of limited use when it comes to identifying transient urban spaces that are created through the agency of individual migrant groups as they make their way into the megacity. This will be illustrated by a brief overview of a variety of transient urban spaces that have been perceived, created or transformed by the different migrant groups considered here, representing their different pathways into the megacities of the PRD.

The perception of their own workplace as an unprotected space was prevalent among migrant workers who had suffered a work-related accident as production workers in small enterprises in Guangzhou. Poor occupational safety, a lack of risk awareness and the frequent absence of accident insurance could quickly lead to an individual financial crisis on top of the injuries. Contrary to the general expectation that they would return to the countryside after an accident at work, these migrant workers stayed in the city. Reasons for this included the possibility of being cared for by family members in the city or the economic pressure to continue earning money in the city. However, there were also cases where victims had borrowed money in their home village to pay for hospital costs and remained in the city because they did not dare to return home without being able to pay the debt. Another important reason for staying in the city was the possibility of taking individual legal action against their employer for compensation for medical expenses or for pain and suffering. Engaging in such individual litigation meant creating spaces of contestation.

These and other migrant workers were supported by NGOs and the dedicated work of their worker and student volunteers. For NGOs, most of which were founded by former migrant workers, the expanding megacities of the PRD, especially Shenzhen and Guangzhou, increasingly offered opportunities to create spaces of care and solidarity among migrants in the city. The proximity to Hong Kong, with its vibrant civil society, was certainly an advantage in this respect. International financial support made the NGOs more independent in their activities. From the perspective of state actors this combination of migrant labour solidarity, strikes, NGO networking and foreign funding was perceived as a potential threat to economic and political stability and existing power relations. New NGO legislation and a policy of securitising the party-state space literally pulled the rug out from under the migrant workers' NGOs. The contradictory dynamics unfolding between state and non-state actors were identified as an example of 'risk entanglement'.

Walking a tightrope between legality and illegality, migrant women working in Shenzhen's entertainment and sex industry sometimes described their situation as living in the *jianghu*, a traditional concept for spaces outside the social order, later applied to urban spaces of uncare, the wild side of the megacity. Although the legal basis for the administrative detention of prostitutes and their clients was finally abolished in 2019, prostitution is still illegal in China, and the debate on its legalisation has been put on hold in recent years. For the mostly very young rural–urban migrant women, who in some cases came to the entertainment and sex industry via a detour through factory jobs, the promise of the megacity of Shenzhen was to reinvent themselves as young ladies (*xiaojie*), part of this modern, young and fast-paced city, with comparatively high earnings, more flexible working hours, fashionable and luxury outfits and an urban lifestyle. The main pathways into the sex industry in Shenzhen, as revealed by the interviewees, were (1) a deliberate decision to work in the sex industry; (2) being tricked into it by "boyfriends" who want to make a living from the young women's sex work; and (3) involuntary and coerced forms of work in the sex industry based on human trafficking, drugs, rape and other forms of violence or threats of violence. At the same time, the megacity of Shenzhen provided the anonymity they needed to keep their sex work a secret from their families in the countryside, although many of the interviewees sent remittances home.

Three types of transnational urban spaces produced or co-produced by African traders in Guangzhou were identified, including business spaces, spaces of care created by a variety of organisations from different African countries, and spaces of intersection between transnational African migrants and internal Chinese migrants. For the group of African small traders in Guangzhou, the priority was their transnational business of trading in clothes and other cheap goods, with little intention of immigration. In recent years, the number of African traders in Guangzhou has declined significantly. The reasons for this were a restrictive visa policy that could easily push small traders into illegality; everyday racism, which increased during the COVID-19 lockdowns; and Sino-African business relations, which have become more diverse, virtual and competitive.

In the imaginations of graduates from rural areas, megacities such as Guangzhou and Shenzhen are difficult to replace with smaller cities, even though official migration and urbanisation policies have long encouraged them to do so. This is because, despite persistently high youth unemployment, they see more opportunities to create spaces for survival and, eventually, careers, not least because Guangzhou and Shenzhen are major centres of educational and research institutions. Moving to a smaller city would hardly be considered a personal success for these ambitious young graduates, who can look back on an educational career in which each change of school was accompanied by a move to a larger city. To enable young graduates to enter the urban middle class and consumer society, active local labour market policies and the access to affordable housing would be essential. In addition, the location and distribution of educational and research institutions could be reconsidered.

For the group of resettlers from the Three Gorges Dam area, the promise of the modern megacity was that they could turn their fate of involuntary resettlement into a success story by settling in the highly developed PRD. However, the resettlement space offered to them as compensation for the loss of their homes had more to do with their rural *hukou* than with their previous practical existence in Sichuan's tourism industry. The legal and institutional framework of their new life in a foreign environment led to numerous misunderstandings and complex negotiation processes with the local government and the administrative host village responsible for their reception. Although they were privileged in terms of access to local public services, in terms of the constitution and appropriation of the urban space allocated to them, they remained largely confined to the resettlement village compared to other migrant groups.

This synopsis of the production of different transient urban spaces shows that the everyday routines and practices of each migrant group reveal specific policy areas that become visible. These include policies as diverse as occupational health and safety, migrant workers' organising and citizen rights, the legalisation of sex work, visa policies and everyday racism, the concentration of educational institutions in China's largest cities, and post-resettlement policies. Obviously, there is a gap between these policy areas, which emerge from and impact on the everyday lives of different migrant groups in the city, and urban migration governance, which focuses on the exclusion and inclusion of particular migrant groups from the perspective of risk calculation and risk prevention by urban authorities. Whether and how these "loose ends" can be tied together in terms of a fruitful integration policy is beyond the scope of this study and may require further research. In any case, it is worth considering that recognition of the diversity of different migrant groups that are actually in the city will require more targeted urban migration governance.

Despite the diversity between migrant groups, a more general pattern of perception and constitution of transient urban spaces emerged in the course of the analysis. This is evident in the observation that perceptions of space are intertwined with perceptions of risk, which can then trigger constellations of risk entanglement. Different urban actors make decisions under conditions of uncertainty and incomplete information. What one actor sees as a risk prevention measure is perceived by another actor as an external danger, which in turn is met with preventive measures or – depending on the power constellation – with pressure on the perceived perpetrators of the external danger.

The theoretical contribution of the study is to bring aspects of migration sociology and risk sociology into dialogue with each other and with urban China studies. The individualisation of risk and its unequal distribution have been identified as a phenomenon of China's transitional society. They have accompanied and are characteristic of the extensive and accelerated processes of rural–urban migration and urbanisation, including the development of more and more megacities. However, this should not be seen as proving that China's development is exceptional. Rather, individualisation of risk and its unequal distribution should be seen in the context of current global migration and urbanisation trends, with the prospect of further urban population concentrations in Asia and on the African continent. The study of migrants' agency in producing transient urban spaces and finding pathways of self-incorporation in Chinese megacities can provide an empirical and theoretical building block beyond China's national development, linking to ideas of world risk society and planetary urbanisation.

References

Buser, M. (2012). The production of space in metropolitan regions: A Lefebvrian analysis of governance and spatial change, *Planning Theory* 11(3), 279–298.

Lin, G. C. S. (1997). *Red Capitalism in South China. Growth and Development of the Pearl River Delta*, Vancouver: UBC Press.

Patchell, J. (2024). *China's Greater Bay Area. Agglomeration, External Economies, Governance and Urbanization*, London: Routledge.

Wu, F. (2017). China's emergent city-region governance: A new form of state spatial selectivity through state-orchestrated rescaling, *International Journal of Urban and Regional Research* 40(6), 1134–1151.

Wu, F. (2020). Adding new narratives to the urban imagination: An introduction to 'new directions of urban studies in China', *Urban Studies* 57(3), 459–472.

Zhao, H. (2023). Understanding Shiminhua in Chinese Greater Bay Area: Internalizing urban identity and negotiating place attachment, *Regional Science Policy & Practise*, 1956–1979, https://doi.org/10.1111/rsp3.12730.

Index

C

D

E

F

www.ingramcontent.com/pod-product-compliance
Lightning Source LLC
LaVergne TN
LVHW011808200926
848484LV00005B/1105